# TexasMonthly ON . . . Texas Women

TexasMonthly ON . . .

# Texas Women

*From the editors of* TEXAS MONTHLY

INTRODUCTION BY EVAN SMITH
Editor, *Texas Monthly*

University of Texas Press Austin

Printed in the United States of America
First edition, 2006

*Requests for permission to reproduce material from this work should be sent to:*
Permissions
University of Texas Press
P.O. Box 7819
Austin, TX 78713-7819
www.utexas.edu/utpress/about/bpermission.html

♾ The paper used in this book meets the minimum requirements of ANSI/NISO Z39.48-1992 (R1997) (Permanence of Paper).

*Library of Congress Cataloging-in-Publication Data*

Texas monthly on— Texas women / from the editors of Texas monthly ; introduction by Evan Smith, editor.— 1st ed.

p. cm.

ISBN 0-292-71327-4 (pbk. : alk. paper)

1. Women—Texas—Case studies. I. Smith, Evan, 1966– II. Texas monthly (Austin, Tex.)

HQ1438.T4T495 2006
305.409764—dc22

2005025203

# INTRODUCTION

There is such a thing as a Texas woman. She's a very particular and recognizable type: independent and courageous, comfortable in her skin, possessed of both frontier survival skills and urban sophistication, fun-loving, forward-thinking, rich in spirit. Such a person may not exist elsewhere—not in the sense of fully embodying the values of the place she calls home—but she certainly can be found here, and she's been with us as long as Texas has. If you don't believe it, you're about to find out.

The stories in this collection, all of which first appeared in *Texas Monthly*, pay tribute to some really extraordinary examples of the species. Over the past 33 years we've had the good fortune to write about first ladies and second wives, writers and ranchers, senators and socialites and strippers, and more than a few moms. To a one, they've been every bit as interesting and exceptional, in ways obvious and not, as their male counterparts. And they've been great material.

Though not all for the same reason. In some cases, the lives and times of our subjects have demonstrated something superlative: Barbara Jordan's groundbreaking accomplishments in politics, Selena's and Janis Joplin's star turns in music, and Hallie Stillwell's long years tending to the lands of West Texas need no explication. In others, it's the arc of the narrative that really moves you: the flowering of Claudia Alta Taylor into Lady Bird, the rearing of three daughters any mother would be proud of by a widowed

Mexican immigrant who spoke little English. A few of the profiles here fall into the category of strange bedfellows: Molly Ivins, meet Laura Bush. And what would Cynthia Ann Parker have made of Candy Barr? (Come to think of it, they had at least one thing in common: men who tried—and failed—to tame their wild ways.)

The writers who brought these and other wonderful women alive are superlative, too. So are *Texas Monthly*'s former editors—Bill Broyles and Greg Curtis—who had the good sense to assign more than half the pieces you're about to read, and its founder and publisher, Mike Levy, who recognizes, as few in his position do, the value of a magazine that's a venue for this kind of great journalism.

Enjoy.

*Evan Smith, Editor*
TEXAS MONTHLY
*May 2005*

# TexasMonthly ON . . . Texas Women

# ALL ABOUT MY MOTHER

*Three daughters, two countries, one life, no regrets.*

CECILIA BALLÍ

**When I first sat down to talk to my mother about this story, I actually interviewed her, with a notepad in hand. I'm still not sure why she trusted a journalist—even her daughter—but what she confided over the course of two sittings and many hours left me breathless. For the first time, she told me her life story as it had unfolded inside of her mind and her heart. Which is to say that she told me the story of herself as a woman, not as my mother. And although I'm sure this piece is tainted with some grain of sentimentality, I am confident that her experiences speak for those of countless Texas women who have made this state what it is today.**

SHE WAS, as they say in the Mexican border city of Matamoros, *del rancho,* from one of the scrappy ranches on the outskirts of town, which should have meant she was so shy she wouldn't even eat in front of strangers. But the boys she met at the dances in the city were always surprised to learn that she had been raised on a ranch, because she wore the most fashionably daring clothes and liked to converse and go to the movies.

He was 23. He didn't know too much about her, only that he wanted to dance with her that night. You see, he was from a ranch too, but from a real one farther down the same road, where agriculture had paid off in big wads of cash that were traded for gaudy furniture. Although they had attended the same elementary school, their backgrounds had set them worlds apart. It wasn't until he was a young man with a trim mustache that he would watch her across the aisle of the bus from town. He was so smitten with her that when she got off, he would take the spot where she had sat, just to feel what was left of her. Sometimes, when he drove by Rancho San Pedro on his way home, he would honk in case she was sitting by the window or wandering about outside and might turn to look.

But she was oblivious. She had promised herself that she would not date any of the young men from the ranches, whose small-town ideas about the world frustrated her. She had grown up admiring the city lights. From her family's property, she could see them winking in the distance if she walked far enough into the fields, and they stood for all the things that couldn't be hers on that little patch of dirt. There, for six years of schooling, she had squeezed an old rag late at night through the top of a petroleum can and lit it, devouring the facts and numbers she had printed as her teacher dictated them aloud, because too many of the schoolchildren couldn't pay for textbooks. She rose to the top of her class and even got to carry the Mexican flag once during an end-of-year assembly, decked out in her cousin's pink *quinceañera* dress since she couldn't afford a school uniform like everyone else.

Then it was over: no free education after the sixth grade in her country, and the young women—especially *las del rancho*—had to get a job or help watch their younger brothers and sisters. But she kept on daydreaming, thrilled when she sat by the radio and listened to it murmur of all the great things man did, like walk on the moon. On infrequent trips to the hospital in Matamoros, she would idolize the nurses in their crisp white uniforms. One day, she believed, she too would live in the city and wear a white uniform—maybe a chemist's lab coat. All she knew about her future was that she wanted to discover new things.

So naturally, when this young man offered her a goofy, hopeful grin from across the dance floor that night in 1969, she didn't understand. And she didn't really care for it either, despite his good looks and his reputation as a charming guy. What could he want? she wondered. To dance, he confessed. She hesitated. But then—who knows why—she said yes.

"I LIKE THE WORD 'WI-DOW,'" my mother told me recently. She was speaking in Spanish, the only language she knows well, but she allowed the precariously pronounced English word to teeter on the tip of her tongue. Then, aware of the stigma of being a woman alone, she added, almost defiantly, "I'm not ashamed. It gives you personality."

She had slipped on her black-rimmed glasses to inspect the naturalization certificate she had just received. At the age of 53, she had finally become a citizen of the United States. Always on the fringe—that had been her biography. I had thought about this as a solemn woman opened the ceremony with a dramatic rendition of "America the Beautiful" and the robed judge thanked the inductees for representing the very best of this country. Even though I, an American citizen by birth, have in some ways become jaded about the meaning of U.S. citizenship, that morning I found myself swelling with pride for my mother. She herself had been a little distracted during the ceremony, flustered by the way everyone raced through the Pledge of Allegiance. But when the vocalist took the microphone one last time and filled the auditorium with glass-shattering strains of "God Bless America," she blinked rapidly and began to fan herself.

It wasn't until we were outside, walking toward her silver pickup under the warm South Texas sun, that she began dabbing sloppily at her red eyes. For the first time, she told me that when she was about eight, she had briefly attended an elementary school in Brownsville, just across the Rio Grande from her Mexican hometown. She wasn't supposed to be there, of course, a child whose family had tiptoed across the border *sin papeles,* "without papers." She and her parents and her little brother, Raul, had squeezed into a one-room, rat-infested shack. At the American school the students had sung "Ten Little Indians" and "God Bless America." She was crying now because the song had brought back bittersweet memories of how tough things had been then for that bony, dark-skinned girl who didn't belong.

Indeed, for most of her life my mother has been only a partial member of her own world. She was taught how to be a woman in rural Mexico during the fifties and sixties. As a daughter, she was expected to shoulder responsibility without questioning. As a wife, she was expected to serve without resenting. As a mother, she was expected to sacrifice without looking back. Soon it was difficult for her to remember the days when she had indulged in making plans, in thinking about what might make *her* happy. Only in recent years has my mother begun to make sense of how life changed her and then brought her old self back. Only in recent years has she begun talking to my two sisters and me about herself—not about who she is in relation to anybody else, but about who she is, plain and simple.

I'M NOT SURE when Mami's dreams vanished, but they must have fluttered out the window on one of those 45-hour drives on Interstate 10 to California. Maybe it was the time she rode a Greyhound alone because she was utterly pregnant with twins and didn't fit on the passenger seat of our uncle's pickup yet would have been equally uncomfortable in the back camper. She still cries when she remembers how—three days into the trip and not far from the city where my father and five-year-old sister, Cristina, were waiting to meet her—the bus stopped for a two-hour layover in Oakland and she walked around aimlessly on swollen feet under miserable skyscrapers.

Antonia Hinojosa and Cristóbal Ballí had begun dating after he asked her to dance that night in Matamoros. He and his first wife had ended their marriage some time before, so he ran off with this improbable ranch girl and married her. His father, a Mexican American who had chosen to make a life on the Mexican side of the Rio Grande, had planned to leave his ranch to him, but my dad was irreverent and reckless and lost his inheritance to an older brother who worked harder. Now that he was ready to settle down, he was forced to begin from scratch. He filed for American citizenship, rented a small house in Matamoros, and was driving city buses in Brownsville when my mother bore a beautiful baby girl.

Once Cristina turned one, he and my mother decided to cast their lot with the migrant workers who made seasonal pilgrimages to California, where there were fields of ripe tomatoes to pick and few labor laws. In fact, when César Chávez and his people came by urging the workers to demand an eight-hour day, my mother wouldn't hear of it. Every extra hour under the sun was an additional brick on the house she and my dad would build when they settled back in Texas. In Davis they tracked down some cousins and rented a tiny two-bedroom in the same migrant camp. It had no living room or air conditioner, but it cost just $60 a month. They figured the sacrifice would pay off in a few years.

She did not fully know yet how to be a woman in Mexico, much less in the United States. But my mother was determined to do her part to make her family's life better. Antonia Hinojosa de Ballí became Antonia H. Ballí, and she tried not to think much about the ranch back home, instead putting blind faith in the idea that raising a good family and working hard in a strange country would get us all somewhere. For the most part, it did. Papi was soon hired to drive a big truck that hauled tomatoes to other cities, which paid far better than hoeing and picking them. And our mom eventually became a cook at the migrant camp's preschool, where she could keep an eye on Celia and me, her toddler twins. They saved every penny they could and watched their three daughters grow.

IN 1981, when I was five, the trips to California finally ceased. Back in Brownsville, we moved into a small wood-frame house in the Las Prietas subdivision while our mother and father built our brick one. There was no contractor involved. Don Lencho, an old carpenter friend from Matamoros, put up the towering frame, and a couple of hired hands helped lay the beige-colored brick. Soon we were living on Clover Drive, across the street from Perez Elementary School, where Celia and I would begin kindergarten and where Cristina, who was ten years old by then, would finally be able to sit in one classroom all year long. Mami took a job cooking for a nursing home, and Papi bought a used 1973 Crown Victoria and painted it egg-yolk yellow, proudly stenciling his cab number—a bold, black "15"—on the front fenders of his new business.

For my sisters and me, household chores consisted mainly of doing homework. Though our mom could not help us with it, every evening after dinner she would wipe off the dining room table that doubled as a desk and often slip us a favorite snack as we worked out long math problems. When the local grocery store offered a cheap encyclopedia in installments, she carefully timed each trip so that she wouldn't miss a single volume, bringing home some eggs and milk and another $2 book full of knowledge. After 31 weeks of patient shopping, the full set stood in our living room bookcase, looking rather dignified. And she never missed the school's open-house nights. She might have barely understood some of our teachers, but she made sure to smile and nod her head as we translated how we were doing in school: *"Dice que soy muy buena estudiante."*

Almost instinctively, she knew that she wanted our lives to be different from hers, yet it took time for her to figure out just what that would require. Because she had been brought up in another culture, where being a child meant something else, at first she wouldn't let us indulge in activities she considered childhood frills, like going to friends' slumber parties and volunteering after school as crossing guards. But we pushed as far as we could. We had to convince her, for one, that extracurricular activities were important. When the troop leaders at an informational Girl Scout meeting began discussing expenses, her under-the-table pinches urged us to leave, but Celia and I held back our tears and refused to get up. In the end, our mom worked out a compromise with one of the troop leaders; our Aunt Letty, who made beautiful wedding gowns, stitched our Brownie dresses with fabric that was only half a shade darker than the official uniform. Trial and error—that was the way my sisters, our mother, and I forged our relationship in the early years of my life.

THE CANCER was eating him up, chewing him from head to toe like an impatient dog. His hair was the first casualty. The chemotherapy left it lying in clumps on his white pillow, so much that you could soon see his pale scalp under the few sad strands that remained. Gone were the days when he would spend hours before the mirror gelling it all in place, even though he would be spending most of the day sitting under a palm tree next to his yellow cab as he waited for customers. The tumor was lodged behind his nose, and all the radiation on his face had made him extremely weak. Now our dad used the mirror to watch himself as he performed the daily jaw exercises the doctor had ordered, forcing him to make exaggerated, contorted faces. Plus, something was rotting inside him, we were convinced, because his disease made him smell very bad. Every morning in the hallway, my mother would have to coax me, quietly so that his feelings wouldn't be hurt, to walk to his bed and kiss him good-bye, as my sisters and I had always done before running off to school.

Two years after we had settled in Brownsville, after our father had turned 36 and his sinus problems had grown increasingly worse, we made that fateful trip to a Harlingen clinic, where the doctor announced that he was seriously ill. Our parents received the news together, and though they said little, they understood that in too many cases cancer meant death. "So much for building my credit," Papi muttered as they walked out glumly. When he saw his three daughters, though, he tried to appear cheerful, and since fast food was considered a special treat, he announced that he felt like eating a really big hamburger.

In reality, he was devastated. He was immediately given a dose of radiation and then went to Houston every few months for checkups at M. D. Anderson, where he could get free treatments. In between, he drank himself to sleep and laughed in cancer's face. *"El cáncer me hace los mandados,"* he would brag. It was the cancer that took orders from him. Once, on his way to a bar after he had been drinking at home, he lost control of his car and took down the fence of our elementary school. He would curse and slam doors and throw things when he felt like it, then try desperately to make amends the next morning. It was his way of coping with his downfall, with the fact that, deep down, he understood life was cruelly slipping away.

For five years our mother bore it all stoically, calmly even. She made the long trips to Houston with him, spending hours embroidering Mother Goose pillows for us while he slept. She was forced to quit her job, leaving us with no income at all. But she tried to stay focused on helping our dad feel better, especially since the doctor told her that he cried when she wasn't with him. One day, when he said he wanted some *caldo de pollo,* she rode the only bus route she knew to a Mexican neighborhood on the other side of Houston, where she found the chicken broth he was craving. "The patient prefers Spanish foods," the doctor had noted in his file. By the time she returned, four hours later, the patient had fallen asleep.

As he lay dying, he wept regretfully and pleaded for forgiveness. Then he was gone, just moments before my sisters and I arrived to see him. A few hours later we were riding back to Brownsville in the darkness, my mother embracing me silently as we nodded in and out of sleep. She asked the mortician to dress him in the only suit he owned—the brown one he had bought at the Salvation Army store he often rummaged through to kill time on his trips to Houston. Though she wept a little, she made sure to greet the many people who came to the funeral home to pay their respects. Even when she closed the coffin, she was surprisingly, almost embarrassingly, composed.

It was weeks later, when she was home and we were off at school, that she cried, letting her pain fill the walls of her empty brick house. She cried for the times the nurses had poked him blue in search of a vein, cried for the days his anxiety attacks had gotten so bad he had sworn his flesh was falling off his bones. In those tears went the long nights by his hospital bed, the hot trips to California, the evening he had asked her to dance. Seventeen years later it was just her, her and three daughters and an undetermined future. No husband. No job. No guarantees. She was so young to be left alone, so old to be starting her life. She was 38.

But after all the sadness had been emptied and God had answered her prayers for peace, my mother's anxieties turned into resignation—then into exhilaration. For the first time in her life, she began to feel like an independent adult, and the sensation was liberating. She knew immediately what she would do: She would work hard and take care of her daughters. That was what she already knew how to do, only now it would be on her own terms.

Slowly, she began to piece herself back together. She had applied for a job cooking in the public schools after my father died; nearly a year later, she was hired. One day she noticed a line of people outside the school district's offices. When she asked them what the line was for, they said they were signing up to take the general equivalency diploma exam. On a whim, she put down her own name, and although she hadn't sat in a classroom in nearly thirty years, she took the test in Spanish and received a high school diploma.

I remember when she bought her first car and posed with us for a Polaroid that would be tacked up on the dealer's wall—four smiling women and an equally proud 1988 charcoal-gray Plymouth Reliant. Her first new car. In her name. That car was her little mobile home for the next six years, the place where she spent many hours in a school parking lot waiting for us to emerge from a late choir rehearsal or student council meeting. When we had a concert or an awards assembly, she always sat near the front, making every effort to appear interested despite the ungraceful sounds of our awkward sixth-grade band. She made only about $7,000 a year working full-time, so when I cried to her that I would be the only clarinet player at the all-state band tryouts with an old, second-rate instrument, she made mental calculations for days. Finally, she charged my $1,300, top-of-the-line Buffet clarinet on a credit card.

"WHEN YOU THREE began to learn is when I began to learn," my mother once told me, oblivious of the fact that the reverse had also been true. In our family, almost everything is a group project, and one person's accomplishment belongs to everyone else. Our mom didn't get to be a chemist after all—didn't even get to middle school—but she has three college degrees hanging on her wall and several graduate degrees coming. And they are all hers as much as they are ours. She is a social worker, a journalist, a lawyer. Even as young adults, we continue to seek her help and her company. It is not just that her experiences help us put our own challenges in perspective; it is that they reside deep within us. It is that a little part of her is with us always, making us the women we want to be.

She has had to swallow the consequences of choosing a different life for her daughters. When Cristina insisted that she had to leave Brownsville to get a degree in social work, our mom was afraid to let her go, but she halfheartedly packed up the Reliant and drove her firstborn to San Antonio. Her heart sank when, walking into the dorm where my sister would be spending the next several years, she saw the students sitting around the lobby. The scene was painfully familiar: They reminded her of sad relatives in a hospital waiting room. Two years later she forced a smile and waved good-bye from the tiny Brownsville airport as her twins flew away to New York and California. She later told me that she had wept the night before as, for the last time, she ironed my long-sleeved cotton shirts just the way I liked them. The way my father had liked them too.

But a new kind of life, one that she had longed to know as a child, opened up to her when we left. In endless late-night phone conversations, she sympathized with our registration hassles, asked about our new friends, reminded us to eat well and sleep plenty. She came to visit me in California, where we climbed the sloping streets of San Francisco and revisited the migrant camp in Davis that had been her first home in the United States. When I spent a semester in Puebla with a Mexican exchange program, she made the eighteen-hour bus trip with me, exploring places she'd never known in her own country. She took lots of pictures, later carrying them in her purse to show her co-workers.

Then, in 1996, Celia took her to New York. She was horrified by the crazy driving and the subways where people stared, so she insisted on walking dozens of blocks at a time to see the city. On a sticky July morning, they decided to visit the Statue of Liberty. Our mom knew little about the scores of immigrants who had passed by the monument for generations, but as a child she had glimpsed it in books and on television, and it had represented the glitzy life of New York—a cosmopolitanism this little girl from the ranch had always wished for herself.

Standing there in her broken-in walking shoes, her unruly black curls dancing as the ferry glided across the cold blue waters to Ellis Island, Mami choked up and tingled all over as she contemplated that majestic woman for the first time. Miles away from the fringes of Matamoros, Antonia Hinojosa felt she had seen the world.

*February 2003*

## CANDY

*Taking the wrapper off a Texas legend.*

GARY CARTWRIGHT

Candy Barr is one of the great ladies in my life. For me, as for thousands of other young men in Texas in the 1950s, she was sexual-liberation-by-proxy. That face, that body, that hair, that *attitude* . . . she epitomized the conflict between sex as joy and sex as danger. I had never met her in person until our memorable night together in the fall of 1976, when she taught me that trust can be better than sex. Or just as satisfying. I don't think any writer ever got that close to Candy, before or after. She talked a lot that night about her plans for the future, getting her fan club organized, maybe making a movie about her life. Those things never happened. Candy and I talked from time to time after my story appeared in *Texas Monthly*, but gradually she drifted away.

Then, in the magic of a Hollywood moment, she reappeared in 2003. An agent from William Morris contacted Skip Hollandsworth, another *Texas Monthly* writer who had once interviewed Candy, and asked if he was interested in writing a book and screenplay on her life. Big bucks were involved. Skip called Candy, who said she might consider it—but only if I was part of the deal. I agreed, most reluctantly: As I wrote, even on her best days, Candy can be like "a hurricane in a Dixie Cup." Thus began a series of frustrating and confusing phone conversations, not unlike the conversations we'd had so many years ago, Candy complaining that writers had told and retold so many awful lies about her, and me begging for her trust, just one more time. In the end, the fears and anxieties that had shadowed Candy all her life won out and

**she killed the project. But I smile every time I remember our final conversation. "By the way," she told me, out of the blue, "I did have panties on!" Read the story and you'll understand.**

ON THE ROAD HOME to Brownwood in her green '74 Cadillac with the custom upholstery and the CB radio, clutching a pawn ticket for her $3,000 mink, Candy Barr thought about biscuits. Biscuits made her think of fried chicken, which in turn suggested potato salad and corn. For as long as she could remember, in times of crisis and stress, Candy Barr always thought of groceries. It was a miracle she didn't look like a platinum pumpkin, but she didn't: Even at 41, she still looked like a movie star.

For once, the crisis was not her own. It was something she had read a few days earlier about how the omnipotent, totalitarian *they* were about to jackboot the remnants of the once happy and prosperous life of a 76-year-old Dallas electrician named O. E. Cole. Candy had never heard of O. E. Cole until she spotted his pitiful tale in the Brownwood newspaper. She didn't know if Cole was black or white, mean or generous, judgmental or forgiving. She only knew he was in trouble. For nearly fifty years Cole had been an upright, hardworking citizen of a city Candy Barr had every reason to hate; then his wife, Nettie, suffered a stroke and lingered in a coma for eighteen months while their savings were sucked away. According to the newspaper account, Cole spent $500 for Nettie's headstone, which left him a balance of $157. Before he could use that money to cover mortgage payments on his home and the electrician's shop at the back, a gunman shot and robbed him. Now, when he was too old to apply for additional credit, *they* were prepared to foreclose.

"This is a goddamn crime!" Candy raged, throwing her suitcase on the bed and barking a string of orders to her houseguests: Scott, her 22-year-old boyfriend of the moment, and Susan Slusher, her 17-year-old niece who had recently come to stay with "Aunt Nita" from a broken home in Philadelphia.

Scott and Susan had been around just long enough to know that when Candy blew—as she often did, without warning—you had to look not for explanations but for something sturdy to hang on to. Try to imagine a hurricane in a Dixie Cup. The laughing tropical green eyes boiled, and the innocence that had made that perfect teardrop face a landmark in the sexual liberation of an entire generation of milquetoasts became the wrath of Zeus. They say she once sat waiting in a rocking chair talking to sweet Jesus and when her ex-husband kicked down the door she threw down on him with a pistol that was resting conveniently in her lap. She shot him in the stomach, but she was aiming for the groin. When she caught mobster Mickey Cohen talking to another woman, she slugged him in the teeth. She carved her mark on a dyke in the prison workshop: This was not a lovers' quarrel, as an assistant warden indicated on her record, but a disagreement stemming from Candy's hard-line belief that a worker should take pride in her job.

Candy had a cosmic way of connecting things, which to the more prosaic mind might appear coincidental. So it was that the ill-fated placement of a Citizens National Bank of Brownwood ad next to the article outlining the plight of O. E. Cole ignited her fuse. The bank ad suggested that had it not been for a Revolutionary War banker named Robert Morris, we might all be sipping tea with crumpets and begging God to save our Queen. What the average eye might take as harmless Bicentennial puffery hit Candy's heart dead center.

"I watched the bastards do the same thing to my daddy," Candy fumed, removing her mink from the cedar chest and raking bottles and jars of cosmetics into her overnight bag. "I sold my hunting rifle three times to help my daddy. It's a crime what they can do to people, a goddamn crime. Don't call me a criminal if *you're* gonna be one."

With the skillful employment of her CB radio, "the Godmother" and her two young companions made the 160 miles to Dallas in less than two hours. Candy hocked her mink for $250, then called on dancer Chastity Fox and other friends to help raise another $150. Then Candy painted her face with soft missionary shades of tan and gold and called on O. E. Cole, introducing herself as Juanita Dale Phillips of Brownwood and presenting the goggle-eyed electrician with $400 and a copy of her book of prison poems, *A Gentle Mind . . . Confused*. Cole couldn't have been more confused if he had found Fidel Castro in his refrigerator. When I spoke with Cole two weeks later, there were still some blank spaces behind his eyes, but the crisis had passed.

"I didn't know who she was till I saw her name on that little book," he told me. "Oh, yes, I knew the name Candy Barr. You couldn't live in Dallas long as I had and not know that name. But it wasn't for me to judge her. What is past is past. It's what a person is now I go on, and she was awful nice. We sat around and talked for hours. In fact, we talked all night long."

Cole hadn't stayed up all night in years. He had never seen Candy Barr's famous blue movie, or watched her strip at Abe Weinstein's Colony Club, or read about her romance with Mickey Cohen, or paid much attention when his fellow citizens gave her fifteen years for possessing less than one ounce of marijuana. In fact, he couldn't remember what he had heard about her, only that it seemed unsavory. "That was a long time ago," Cole seemed to recall. Roughly twenty years.

To place her properly in time you had to go back to Sugar Ray Robinson, James Dean, Marilyn Monroe, Bridey Murphy, Joe McCarthy, John Foster Dulles, the Kefauver Committee, RAF Group Captain Peter Townsend, Mort Sahl, and Sputnik. Texas was still the largest state in the union, and Elvis Presley's "Don't Be Cruel" was the number one song. *Playboy* magazine was an under-the-counter novelty, less than three years old and tame as a pet goose. Brigitte Bardot was being banned in Philadelphia, Fort Worth, and Abilene. The Dodgers were in Brooklyn, Russian tanks in the streets of Budapest, Fidel Castro in the jungles of Cuba. It was a time when the National Organization for Decent Literature was putting pressure on bookstores and enlisting local police to threaten booksellers who were too slow to "cooperate" in removing from their shelves such filth-spreaders as Hemingway, Faulkner, Dos Passos, Zola, and Orwell. Thirteen million Americans spent Tuesday nights watching a TV charade called The *$64,000 Question*. Someone with a dark sense of humor labeled it "the Age of Innocence."

Candy Barr was a household word then, an authentic Texas folk hero. To the absolute surprise of hardly anyone, Candy Barr would still be a name twenty years later. What precipitated a revival in her long-dormant career was a photo layout and interview in the June 1976 issue of *Oui:* How many 41-year-old grandmothers ever posed for split beaver shots? Now Candy was talking of college fan clubs, of posters and T-shirts. "If I don't get into it, somebody else will," she said. "I'm tired being ripped off. I'm not even aware of how to be a star, I just am one." It was time to move ahead with her autobiography. "All the lies and tackiness that have been written about me . . . now I'm going to set the record straight." She calls her as yet unwritten memoirs *Bits and Pieces,* and speaks of "leaving my legacy for my daughter and granddaughter."

In the three months since the *Oui* photographs, Candy had received maybe five hundred fan letters, from all across the United States, from Mexico, from Canada, from Puerto Rico, from the National Organization for the Reform of Marijuana Laws, from members of the U.S. Navy stationed on Diego Garcia somewhere in the Indian Ocean. There was the usual sprinkling of nut mail—a man in Syracuse sent a tracing of his private parts—but the vast majority of the letters were from true fans, properly reverent and begging only to speak, just once, of loneliness and isolation, of dark fantasies and repressed urges and wives that would never understand, of their recurring feeling that life had them by the nose and would never let go. An Indian from a place called Bull Mountain sent her a flower. A Los Angeles Dodger invited her to a doubleheader. A retired firefighter from California wrote that he had pasted her picture to his locker years ago and there it remained "until my last days of fighting fires." A man from New Jersey accompanied a gentle note of adoration with three pair of sheer panty hose. The president of the chamber of commerce of a small Southern town wrote: "It seems rather bizarre to me that a 36-year-old man with a responsible job, family, and being reasonably well adjusted would sit down and write a fan letter to someone he has not met, and never will meet. Yet, that is exactly what I find myself doing."

Maybe half the letters came from men, and a few women, in prison. One convict wrote that Candy's picture had once sustained his father during a long prison stretch and "now I can understand why." It was these letters from men inside the walls that moved her most. She intended to answer every one of them, although she was uncertain how she could afford to mail pictures to all those who requested them. She would have to find a way. "Nobody is ever going to make me feel dirty and cheap and ugly again," she swore.

To Scott and to Susan, neither of whom was born when Juanita

Dale Slusher was transforming herself into Candy Barr, this whole episode must have seemed like a pilgrimage to a mystical shrine. Scott had forsaken his first passion, mountain climbing, to sit at the feet of Candy Barr and follow orders explicitly. Susan walked around with a glazed expression, saying "far out" and rubbing her fingers over the fading newspaper clippings as though to verify they were real. "I never really knew who Aunt Nita was, just that she was someone famous," Susan Slusher said. "When I was about nine or ten she visited us in Philadelphia. She was so beautiful in her mink coat and high heels and all. She wasn't like an aunt, she was someone I could talk to." Susan had been in Brownwood less than one week when the O. E. Cole mission cleaved the pattern. Now she was wondering if maybe she ought to move to Dallas and look for a job. When you got past the talking, there wasn't a helluva lot to do in Brownwood.

Scott did the driving back to Brownwood, mountain climbing never far from his mind. Candy thought of biscuits and talked on the CB. The only thing those good buddies out there knew about "the Godmother" was that she had a husky, rapid-fire Loretta Lynn voice and a way with the double entendre. Could anyone look as good as that voice sounded? Candy Barr could. She still had it. What to do with it, that was the problem. That had always been the problem.

JUANITA DALE SLUSHER encountered the joy of sex at age five with the aid and comfort of an eighteen-year-old neighbor named Ernest. She remembers that he was gentle, and not at all unpleasant. It wasn't until she encountered the Dallas police force some years later that Juanita Dale associated sex with guilt.

When she was nine her mother died and her father remarried: Doc Slusher, brick mason and handyman, a whiskey-drinking harmonica player and all-around rowdy, already had five kids, and right away there were four more, then two more after that. With all those Slushers around, you'd think the work would get done, but it never seemed to.

"I know in the fourth grade I was a real good student," Candy recalled. "I got to hand out the spelling and Spanish exams." After school it was three or four hours washing bedsheets over a rubboard next to a boiling iron kettle under a chinaberry tree. "When girls ask me about breast development, I say, 'Honey, get yourself a rubboard.'"

At age thirteen and painfully confused, Juanita Dale took her babysitting money and grabbed a bus out of Edna, an independent decision that would become socially acceptable, even laudable, to future generations, but an act worse than rebellion in those days: It was the act of a *bad girl*. For a while she lived with an older sister in Oklahoma City, then a year or so later moved to live with another sister in Dallas. The Dallas sister soon hooked up with a man, and Juanita Dale was on her own.

Many talent scouts have taken credit for discovering Candy Barr: Barney Weinstein, who paid her $15 to act as a shill for his amateur night at the Theater Lounge; his brother Abe, who hired her away to become his headliner at the Colony; Joe DeCarlo, a Los Angeles entrepreneur and pal of Hefner and Sinatra, who got her away from Abe; and Gary Crosby, who once advised Mickey Cohen: "Goddamn, one thing about that broad, she can make ya feel like a *real* man."

To be technically correct, it was the old Liquor Control Board (LCB) that first discovered the girl who would become Candy Barr. They discovered her posing as an eighteen-year-old cocktail waitress—the minimum legal age. She wouldn't be eighteen for another four years, but girls from tough backgrounds develop early, or they don't develop at all. She kept changing jobs, and the LCB kept discovering her. Once they sent her home to Edna, but she caught the next bus back to Dallas.

The only place a teenage runaway could count on steady work in Dallas was at the Trolley Courts, or the other hot-pillow motels located out Harry Hines Boulevard, or along the old Fort Worth Highway. Pimps, thugs, and night clerks traded around young girls as they pleased. Candy's arrangement with the hotel consisted of making beds by day and turning tricks at night. There were buses out of town, but they went nowhere. There were other jobs, but she had already put in her time on the rubboard. An old crook named Shorty Anderson decided she had too much class for the Trolley Courts, so he claimed her as his own and took her to live in his trailer under a bridge where he ran a school for young burglars.

Candy's first husband, Billy Debbs, was a graduate of Shorty's academy. Billy was a good lover but a poor student. He went to the pen, got out, then got shot to death. Somewhere in there—she can't fix the exact time—a pimp spotted her jitterbugging in a joint called the Round-Up Club and launched Candy's movie career. She must have been about fifteen when *Smart Aleck* was filmed. The thousands (perhaps millions) who have seen this American classic will recall that she was a brunette then. *Smart Aleck* was America's first blue movie, the *Deep Throat* of its era, only infinitely more erotic and less pretentious. It was just straight old motel room sex; the audience supplied its own sounds. I remember seeing *Smart Aleck* at the Wolters Air Force Base NCO Club in Mineral Wells about 1955. There had never been anything like it, and for my generation there never will again. All of us had seen stag movies before, threadbare hookers sweathogging with some jerk hung like Groggin's mule, but this was different: This was a beautiful fifteen-year-old sweetheart type and you could just tell she was enjoying it.

Candy claims that she had never seen her movie until she went to Chicago to pose for *Oui*. When I asked how it felt watching herself perform, she said it felt like nothing. "It didn't turn me on," she told me. She could barely remember having performed.

"They may have drugged me, or maybe I blocked it out of my mind," she said. "I suppose they took me to a motel, I don't know where. In Dallas, I guess. I had been forced into screwing so many times I wasn't really aware that this was different. I don't think they even paid me. I've read that that movie made me Candy Barr. That movie made it because I *became* Candy Barr."

One of the fringe benefits of being in films was that Candy got invited to all the best stag parties. Several prominent and wealthy Dallas business and professional men, on my oath that their names would not be revealed, recalled a junior chamber of commerce stag where Candy was the star attraction. One auto dealer told me, "She went for two hundred, three hundred, even five hundred bucks. There was a banker who paid five hundred every time he put a hand on Candy." Bill Gilliland, the manager of the Doubleday Book Store in downtown Dallas, recalled that when he was a student at SMU in the mid-fifties Candy was the sensation of the Phi Delta Theta stag held at the Alford refrigerated warehouse.

"What I remember most about Candy was her enthusiasm," Gilliland said. "Later, when she was stripping at the Colony, I saw her many times. Sometimes my wife went with me. A lot of women were turned on by Candy. Here was one woman willing to flaunt it."

"She made me a lot of money," Abe Weinstein freely admitted. "The biggest draw I ever had at the Colony was Rusty Warren. What a sweetheart. But Candy ran her a close second."

Abe, who lives alone now in a north Dallas townhouse, enjoying the fruits of retirement, actually "discovered" Candy Barr, as opposed to Juanita Dale Slusher. The first time he watched Candy upstage the amateurs at his brother Barney's Theater Lounge, he said to himself, "That's raw talent." The name Candy Barr was Barney's inspiration (she really did eat a lot of candy), but it took Abe's sound business philosophy and promotional acumen to bring Candy uptown where she belonged. The Colony was the Stork Club of Dallas, the Coconut Grove, the butterfly of the Commerce Street neon patch where Jack Ruby ran the sleazy Carousel and conventioneers intermingled with cops and hustlers and drug merchants.

"I didn't make Candy a headliner," Abe told me as we drank coffee in the living room of his townhouse. "She made herself a headliner. Of course those stag parties and that famous movie—it made a flat million over the years—that didn't hurt her image, but Candy was a real pro from the start, one of the best strippers to ever hit the stage. I don't want to say anything about how she was offstage—she'd probably come up here and kill me—but onstage she was number one, the best. She drove 'em crazy, women too. No, I didn't make her a headliner, but I can say this without bragging: I knew how to make the most of what she had to offer."

Abe cited several examples of his promotional genius, including daily newspaper ads ("I called her my Sugar and Spice Girl"), the life-size cardboard cutout of Candy with her cowboy hat and cap pistols outside the Colony, and a deal Abe negotiated whereby Candy got a percentage of the door for playing the Jayne Mansfield role in a local production of *Will Success Spoil Rock Hunter?* She memorized the script in three days, and opened after one rehearsal.

Another example, which Abe failed to mention, was how he seized the moment when Candy shot her ex-husband, Troy Phillips. State Senator Oscar Mauzy, the attorney who represented Candy in that case, filled in the details: "They set the normal bond in the case, about five thousand, as I recall. There wasn't much chance the grand jury would indict: Troy had a bad habit of getting drunk and kicking down her door, and he wasn't hurt very bad anyway. When Abe heard the bond was only five grand, he hit the ceiling. He called his friend [Sheriff] Bill Decker and got it raised to $100,000. Then he paid it and called a press conference. I heard about it and got the hell over to the Colony Club. There was Candy in her costume with the toy pistols and every TV and radio newsman in town. They were just about to start when I grabbed her and got her out of there."

Abe recalled that the Colony did near-record business in the days just after the shooting. When she got popped for marijuana twenty months later (in October 1957), the place was packed every night. And when Candy was released after serving three years and four months of her fifteen-year sentence, it was standing room only. By then Candy was making $750 a week. "I don't know how much money you make," Abe told me, "but I only wish you had half the money she brought in those three weeks." Abe showed me a copy of Candy's poetry, which, I gathered, had been placed on the coffee table for my benefit. It was inscribed: "Nov. 27, 1972. To Abe, dear Abe."

Abe shook his head sadly and said, "I read an article where she said nobody ever visited her in prison and it really irritated me. My late wife, Ginny, God bless her, and I visited her twice a month, which was all that was allowed. Never once missed a visit. Not in the whole time she was down there."

He refilled my coffee cup and asked a question he had been leading up to. He asked me what Candy had to say about Abe Weinstein.

"Nothing very unkind," I said. "I don't think she's bitter. At least she says she isn't."

"Then you've seen her."

"Yes," I said. "It took me twenty years, but I finally saw her." I told Abe that I remembered the first time exactly: It was February 1, 1956, the night after I got out of the Army. Jim Frye and I were walking down Commerce Street toward the Colony Club, toward that life-size cardboard cutout which was so close to the real thing I could smell it. I had dwelled on it many times: a fat cook in our barracks who later got sent up for armed robbery had a smaller version pasted to his locker. In the age of innocence that was the face and the body and the telltale blond hair that seemed to focus all the guilts and fantasies of the fifties. She epitomized the conflict between sex as joy and sex as danger. The body was perfect, but it was the innocence of the face that lured you on. *I know the secret,* it said. *I can enjoy sex without guilt.* But the cap pistols in her hand were a clear warning of danger. Three days earlier Candy had thrown down on poor Troy. It was front-page stuff. Now those cap pistols had a frame of reference: They were directed at me.

"How did you like the act?" Abe asked.

I told him I never saw the act. One block before Jim Frye and I reached the Colony Club two Dallas cops jumped out of their car, wrestled us to the sidewalk, clapped us in handcuffs, and took us to jail. They said we were drunk. We weren't drunk, though that was certainly our intention. Those were the days of the old How Dare You Squad in Dallas: Intent was sufficient cause for arrest and confinement. Candy knew that a lot better than I did, but I bygod knew it, too. All those women's clubs and all those wives of all those fine men who paid $500 to get their hands on Candy Barr were actively applying pressure to the powers that were, most particularly to the Dallas Police Department's special service bureau and its hard-line director, Captain Pat Gannaway, scourge of the drug peddler and sex merchant and guardian of community sensibility. I wanted to ask Abe Weinstein, master of media manipulation, if he had ever considered that maybe he did his job of promoting Candy Barr too well. Had he ever considered that at least 10 percent of that fifteen-year prison sentence rightly belonged to Abe Weinstein?

OLD MEMORIES are masters of deceit. It wasn't that hard growing up on a farm, and John D. Rockefeller didn't ride around Central Park on the backs of orphans. Japs weren't all that evil, Harding wasn't that dumb, and Lindy wasn't that lucky. If we cared about the truth, Alan Ladd had to stand on a soapbox to kiss Maria Montez, and Mickey Rooney couldn't walk under a billy goat's belly. I mention this because now, twenty years later, when they should feel remorse and more than a little guilt, the nabobs and psalm singers of Dallas still remember Candy Barr as an epic force of evil.

As far as I am able to determine, Candy made only one blue movie, *Smart Aleck*. Yet many of the men I spoke with put the number at eight or ten or even fifteen. The prominent auto dealer seemed to recall that her costar in one flick was an Army mule. District Attorney Henry Wade had a recollection that she once went before a camera with a black man, which didn't help her image, especially with the police. An old-time police reporter recalled that "everyone knew she was chipping around with the stuff," meaning drugs. One of her defense attorneys in the marijuana case, Bill Braecklein, now a state senator from Dallas, didn't remember the quantity of grass she was charged with possessing, "but it looked like one hell of a lot in that courtroom."

In fact, the Alka-Seltzer bottle of grass that Candy surrendered to Captain Pat Gannaway and his armada of undercover agents weighed 375 grains, or 24.3 grams. Less than one ounce—a small-time misdemeanor today. We would call it a short lid. If, as Lieutenant Red Souter testified, this was an amount sufficient to roll 125 joints, I would like to invite Red to my next birthday party.

Nobody in the Dallas Police Department wanted to talk about a marijuana case from twenty years ago, and Pat Gannaway, who retired a few years ago to join the Texas Criminal Justice Division, wasn't available for an interview. But I know this: Pat Gannaway spent a lot of man-hours bringing one stripper to justice. The confluence of these two forces—Candy Barr, desecrater of all that is decent, and Pat Gannaway, the terrible swift sword—is surely the quintessence of a morality frozen in time. Captain Pat Gannaway was referred to in newspaper accounts of the time as "Mr. Narcotics." As a lad he had been so eager to join the Dallas Police Department that he lied about his age. For twelve years, until he was kicked upstairs (he was put in charge of rearranging the Property Room) in the 1968 department shake-up, he ran the special services bureau as his private fiefdom. He reported only to the chief. "His passion," reporter James Ewell wrote in the *Dallas Morning News* on the occasion of Gannaway's retirement, "was police work, down on the streets with his men." He loved the Army, too. He served in Army intelligence and was an expert wiretapper. When he wasn't swooping down on the vermin that afflicted his city, Gannaway and his entire force were making speeches to civic clubs, warning of the peril. Those recent thousand-year sentences that made Dallas juries such a novelty may have been the direct result of Pat Gannaway's tireless crusade. Gannaway told James Ewell: "It was always a good feeling to see someone on those juries you recalled being at one of those talks. We always told our audiences if you got rid of an addict or pusher, you were also getting rid of a burglar, a thief, or a robber."

In the autumn of 1957 Gannaway assigned Red Souter (now an assistant chief) and another of his agents, Harvey Totten (now retired), to rent an apartment near Candy Barr's apartment and establish surveillance. A telephone repairman would testify later that he discovered a "jumper tie-up" connecting Candy's telephone to the telephone in the apartment occupied by Souter and Totten, but the jury either ignored this or didn't believe it. A few days after the surveillance began, Candy received a visit from a friend, a stripper named Helen Kay Smith, who laid out a story about her mother coming to visit and asked Candy Barr to hide her stash—the Alka-Seltzer bottle of marijuana. Candy agreed and slipped the bottle inside her bra, next to her big heart. Two hours later, as Candy was talking on the telephone to a gentleman friend (and therefore obviously at home, in case anyone with a search warrant wanted to drop in), there was a knock at the door. Candy's defense attorneys claimed the search warrant was a blank that Gannaway filled in after the arrest, but the court didn't buy that either.

Candy's gentleman friend, who asked to not be identified, told me what happened next:

"Candy said hold on, someone is knocking at the door. I heard some noises and someone hung up the phone. All I could think of was she's in some kind of trouble. I got over to her place. When I walked in I saw Gannaway, Totten, Red Souter, Jack Revill, and I think one other narcotics officer. Gannaway picked up a chair and said something like, 'Well, well, that looks like a joint on the floor.' I swear to you, it was the first marijuana cigarette I ever saw. That's when Candy, God bless her, said to Gannaway, 'He's just a square john kid. He doesn't know anything about this. If you let him go, I'll give you what you came for.' She reached in and pulled out the bottle. Gannaway decided he would take me in anyway, and that's when Jack Revill said, 'Captain, if you do that, I'm turning in my badge.' So they took her away."

Candy's four-day trial the following February was a farce, which didn't prevent it from also being a sensation. In its year-end review the *Dallas Morning News* headline read: "Candy's Trial Led '58 Scene." Judge Joe B. Brown, who would later make his mark as the buffoon judge in the Jack Ruby trial, borrowed a camera and during one of the recesses snapped pictures of "the shapely defendant." Defense attorneys Bill Braecklein and Lester May realized from the beginning that their problem was much larger than a bottle of marijuana, although, as May explained, "In those days marijuana was worse than cancer."

"It was a time when the pendulum had swung far to the right," May told me. "If the police decided you were guilty of something, they made a case and you were found guilty. It was just that simple. Candy's real crime was she wouldn't cooperate with the vice squad."

No, the real problem wasn't the marijuana, it was Candy Barr herself. It wasn't merely her reputation—though God knows that was strong enough to kill a rogue elephant; it was that combative stubbornness, that unwillingness to throw herself at the feet of the jury and beg forgiveness. Chief prosecutor James Allen offered her two years for a guilty plea, and if Les May hadn't got her out of the room she would have spit in his eye, or worse.

They decided not to put her on the stand; without her testimony, of course, it would be almost impossible to challenge state witnesses: She was in possession of marijuana, regardless of Helen Kay Smith's testimony. That mysterious cigarette on the floor, though, was something else entirely. The attorneys worked out a way to let Candy make a statement to the jury without actually testifying, which meant that she could not be cross-examined. No one remembers Candy's exact words, but it must have been a stirring oration. When she had finished, the jury just retired and voted her fifteen years in the Big Rodeo. It was Valentine's Day 1958.

"She was a very naive young lady," Braecklein recalled. "While we were waiting to come to trial, she was out in Las Vegas, doing her act. Just one *week* before we came to trial, I got word that she was going to be a bridesmaid in Sammy Davis Jr.'s wedding [to a white actress]. Anyone who grew up in Texas knew you couldn't do that right before a trial."

In retrospect, observers on both sides acknowledged that the strategy to pick an all-male jury backfired. In his book *The Super Americans,* John Bainbridge quotes "a native of Dallas who is possessed of a philosophical cast of mind and a family pedigree going back to Sam Houston" with a theory that, in one form or another, I heard many times: ". . . those eleven men [there was one woman], they got a chance to go home that night and say to their wives: 'Well, Maude, you can brag on me for what I did today. We put that shameless creature away for a good long spell.'"

Although they didn't anticipate anything approaching fifteen years, the defense team had braced itself for a verdict of guilty. They had already drafted a list of reversible errors that would have choked the Star Chamber. The real shock came when they lost a 2–1 decision in the State Court of Criminal Appeals. In the eleven months that separated the trial from the appeals verdict, Candy had reinforced her public image by moving in with hoodlum Mickey Cohen. One assumes justice is blind, but just how blind is an open question.

In a hotly worded fourteen-page dissent, Judge Lloyd Davidson wrote: "If that is equal justice under law, I want no part of it. If a conviction obtained under such circumstances is due process of law, then there is no due process of law."

District Attorney Henry Wade, who took no part in the most sensational trial of 1958, beamed serenely when I asked him twenty years later if it was possible Candy Barr had been railroaded into prison. "Far as I know," he said, "that wasn't the case." One of the jurors told Wade some time later that the reason Candy's fellow citizens slapped her with so much time was something she said. She called chief prosecutor James Allen "a liar." "That's when her true colors came out," the juror told the district attorney.

"At that period in time," Wade told me, "it wasn't unusual to get life for one cigarette. I recall we had a letter from the governor's office, inquiring into the severity of her sentence. The governor asked us to check our records and find out what was the average sentence for a marijuana conviction. So we did. It turned out the average sentence at that time was eighteen years. So she received less than the average sentence."

Referring to my notes, I told the district attorney that in 1960 shortly after the final appeal had been exhausted and Candy had gone inside, a survey conducted by the *Dallas Times Herald* revealed that nine defendants recently convicted of the same crime had received much shorter sentences for substantially larger quantities of killer weed.

"I think that if you'll check that again," Henry Wade smiled benignly, "you'll find that all nine of those defendants were women."

I checked again. Damned if Henry wasn't right.

I SPENT THREE WEEKS trying to arrange an interview with Candy Barr, and although I was now calling from a telephone booth beside a Brownwood liquor store less than seven miles from her lake cottage, I had the recurring feeling I wasn't even close. She told me to call back later. I had already called back five times. She told me that her mind was too scattered to talk right now, the house was a mess, she hadn't been able to locate the scrapbooks she had promised to show me, she was still worried about O. E. Cole, she hadn't even had time to shower and wash her hair.

"Why don't you look over the town," she said, not very convincingly. "Call me back after a while."

I had already experienced the pleasure of touring Brownwood. It's a pleasant, folksy little town where men wear business suits and women dress up to shop at the Safeway and motorists park in the middle of an intersection to exchange gossip with pedestrians. Big church town. Trees. Home of Howard Payne College, the Douglas MacArthur Academy, and the onetime golden boy of Texas politics, Ben Barnes, as well as small industries untroubled by labor problems, some ranches, a pecan research station, a model reform school, and a farm where little pigs—potty trained and dressed in plastic boots—never touch the ground from conception to skillet. In the summer, people play softball all night long. The remainder of the year they talk about their high school football team, which is usually one of the best in the state. Hardly a coffee break passes that someone doesn't remember 1940 when a wee halfback named Chili Rice personally defeated archrival Breckenridge for only the second time in 36 years. Every Friday during football season, the town shuts down.

The people were friendly and proud to be right there. They all knew Candy Barr of course; but, of course, they didn't *know* her. There is a custom among the businessmen of Brownwood that the first thing you say on meeting a stranger inquiring about Candy Barr is: "For Godsake, don't use *my* name." "My wife would leave me if she knew I'd even spoken to her," one businessman told me. "Not that I've ever fooled around. But just try telling that to my wife." Another man told me, "If you want to know about Candy, ask my son." It was the young men who knew her best, and if they refused to talk about her it was not peer pressure but respect for her privacy. "She's been through enough," a college-aged man said. "She just wants to be left alone."

"People here know how to forgive and forget," Sheriff Danny Neal said. "Not just Candy . . . anyone who paid a price and is back on the street. Nobody here gives her a hard time."

"She comes in here and shops just like anybody else," a druggist said. "No, I can't think of anything special about her. She buys a lot of cosmetics that I wouldn't ordinarily stock, that's about all."

Though Candy lives her private life in her lake cottage with no visible means of support, she arouses little curiosity. The menfolk assume she is supported, at least partially, by a certain Brownwood banker, or by a former member of the Texas Board of Pardons and Paroles who at one time "kept her." The women just naturally assume she is a hundred-dollar-a-night hooker. Candy has learned to live with the whispers. "That's a hundred dollars an *hour*, man," she jokes among friends. Recently, Candy made an unexpected appearance at a fundamentalist church, where she gave a brief testimonial to Jesus as a "superstar." Nobody was shocked.

But, why Brownwood? She had tried Dallas, L.A., Vegas, New Orleans, Mexico City, Huntsville. She had seen their bedrooms, their bars, their jails. When Candy returned to Edna after her parole in April 1963, overweight and overwrought and badly jolted by the experience, she met a woman named Gloria Carver and they became fast friends. When Gloria moved to Brownwood a few years later, Candy followed. "I felt safe here," she had told me in one of our telephone conversations.

That feeling of security didn't last too long. In 1969, she made headlines again when a Brownwood cop acting without a search warrant found a handful of seeds and stems in a shoebox in her apartment. Candy was out of town at the time. The case was dismissed, to the great relief, I gathered, of almost everyone. Brownwood wasn't *that* kind of town.

Certainly those were difficult times: Sewing men's trousers in a prison workshop and appearing once a year at the rodeo hadn't exactly prepared her for a new career. Old friends like Mickey Cohen and Sammy Davis Jr. had their own problems now. Under the conditions of her parole she couldn't even set foot in a place that sold alcoholic beverages. "What was I supposed to do, work in a root beer stand?" she had said. "They were pushing me into a corner all over again. It was either get on my back or do something silly." The one old friend who did help was Jack Ruby. Jack gave her $50, an air conditioner, and two breed dogs "so you won't have to go out and sell yourself."

After Abe Weinstein pulled a few strings in Austin, Candy made a brief comeback at the Colony, then she just sort of wandered off. There had been a lot of talk about movie and recording offers in the weeks following her parole, but all of it came to nothing. Abe, who was still technically her manager and agent, tried to hustle her prison poetry—scrawled, overlabored cries on sheets of paper decorated like some fifth-grade art project with glossy photographs clipped from *Vogue* and *Ladies' Home Journal*. Abe even spread the word that the poetry was "in the hands of Doubleday right this minute." To Abe's way of thinking, this was true. He had stashed the pages with his friend Bill Gilliland at the Doubleday Book Store in downtown Dallas.

After Candy had saved and borrowed enough to publish her poems, she would make brief, unannounced appearances at events such as the chili cook-off in Terlingua, trying her best to promote the book. Even then, she played the star. She would wait for a crowd to gather, then she would pop from a trailer, looking sexy and posing for pictures with the book in her hand. Some people bought out of curiosity, but most of them just gawked and waited for something else to happen. Nothing did.

She made many tentative agreements with writers and editors

to do her life story. "She must have sold ten percent of herself about two hundred times," writer Larry King says. Then, unexpectedly, in October 1975 *Oui* offered her $5,000 to pose and be interviewed. The idea originated with writer Gay Talese, who suggested to a friend at the magazine, "Instead of those teenybopper dipsos, how about some pictures of a mature woman?"

Talese's motive was not altruistic. A year earlier he had visited Candy in Brownwood, hoping to do research on his own long-awaited book on sex, society, and the law. The interview had been a disaster. Candy refused to talk into a tape recorder, and when Talese asked specific questions about Jack Ruby, Mickey Cohen, Joe DeCarlo, prison, and Dallas in the fifties, she wouldn't talk at all. Instead, she wanted to talk about her memoirs, which she assumed Talese wanted to write. Talese tried to explain that he had enough problems with his own book, which he had been working on for several years. After a day and a half of wrangling and getting nowhere, Candy did one of her dramatic flip-flops. She stripped naked and positioned herself on the floor, as she had so many other times when there didn't seem to be another choice. What happened next depends on which party you care to believe, but shortly afterwards Talese grabbed the first plane out of town.

The purpose of the *Oui* offer then was a second chance for Talese. Unfortunately, it developed pretty much as it had a year earlier. Candy still refused to answer questions. The interview, such as it was, was finally accomplished by flying Candy and her companion Gloria Carver to the Chicago offices of the magazine. Talese told me that he accepted no fee, other than expenses, for his troubles. He wished Candy well and hoped that the $5,000 and publicity helped.

"Good luck with your own story," he said.

WHEN I TELEPHONED for what I already knew was going to be the final time, Candy invited me to come for supper and spend the night.

I thought of Commerce Street and my old Army buddy Jim Frye as I stood in front of her small, white clapboard cottage, shielded from prying eyes by an unpainted plywood fence and a yard of junk. She called her cottage Fort Dulce, dulce meaning sweet. Like Candy. The license plate on the Cadillac was Dulce 1. Dulce Press, Inc., was the publisher of her poetry. On the shelves that separated the living room from the kitchen there were many jars of candy—candy kisses, lemon drops, jelly beans, peppermints, candy corn. Twenty years of waiting and I felt like a character out of a fairy tale.

Susan, three dogs, and four cats met me at the front door. She said Candy was still dressing. Two hours later, Candy was still dressing. When she finally made her appearance, shortly before 10 P.M., she hit the room like one of Sgt. Snorkel's ping-pong smashes. Her blond hair was in curlers. She had scrubbed her face until it was blank and bleached as driftwood. Her green eyes collapsed like seedless grapes too long on the shelf. She wore a poor-white-trash housedress that ended just below the crotch, and no panties.

"Don't think I dressed up just for you," she told me.

The next twelve hours were like being trapped on the set of a Fellini movie, without Fellini. On one level Candy was doing her best to cook supper, and on another I was trying to interview her. The stereo blasted top volume with rock and Jerry Jeff and the kind of blues you heard in the black hovels of Dallas in the fifties; dogs and cats prowled underfoot; a pet spider named Brutus spun a web above a portrait of Jesus saving New York City. I was confused because I couldn't hear what she was saying, and she was angry because I wasn't listening. I asked questions about her life as a teenager on the streets of Dallas, and she rambled about Jesus, Daddy, and Lord Buckley, three of the men she found worth remembering. She accused me of having a secret tape recorder, and when I told her I hated tape recorders, she scolded me for using the word "hate" in her presence.

She smoked Virginia Slims and made bad puns about "coming a long way," and sometimes she broke out with a few lines from a song that happened to cross her mind. Susan watched the TV set with the sound turned off, and every ten or fifteen seconds walked to the front door to let the dogs and cats in or out. Scott attempted to make himself obscure.

"My God, what have you done!" she shrieked, lifting a dripping black iron skillet from the sink where Susan had put it to soak. "Don't ever, *ever* put that skillet in dishwater. And I told you to sharpen this knife. Look at it!" Candy whacked the knife blade into a tomato, disfiguring the inoffensive fruit. Susan said she would try to do better.

"Before my mother died," Candy said as she dipped pieces of chicken in flour, "she instilled in me a lot of wonderful things like tolerance and patience. After she died, I talked to Jesus a lot. I wanted to be a missionary."

"Then tell me about that," I said.

"I walk around talking to the Chief a lot," she went on. "I tell Him: you're a groovy cat. He was far ahead of His time. I argue with Him. I ask a lot of damn questions and get some answers. Sometimes I don't agree. Sometimes He seems too severe. Hey! Give me some slack! Daddy never gave me pain seven days and seven nights. But nobody is gonna make me change what I feel about Him. Not even Him."

She started to tell me about "an incident that scared me for years, something that happened a year or two after Mama died," then she got interested in mashing potatoes and refused to think about it. Instead, she talked about what a luxury it was to visit her grandmother, the big feather bed, the indoor plumbing, the jars of candy, being able to go to church, and the unexcelled biscuits her grandmother made. Those biscuits will never be duplicated, Candy said, taking a can of store-bought biscuits from the refrigerator and cracking it against the corner of the table.

She looked straight at me and her green eyes swam. "This is very, very hard for me . . . talking to you," she said in a little girl's voice. I could see that it was. Candy's necessary illusion was control. No matter how chaotic or predoomed the situation, Candy required the illusion that she was in control. No matter how counterproductive it appeared, when Candy detected the irresistible forces of logic and authority, she became the immovable object. When Pat Gannaway put the heat on, *she* threatened to sue *him*. She remembered that when she was a child, "I kept my eyes closed so nobody could see me."

"Let's go in here for a while," she said, leading me to the bedroom with the pink wallpaper and the elaborate dressing table. It was the bedroom of a star, though one fallen on hard times. The floor was carpeted and old publicity photographs collected dust on the wall by the screened porch. The bed was extra large, and so was the bathtub. Carefully crossing her legs, Candy seated herself in front of the dresser mirror, so that the face I saw was her reflection. She raked the clutter of tubes and jars and cosmetic brushes aside.

I offered her one of my cigarettes and asked about Mickey Cohen. Cohen had personally guaranteed her $15,000 bond while the marijuana appeal ran its course. In a cruel way, those were the peak years for Candy Barr. She lived in a villa in the notorious Garden of Allah on Sunset Boulevard in L.A. and earned up to $2,000 a week stripping there and in Vegas. Simultaneously, a pack of lawmen and profiteers howled like hungry dogs in her shadow—FBI agents, CIA agents, Treasury agents, IRS agents, L.A. cops, Vegas cops, Dallas cops. The pressure was so enormous that the El Rancho Vegas had her replaced with Nelson Eddy. She was also in and out of the hospital with hepatitis. Candy recalled that the first time she ever *heard* of Mickey Cohen was when he sent an orchid in a champagne glass to her hospital room in L.A., along with this note: "Don't worry, little girl, you got a friend."

I had heard from good sources that the reason that Cohen got rid of Candy was she was giving him a bad press. The vast majority of those agents were interested in Mickey Cohen, not his girlfriend. Word came down from "the Eastern organization" that if Cohen didn't drop Candy, they would. Somewhere between Catalina Island and Hawaii.

"When I finally went to prison," she said, and I realized now, watching her face in the mirror, this was the only way she could answer the question, "it was with a great sense of relief. Otherwise, I would have been dead or laying on some gangster's couch. Of course I didn't know what prison was. I guess I thought it was a private club. I ordered all these new clothes from a place in Florida—ten dresses, twenty bras, cosmetics—hell, I was gonna be there a long time. The only thing I didn't think to take with me was the only thing I needed—money. Everything else they took away."

She reached for another cigarette and said, "I started to tell you a story earlier. About something that scared me for years. It was one night when I was babysitting, I was dead tired from washing bedsheets all afternoon and trying to study and the baby was crying. I walked over and put my hand on the baby's nose. That's all there was to it, a moment of darkness, but just for a moment I knew I was capable of killing. I thought about that many times in prison. Women who had killed or harmed children were horribly ostracized in prison. I could understand why they struck out at me, but those poor women—didn't they understand how those women hurt inside? Couldn't they tell by the depth of their tears? Didn't they understand that brief moment of darkness?"

Scott attempted to slip through the bedroom carrying an armload of clothes from the dryer, but Candy froze him with her eyes. She stood him in the corner by the blasting stereo and barked five or six terse, no-nonsense commands: Bring in some fresh drinking water, go into town and pick up the mail, check the tires on the car. "Now repeat all that back to me," she demanded, holding him with her eyes. Scott repeated it all, a trait, I gathered, that was recently acquired.

"Goddamn," Candy snapped at me, "I'm supposed to be in there cooking supper. See what you're doing to me!"

I mixed a drink from a bottle of Scotch I had brought for just such emergencies (Candy doesn't drink) and studied the modest collection of books on her living room shelf. There was *The Complete Works of Emily Dickinson, Dream Dictionary,* a book of *Living Magic,* a book called *Oddities: A Book of Unexplained Facts,* and another called *Enigmas: Another Book of Unexplained Facts.* There were random copies of *Reader's Digest* and *Ladies' Home Journal.*

A collection of men's hats hung like trophies from antlers. A rack containing seven or eight briar pipes sat solemnly beside a large can of Prince Albert.

It was after 4 A.M. when we sat down to a meal of fried chicken, potato salad, corn, red beans, sliced tomatoes, canned biscuits, and iced tea. Candy's spirits improved with each mouthful. She winked and asked was everything OK. Clyde McCoy blew his bluesy harmonica on the stereo and Candy began a monologue recalling her daddy, old Doc Slusher—how the deputy back in Edna used to ride into the yard on a white horse to question Doc about some groceries that had disappeared from the local market; how when they came to repossess his car Doc sloshed a ring of gasoline around it, struck a kitchen match on the seat of his pants, and invited them to come ahead.

"Ride the rhyme, that's what Lord Buckley taught me," she said. "I learned to dance when I was two . . . on my daddy's knee. Daddy played the French harp. He was a blues man. Saturday was his blues day. He'd set a bottle of whiskey on the table for anybody that came around and he'd play the blues on that harp."

She went on about how she picked cotton and made soap and bacon for the family, the big black wash pots in the yard, hunting with the hounds, the taste of possum, which she couldn't stand, and fried armadillo, which was still a favorite.

Candy showed me her fan mail and some old publicity pictures. Maybe it wasn't much of a legacy, but it was a start. There were those who remembered her well, many more than you would ever think. "I know my kids have been hurt by what's been written about me," she said. "I'm not saying it's totally incorrect, it's the way they say it." Sure she'd done a little dope, and turned some tricks. She'd never stolen or hurt anyone, except when it was necessary. "I've rebelled," she said, "and I've learned that in rebellion you can become what you're rebelling against." Even now there were moments when she wasn't all that certain she had it together. Not too long ago a sheriff from Bell County had called and said he'd heard Candy was working his area. "I just cried," she told me. "Then I got it together and told him, 'If and when I do, you'll know it all right. I'll be there in my Cadillac blowing your doors off.'

"I almost let them make me feel ugly," Candy said, studying the twenty-year-old photo of the young girl with the toy pistols. "I look at these old pictures, and what I see is people grabbing my ass. From five years old on. I had my heart broke many times. I didn't even know why people were snotty to me. I was making a living. But it was like they had a bleeper on my ass. I was making $85 a week as a cigarette girl at the Theater Lounge, and all I could think of was, I had a car, a place of my own, and now nobody could throw me back in a motel with a night porter.

"But they wouldn't let up. Do you know what it's like working onstage with a couple of harness bulls sitting two feet away? Why did *I* have to take them to the backseat? Why did I have to call them *sir* when they were watching me take my clothes off? They were on my level then."

It was nearly dawn when Candy made a bed for me on the living room sofa. She covered me with an imitation bearskin rug and tucked it in. An early autumn cold front had passed through West Texas: The thin walls of Fort Dulce rattled, and I lay there in the changing shafts of light thinking not of the woman whose essence filled the room but of a life-size cardboard cutout of Candy Barr. I knew what Jim Frye would ask. He would ask: *Did you get any?*

It was all a fantasy. Twenty years ago Candy Barr was forbidden fruit, a symbol for the agony of our tightly corked libidos, a martyr to repressed yearnings for violence and identity, a solitary being bending into the prevailing winds of injustice and insensitivity. When you got right down to it, Candy Barr did not apply to be our symbol. Like Patty Hearst, she just got carried away.

AFTER A FEW hours' sleep we all felt better. The sudden cold snap had turned the lake bronze as the warmer bottom water floated to the surface. I walked down by the lake and watched Scott dig the cottage intake pipe from the mud and blow it clean so there would be clear water for Candy's morning shower. After her shower, Candy seated herself at the dressing table and, like one of those time-lapse Disney films where a desert flower appears to blossom before your eyes, performed the ancient miracle of her sex. The blond hair brushed out soft and glossy. Mascara arches defined the eyes, which sparkled now like polished turquoise. That cave-dweller's pallor that had appeared so unflattering in the harsh light of the kitchen took on tones of finely dusted nutmeg. In her tight hip-hugger jeans and red halter she looked like a young girl ready for a hayride.

Momentarily, she reappeared as Candy Barr, a lost vision of great beauty, warmth, and charm.

She popped open a can of biscuits and asked me to sit beside her.

"Now we can talk," she said. "What do you want to know?"

"I want to know how you feel," I said.

"I feel like . . . like I'm not vulnerable anymore," she told me.

*December 1976*

# THE EDUCATION OF LAURA BUSH

*She has learned what is expected of her, and she'll do what she has to do.*

PAUL BURKA

This story was the first magazine profile of Laura Bush to be published after she became first lady in January 2001. When I interviewed her in the Map Room of the East Wing of the White House, barely five weeks after the inauguration, she seemed very different from the Laura Bush I had known back in Texas who was completely comfortable with her nonpolitical role as first lady of Texas. The day before, I had seen her visit an elementary school in Maryland, where she had plugged her husband's education policies. In the interview, I found her to be wistful about the days when she was not in the public eye and, when she talked about her twin daughters, who were off at college, a bit sad. I left the White House thinking that the essence of the story wasn't "Laura Bush, First Lady," but "Laura Bush, Empty Nester." I did not foresee that terrorism and war and the criticism of her husband would transform her into a more enthusiastic and effective campaigner than I could have imagined.

I MET LAURA BUSH for the first time in early May 1995. An interview I had scheduled with the governor had to be changed from afternoon to evening and from the Capitol to the Governor's Mansion. I was invited to a casual dinner, along with my wife. Mrs. Bush would be there. The interview was a lost cause, but the evening wasn't. Most of the conversation is lost to memory, other than that it consisted mainly of nonpolitical small talk and the governor's reports of phone calls from aides updating him on the progress of House floor action on his education bill, but at one point the antics of a prominent Texan popped up in the discussion—sorry, no names. I observed that he had once accused the Republicans of a nefarious plot to embarrass his family.

Suddenly Mrs. Bush leaned forward in her chair. "Not the Republicans," she said. "Us! The Bushes!" It wasn't just her words that made the moment embed itself in my memory, but the force with which she delivered them and her body language, which conveyed solidarity with her husband across the room. That brief exchange provided a rare glimpse into the private world of the Bush clan; its power and intensity, its unity and sense of loyalty, flashed before our eyes.

Soon afterward, she excused herself to put her twin daughters to bed. She returned later to say good night, having changed into pants, and she was barefoot. You may not find this reportorial detail particularly newsworthy, but in the home in which I grew up, to come downstairs with feet unclad was an action that would draw my mother's worst epithet: "Tobacco Road," the title of a thirties novel about the unimaginably low-class life of sharecroppers in the Deep South. My wife and I exchanged approving glances: The first lady of Texas was a woman who, literally and figuratively, was comfortable in her own skin.

Now, six years later, Laura Bush is the first lady of the United States, one of the most visible and important women in the world. Yet the two sides of her that I first saw in 1995 still define the person she is today. You could call one side Laura and the other side Bush. Laura remains a woman who is down to earth, without affectation or pretension—someone who, as she once said, would be just as happy puttering around in her garden as being first lady. Her reluctant attitude toward public appearances hasn't changed much since the time, early in their marriage, when he was running what would be an unsuccessful race for Congress in West Texas, and he asked Laura to make an appearance for him. "My husband told me I'd never have to make a political speech," she told a group of supporters in Levelland. "So much for political promises." But the other side of her is that she is totally a Bush. Not all of her education has come from reading the succession of books that the former teacher and librarian keeps stacked on her bedside table and on the floor beneath it. Being a member of the clan has also been a central part of the education of Laura Bush: She has learned what is expected of her, and she will do what she has to do.

The job of first lady has not always been what it is today. Indeed, before the Civil War, when presidential spouses served mainly as hostesses, the title did not exist; a British correspondent, ever mindful of royalty, was the first to apply it, in reference to Mary Todd Lincoln. (This distinction has not saved Mrs. Lincoln from historical opprobrium. Her eccentricity, her free spending on the White House in a time of war, and her family's divided loyalty—several of her brothers fought for the Confederacy, leading to baseless rumors that she was a traitor—relegated her to the bottom spot in the Siena Research Institute's 1982 and 1993 rankings of first ladies, based on a survey of historians at 102 universities.) With the rise of mass-circulation newspapers and magazines, the first lady became a public figure. Some were fashion trendsetters; others took political stands, most notably Eleanor (Mrs. Franklin) Roosevelt, the nation's foremost civil rights activist and the leader in the Siena Institute surveys. In recent administrations, it has become customary for first ladies to promote a worthy cause, from beautification (Lady Bird Johnson) to literacy (Barbara Bush).

Laura Bush's cause is reading, particularly early childhood reading. It brought her to Cesar Chavez Elementary School in Hyattsville, Maryland, on a mild morning in late February. Motivational signs occupied the cream-colored cinder-block walls of the small auditorium where she was to speak: "Today is a great day to LEARN something new"; "Turn the pages of your imagination—READ"; and on the podium, the name of the program Mrs. Bush would unveil that day, "Ready to Read. Ready to Learn." Her appearance was scheduled for ten-thirty in the morning, but the room was filled to capacity more than an hour earlier. Despite the new Hispanic name of the fifties-era school, which reflected an ongoing demographic change in the surrounding neighborhood, the audience included a large number of African Americans—educators and dignitaries, along with some parents, from Prince George's County, the largest and most affluent African American suburban community in the country. The women sported business suits and stylishly coiffed hair. Prince George's is overwhelmingly Democratic country, but this event was, for this audience, more social than political.

The first lady arrived precisely on time, as is the Bushes' way. ("Mr. and Mrs. Prompt" was her description to me in our 1999 interview.) She wore a light blue suit, shaded a bit toward lilac, and minimal jewelry: a wedding ring and earrings all but hidden by her hair, which had hints of red under the bright lights set up for the television cameras. Her speech was serious and self-effacing; the text was laced with references like "President Bush and I support . . . ," "President Bush has a plan . . . ," "I am proud to be a part of President Bush's effort . . . ," all designed to underscore that the reading initiative was not hers alone but also her husband's. Otherwise the speech was nonpolitical: no jokes, no made-for-TV sound bites, no rhetorical flourishes, no applause lines (although the audience did clap once, when she said, "Television is no substitute for a parent"). This was a speech for educators; she spoke of recruiting more teachers, of spotlighting early childhood programs, and of encouraging parents to read to their children. Her demeanor was earnest, but her emotions—and her motions—were reserved, which is how she always is in public. As she read the speech, she clenched the sides of the lectern with her hands, letting go only twice to make a slight gesture of turning her left palm upward. She could have been at a lyceum, presenting her annual research paper to her fellow members.

After the speech, the first lady went off to read to a group of kindergarten students while I waited in a hallway to talk to the principal. Among the many posters on the wall was one titled "If We Met President George Bush," and underneath were three questions that students wanted to ask. "Do you work on projects?" "Do you help people?" "Do you fly airplanes?" Later I would ask the principal how the reading went. "Oh, she connected with those kids right away" came the answer. "I could tell she had been a teacher, because she had them sit around her, and she read upside down." I didn't get it. The principal explained, "So they could see the pictures." Then she picked up a Styrofoam coffee cup from the table beside her and held it aloft, like a trophy. "Look!" she squealed with excitement. "Mrs. Bush drank from this cup!"

The position that Laura Bush occupies is at once great and small, a truth recognized by a 1989 cartoon in the *New Yorker* labeled "Ms. Rushmore." The faces of Martha Washington, Martha Jefferson, Edith (Mrs. Theodore) Roosevelt, and Mary Lincoln appeared in place of their presidential husbands. The genius of the cartoon is its ambiguity: Is it making the straightforward point that first ladies are just as deserving of a memorial as their husbands or the ironic point that they are not? The ultimate arbiter, history, has not been kind to first ladies. Presidents are remembered; their wives are not. Who recalls today that Dolley Madison was the first American woman to influence fashion and manners? Who knows that Edith Roosevelt oversaw the construction of the West Wing, providing the title for a popular television show? Who reflects upon whether the Civil War might have been avoided if that most obscure of presidents, Millard Fillmore, had heeded wife Abigail's advice not to sign the Fugitive Slave Bill into law? Few first ladies have continued to generate public fascination beyond their tenures in the White House. Before Hillary Clinton, Jacqueline Kennedy was the most obvious exception, though the obsession was largely with her celebrity status, first as the widow of an assassinated president, then as the wife of one of the world's richest men. Her substantial achievements in historical preservation and the advancement of the arts have receded in public memory, leaving only her restoration of the White House, which is usually misdescribed today as "redecorating."

If the fame and achievements of first ladies are fleeting, their role in their husbands' lives before reaching the White House tends to be relegated to history's dustbin. In the case of Laura and George W. Bush, that will be a big omission. For no matter what she accomplishes as first lady, she will be hard-pressed to have as much influence over his life and career as she has already had. Without her, he would not be where he is.

The beginning of the story is well known. They grew up in Midland, he the son of an oilman, she the daughter of a developer; they were the same age and went to the same school but did not know each other. Their paths diverged in junior high, when the Bushes moved to Houston. She went to Southern Methodist University; he went to Yale. Their paths converged but did not cross when they lived in the same apartment complex in Houston. He moved to Midland to try his hand at the oil business. She moved to Austin to get a master's degree in library science and stayed on to teach, but she went home frequently to Midland. They were both in their early thirties and single, and their mutual friends Jan and Joe O'Neill wanted her to meet him. In an interview in 1999, portions of which were used in a *Time* magazine article, Laura Bush recalled her initial reaction: "Oh, gosh, somebody who is probably political, and I wouldn't be interested." Finally, in 1977, she agreed to dinner at the O'Neills'. What happened next must have resembled the romance of Professor Harold Hill and Marian, the Librarian, in *The Music Man:* fast-talking, wisecracking, lovable scamp meets unassuming, firmly grounded woman who values the life of the mind. They were married in three months.

The turning point of their lives came in 1986, their ninth year of marriage. He had gone back to the oil business, but the bust had hit Midland hard. His oil company wasn't successful, and he was drinking too much. The oft-printed story is that he came to breakfast on his fortieth birthday and announced that he had decided to quit drinking. Later he would say that she had laid down the edict: her or the bottle. In the transcript of her *Time* interview, she disputes that version. It happened around three weeks after his fortieth birthday, she said. They had gone to the Broadmoor in Colorado Springs as part of a group celebrating the birthday of Donnie Evans, now the secretary of commerce. "I'd been talking for a while about him quitting drinking," she said. "I don't remember any announcement. I actually remember it more at home than at the Broadmoor. We joked later about it, saying he got the bar bill and that's why he quit. There were a lot of jokes that I said it was either me or Jack Daniel's. I didn't really say that. I think George said that. He made it into the funny story."

But she had been the catalyst. He did not stop drinking to become president, of course, but he would not have become president, or even governor, had she not gotten him to stop drinking. "He was very disciplined in a lot of ways except for drinking," she said in the interview, "and I think when he was able to stop drinking, that gave him a lot of confidence and made him feel better about himself."

The second time that Laura Bush would play a central role in making it possible for her husband to win the presidency came last year, at a critical moment in the race against Al Gore. In the weeks following the Democratic convention—a period known in the Bush camp as "rats, moles, and bad polls," referring to various items of bad news for the home team—Gore had all the momentum on his side. Worse, the Republican nominee wasn't performing well. Behind the scenes, he was trying to keep everyone else's spirits up, but in public he looked wooden. Husband and wife were campaigning separately at the time, and the consensus in the Bush campaign was that she needed to travel with him. She knew it too. "She has a really good sense of how he is doing," says Mark McKinnon, who handled the media advertising for the campaign and frequently traveled on the Bush airplane. "She's the first one to hear the creaks in the submarine when it goes too low."

Once she was next to her husband on the airplane, McKinnon could see the difference. "She brought calm and serenity to his bearing," he says. "He was happier, more at ease, less distracted. Even on the airplane, he was more likely to relax. If she wasn't there, he'd bounce around the plane." With her present, he engaged in his favorite sport, which is joking around with her. Another staffer remembers Bush flying back from a trip to West Texas where all the food at the event was fried. "Ohhh," he said to her, "I had too much chicken-fried. I'm going to have to . . ."—well, for the sake of politeness, let's say "burp." "Oh, no you're not," she said. "Oh, yes I am," he rejoined, a big grin on his face. On the campaign plane, he liked to tease her when she was reading, testing the limits of her patience. "Hey, Bushie"—their pet name for each other—he would say. "What do you think about [such and such]?" She'd answer and go back to reading. Then he would start over again. "Hey, Bushie."

The decision to bring Laura aboard the campaign plane marked the beginning of Bush's comeback. Her role went beyond moral support; she saw most of the TV spots before they aired and wanted the end-of-the-race ads that had been filmed at their Central Texas ranch redone because of poor lighting. "She doesn't say anything unless she feels strongly about it," McKinnon says, "and she was right." But mainly, he says, "She's his safety net for life." Some first ladies have hungered for the power and prestige that come with the position. Laura Bush is not one of them and neither was Martha Washington, the first first lady. As America prepared to choose its first president, Mrs. Washington wanted nothing more than to have her husband to herself for a change, but it was not to be. Nor was she to have her own life as she wished it. The president insisted that they entertain formally—dinner parties for government officials and various foreign plenipotentiaries on Thursdays, a drawing room reception with her as hostess on Fridays. But, he decreed, they would not attend private gatherings at the homes of their friends, as she wished to do. "I am more like a state prisoner than anything else, there [are] certain bounds set for me which I must not depart from," she once wrote. Now it is Laura Bush who is in the gilded cage, having left behind in Austin a life that could not have been more to her liking. A year ago her children were at home, some of her oldest and closest women friends from her hometown of Midland had set down roots in Austin, and her husband had a job that did not place great demands on his time. She belonged to a book club, which was really more about friendship than books, and a garden club, both of which included old and new friends. She could stroll out the front door of the Governor's Mansion and down Colorado Street for a walk along the lakefront. On most Sunday nights she and George W. ate dinner at Manuel's on Congress Avenue; on pleasant spring afternoons they could even slip away to watch a ball game at Austin High, where their daughters went to school.

Her pet project was the Texas Book Festival, an idea that had been moribund until she came along and helped found it. The festival became an annual showcase for Texas authors, most of whose works she had read. She served as the honorary chair but was no figurehead; she attended committee meetings (including one last December that started a little over three hours before the president-elect made his acceptance speech with her at his side), participated in the selection of authors, signed letters to donors and authors personally rather than use a scanner, and sat in on the panels at the festival. When she was in the world of books—whether at the book club or working on the festival—she was much more Laura than Bush. The inner circle had as many Democrats as Republicans, which didn't matter, since no one discussed politics anyway. Among the authors invited to participate at book festivals were Garry Mauro, who was Governor Bush's Democratic opponent in 1998, and Jim Hightower and Molly Ivins, both liberal critics of the governor. That life has vanished. Now she is something of an empty nester: children gone to college, friends far away (although some have come along to Washington), husband surrounded by aides, freedom restricted. Last November she couldn't even attend the panels at the book festival because of Secret Service concerns.

"I had the perfect life for myself in Austin," Laura Bush acknowledged. She was sitting on a sofa in the Map Room of the East Wing of the White House, wearing another blue suit, this one sky blue. It was a few minutes after seven o'clock in the morning, and the first lady had already appeared on *Good Morning America*, from an adjacent room. With Austin now behind her, she talked instead about the ranch in Crawford, close enough for her Austin friends to visit, where she spent two weeks in February. "It has the best walks ever," she said, "steep walks into canyons by the creeks. Condoleezza Rice [the president's national security adviser] explained the Balkans to George walking up one of those canyons. We congratulated her for never stopping to catch her breath or even breathing hard. Now we call it 'Balkan Hill.'" The story was a reminder of something we don't think about very often, that presidents and first ladies and august advisers are, after all, just people. "There are lots of native redbuds," she went on. "A huge field of prickly pear. We're going to have fields of wildflowers this spring, all native. I planted wildflowers on the dam—it's not as easy as you think to get wildflowers started." I asked her where she got her love of gardening. "It's very relaxing," she said. "When Barbara and Jenna were babies, I'd still have a few hours of light after they went to bed. One night I was in the garden, the babies were asleep, safe in their beds, and I remember thinking, 'This is the life.'"

It is not surprising, given Laura Bush's love for wildflowers, that Lady Bird Johnson is one of her two role models as first lady. (The other—even less of a surprise—is Barbara Bush.) "The American people look back and think, 'Oh, she did flowers.' But she was really radical for the time. She said we should use native plants that require less water. She really started the modern environmental movement."

"How do you learn to be first lady?" I asked. "Do you go to 'first lady school' after you get here?" "I had a huge advantage," she said. "George and I both did, from watching his father and mother. But the first lady can create the job as she wants it. I plan to work on what has always interested me, which is reading." She has a social secretary to assist her with White House matters. Mrs. Bush's biggest problem might be her own husband, who doesn't like formal dress or staying up late for social occasions and might have to be reminded occasionally that these things are part of the job description of the president.

A lot of first ladies become political advisers to presidents, and I wondered if she would do the same. "I don't presume to be one of my husband's advisers," she said. "Do we talk about issues? Sure. But not all the time. I've looked at speeches some. I might say something like, 'Oh, I don't think you ought to say that.'" I asked if she was responsible for his deep interest in education. It was the wrong question. Laura Bush is one of the most measured people I have ever interviewed. She answers questions politely and completely but without betraying emotion. She is always under control, hardly ever shifting position, much less changing her facial expression or waving her hands about. So when she made a bit of a fidget when I asked about education, I knew she didn't like it. "People aren't giving George the credit for being interested in education," she said. "He knows how federal policy affects the states. He talks about how important local control is. You're from Texas. You know how interested he was."

Across the room, her press secretary made a motion that time was running out. I tried to avoid eye contact. "What are you reading?" I asked. "On my bedside table is Katharine Graham's autobiography—we went to dinner at her house—and Edith Wharton's biography," she said. "I read the *New York Times Book Review.* But it's hard to find time to read. I didn't move my books here. I built a lot of bookshelves in Crawford." I had the sense, then, that the times when Laura Bush will be happiest are the times that she is away from the White House. "The hardest part for me," she went on, "is that the children don't think of Washington as home. I have tried to get them to come here for spring break—one of them has two weeks—but they don't want to come here. They want to go to Austin. I hope they realize," said the first lady, "how much their mother misses them."

*April 2001*

## THE WITNESS

*Nellie Connally is still alive, alone with her memories of the day that defined the rest of her life.*

MIMI SWARTZ

**Nellie Connally is the last living soul directly involved in the formative event of my youth—the assassination of John F. Kennedy. Interviewing her was a real treat. She is a classic Texas woman—smart, feisty, and intensely loyal to the memory of her husband, the former governor of Texas. What struck me so profoundly about the story was how that event had also shaped her life, and with the deaths of other people in the car—her husband, Jacqueline Onassis, and, of course, JFK—telling and retelling the story became her life. Each person she met while I was with her wanted to hear about that day, and Nellie, who had wanted to be an actress as a college coed, obliged. I came to see what a burden it was, to have been a witness to such an event, as time passed and its importance faded. At one point, she was telling the story to a young man in his thirties, and his response was, "Wow, when was that again?"**

EVERY NOVEMBER, as she has done for almost forty years, Nellie Connally readies herself for the reporters' calls. She has her hair done in preparation for the cameras, and she buys flowers—yellow roses, typically—to freshen her home, a sun-washed two-bedroom condominium on the twelfth floor of a luxury high-rise, the Four Leaf Towers, in Houston. Because the story is always present in her memory, she doesn't have to brush up for the interviews, and because she is a trouper—she wanted to be an actress, a long, long time ago—she always sounds as if she is speaking on the subject for the first time. The story she is perpetually asked to tell, of course, is the tale of that fateful day, November 22, 1963, when she rode in an open Lincoln convertible with the president of the United States, John F. Kennedy; his wife, Jacqueline Bouvier Kennedy; and her husband, John Connally, the governor of Texas.

Every Texan of a certain age recalls the events that swept Nellie Connally into history: the fury of Dallas toward Kennedy's liberal politics, the bitter, full-page ad in the *Dallas Morning News* addressed to the president that essentially accused him of treason ("Why have you scrapped the Monroe Doctrine in favor of the 'Spirit of Moscow'?"), the adoring crowds that lined the route of the motorcade. "Mr. President, you certainly can't say that Dallas doesn't love you," Nellie Connally said to Kennedy, turning around in her jump seat to fix him with a broad, proud smile as she uttered what has become the most famous line of her life. And then, three shots rang out within all of six seconds, changing the country forever. Of the survivors in the car, John Connally, seriously wounded, lived until 1993; Jacqueline Kennedy Onassis died in 1994. So it has come to pass that Nellie Connally is the last living soul to have experienced, firsthand, one of the seminal events of the twentieth century.

Nellie, as she likes to be called—you really can't call her anything else after meeting her—makes an unlikely sage. At 84, she still moves with the hurried step of a happy sorority girl (which she once was); her blue eyes are unclouded and sly, as is her mind. She still wears a variation of the bouffant she wore in the sixties, and she has a closetful of sharp suits by Armani and Yves Saint Laurent, which she wears with aplomb; she enjoys sweets and the occasional cocktail, despite her doctor's orders, and if you get her talking off the record, she will pretend to stick her finger down her throat to describe her feelings about certain former first ladies of the United States. This is a woman who wields the word "jackass" with complete confidence. "I have always been full of fun and full of the joy of living," she explained to me, showing off her dimples. "I just restrained myself when I represented you."

If this is the way Nellie Connally sees herself, others see her as a tragic figure, a witness to America's loss of innocence. As Julian Read, John Connally's longtime public relations adviser, elucidated, "The thing about Nellie you need to know is that she's a survivor." On the day he imparted this information to me, he was seated in Nellie's living room under one of many portraits of the former governor that adorn the apartment. (This one had Connally surrounded by Texas symbols: oil wells, the Capitol, the state flag, Herefords.) Nellie listened attentively to Read's pitch from a comfortable chair across the room, nodding and occasionally supplementing. She knew the Job-like recitation was coming, which in chronological order includes: the suicide in 1958 of her eldest daughter, Kathleen, at age seventeen; the assassination of the president and near death of her husband in 1963; John Connally's failed quest for the presidency, which lasted for the entire decade of the seventies; the collapse of his real estate empire and subsequent bankruptcy in 1987; her battle with breast cancer in the late eighties; and finally, the death of her husband, whom she loved deeply for more than fifty years. "We had everything we ever wanted," she told me simply. "We just lost it all."

Except for her memories, with which she has had a long and ambivalent relationship. They are like the forty-year-old suit shrouded in dry cleaner's plastic in the farthest reaches of her closet, the one she wore on November 22, 1963. It's a jaunty pink tweed, with cheery oversized buttons, and she could still get into it if she wanted to. Nellie can't bring herself to part with the suit, but she can't quite hold on to it either, as time frays the seams and weakens the fabric.

John Connally has suffered a similar fate. For Texans who lived through his governorship, which paralleled almost all of Lyndon Johnson's presidency, it is hard to believe how quickly and harshly time has erased his memory from the public imagination until, like Nellie's suit, all that remains of his role in history is a single day in Dallas. In his day, he was powerful and popular and something of a visionary, who brought state government into the modern era. He was spoken of as a future president. An unauthorized biography of him by James Reston Jr., titled *The Lone Star: The Life of John Connally*, published in 1989, ran almost seven hundred pages and seemed to herald an enduring legacy. But the latest *Encyclopaedia Britannica* dispatches Connally as "an ambitious political figure" who helped elect three presidents and was "indelibly identified as the seriously wounded front-seat passenger who was riding in the presidential limousine in Dallas, Texas, when Kennedy was assassinated on November 22, 1963." A seventh-grade history text published earlier this year, *Texas and Texans*, mentions Connally only once, in a reference to a 1966 meeting with farmworkers who were marching toward Austin to protest working conditions in the fields: "His actions did not satisfy the unhappy workers, and they became more active in politics." That is hardly the grand place in history that he and his followers—and Nellie Connally—believed he was due.

Now, it is through telling the story of the assassination that she keeps the memories alive. She has recorded them in a new book, *From Love Field: Our Final Hours with President John F. Kennedy*, with help from the Texas coauthor of choice, Mickey Herskowitz (who also helped John Connally with his autobiography, *In History's Shadow*). But in Texas, there are now more people born after November 22, 1963, than before it—Michael Dell, Lance Armstrong, Beyoncé Knowles, just to name a few. That the assassination has been subjected to the crushing callousness of history was brought home to me the day I sat with Nellie while she was having her picture taken.

I arrived to find her bossing the photographer around good-naturedly—"You've called me 'beautiful' more in the last hour than John Connally did his whole life," she cracked. As the shoot wound down, she served coffee and candies, and the conversation turned, as it almost always does with Nellie, to that day in November 1963. With little prompting, she told a version of her story, and as she did, the living room, crowded with the photographer, his assistant, and a makeup artist—all decidedly youthful—grew deathly quiet.

"Wow," someone said when Nellie finished. "When did you say that happened?"

NOVELIST CHARLES BAXTER has called the Kennedy assassination "*the* narratively dysfunctional event of our era" because "we cannot leave it behind, and we cannot put it to rest, because it does not, finally, give us the explanation we need to enclose it." This is not Nellie's view of the event; the speculation and conspiracy theories intrigue her not at all. People looking for any new insights into the assassination—some clue that Oswald didn't act alone or that the mob, Fidel Castro, Lyndon Johnson, or even John Connally was behind the killing—should look elsewhere. As Nellie carped one day, "Some of these people think Johnson did it. Some people think John did it. What kind of idiots do they think we were to plan that and then get in the car and sit there?"

By nature, she's not a skeptic. Her narrative is instead more intimate, more feminine, and somehow, more frightening. Four decades of investigations and conspiracy theories have diluted the horror of that day, which she makes vivid again in her book. But more to the point, her book is a way to secure her life with, and love for, John Connally for posterity. In one way or another, that is the story she has been telling, over and over again, since the day they met.

"We were indeed a happy foursome that beautiful morning," she wrote. They were all in their thirties and forties, ready to take on the world: the handsome young president, who promised the dawn of a new era; the governor, fresh from his role as secretary of the navy, who had been in office for only ten months; Jackie, glamorous and, to Nellie, a little intimidating, dressed in a pink Chanel suit and carrying a bouquet of red roses; and Nellie, also dressed in pink, carrying yellow roses. She'd been fretting for days that her suit would clash with the first lady's, that the Governor's Mansion wouldn't measure up to the sophisticated first couple's scrutiny, and that, in general, the Kennedys would find Texas lacking. The warm response in Dallas, then, was an enormous relief. "John and I were just smiling with genuine pleasure that everything was so perfect," Nellie wrote. Suddenly, "a terrifying noise erupted behind us." From her spot on a jump seat, she turned back to look at the president just in time to see his hands fly up to his throat. Then, Nellie turned back to meet her husband's eyes. John Connally had fought in World War II and was a hunter; he knew that sound had come from a gun, but it was too late. A second shot rang out, and Connally uttered what has become one of the most remembered lines of that day. "My God," he cried, his rich, stentorian drawl taut with fear, "they're going to kill us all!" Then he collapsed. The second bullet had hit him in the back.

What happened next was, for Nellie Connally, a defining moment. As she wrote in her book: "All I thought was, What can I do to help John?" Her husband was a big man—he stood six feet two inches—but she pulled him onto her lap and covered him with her body. "I didn't want him hurt anymore," she explained, and so, when the third shot hit its mark, exploding Kennedy's head and showering Nellie with bits of blood and flesh, she was exposed but her husband was not. Nellie felt her husband move underneath her, bleeding heavily but alive. "I felt tremendous relief," Nellie wrote, "as if we had both been reborn." She pulled his right arm over his chest to draw him closer and comforted him as if he were a frightened child: "Shhhh. Be still," she said. "It'll be all right. Be still. It'll be all right."

The driver pulled the Lincoln from the motorcade and raced to the hospital. "We were floating in yellow and red roses and blood," Nellie told me. "It was a sea of horror." While a team of doctors worked on the president, Nellie Connally wondered what to do. Who was treating John?

She became increasingly more frantic as everyone concentrated on Kennedy. The question racing through her mind was this: "How long do I have to sit here in deference to my president, who is dead? All this time I was trying to be so nice when that was the last thing I ever wanted to be. I was as alone as I'd ever been in my life," she wrote. The only consolation was that her husband continued to moan in pain. "That was the best thing I heard, because I knew he was still alive," she continued.

The doctors finally cut John's clothes from his body and began to repair the damage. Nellie sat numbly by while the death of the president was announced, barely able to speak with her three children by phone, unsure what to tell them except that their father was still in the operating room. She broke down only once, when Lady Bird Johnson, a friend of more than twenty years who would soon become first lady, burst through the swinging doors of the emergency room. "She opened her arms wide and I flew into them," Nellie wrote. "And I cried and cried for the first time."

It was many agonizing hours later that Nellie got the news that her husband would live. A doctor told her that by pulling John over and covering him, she had inadvertently closed his baseball-size wound and, most likely, saved his life. Seeing her husband for the first time, pale but alive, Nellie leaned over the hospital bed and kissed him. "We had been through so much and had been spared," she wrote. "We still had each other and could go on and fulfill whatever mission fate had in store for us."

The Nellie who appeared on television in those horrible hours did not look like a woman in control of her destiny, nor did she look like the confident woman people know today. She was a very young-looking 44, drawn and almost unbearably fragile. She stood anxiously by her husband's bedside when he was well enough to talk to reporters, not meeting the camera's eye, steadying herself with the bed rail one minute, fidgeting the next, her bottom lip quivering, her chin tucked. She had still not recovered from Kathleen's death; now she had nearly lost her husband in a terrible crime, and the signs of shock were unmistakable. Even so, she understood on some level that she had become a part of history. Two days after bringing her husband home from the hospital, Nellie went to a quiet corner of the Governor's Mansion, picked up a legal pad, and recorded her account of the events, thinking that maybe her grandchildren and their children might want to know what had happened on that day. "I left Austin at noon on Thursday, November 21, 1963," she began, with the harrowing account to follow.

Then she put her memories in a drawer and began to fashion the kind of story a woman of her time and place could make sense of. As she wrote in her book, she went to the beauty salon:

> *In those days, that's what ladies did when they felt worn down and worn out: They got their hair done.*
>
> *My hairdresser in Austin put me in the chair, looked me over like a Parkland surgeon, then gave a low whistle.*
>
> *"Mrs. Connally," he said. "Did you know there is a streak of white hair, two inches wide, down the back of your head?"*
>
> *I sat bolt upright and reached for the mirror. "No, I didn't! It wasn't there three weeks ago!"*
>
> *Shortly thereafter I made an appointment with our family doctor. During the routine physical, I asked him what might have caused the white streak.*

*"Shock," he said matter-of-factly. "From what you say, you never screamed or even cried until after the event. You kept everything inside. That's what happens to good little soldiers."*

That description is still the best characterization of Nellie Connally. She's stalwart and dutiful and displays a well-developed sense of the absurd only when she's sure the coast is clear. Her friends talk about her affectionately but with the care and concern of diamond cutters; maybe they see her as the perpetual political wife (never say anything that could hurt the campaign, which is ongoing), or maybe they simply do not wish to inflict, even by accident, one more scintilla of pain. Nellie becomes, in their accounts, a virtuous and devoted martyr, albeit one with a madcap sense of humor. Only occasionally will anyone admit that there's been an enormous price to pay for her life, that just as there were enormous rewards for being married to the most classic of Texans, there were also enormous sacrifices. They leave that part of the story to her, and she recounts it with the facts but not the details. "A political wife has a hard go," she told me, as she has told other reporters and friends in the past. "When people ask me who I admire, I say the political wife who has managed to get through her husband's term without becoming a drunk, having affairs, or getting a divorce."

Nellie managed. No one close to the couple has ever doubted that John Connally loved his wife—former lieutenant governor Ben Barnes was sometimes embarrassed when they'd smooch like teenagers in the back of a car he was driving—but Connally was a narcissist, and there were always other women around, the bored wives of very rich husbands, the political groupies. "Nellie was realistic about the kind of husband she had," Mickey Herskowitz told me. "She knew early in her marriage she had to have a philosophy about it." She has repeated that philosophy in countless interviews and repeated it to me, as a shield against further inquiries: "As long as he came home to me at night, I didn't ask any questions," she said. "And he did." She was, after all, his wife, the mother of his children, the one with whom he took long drives in the Hill Country and the one with whom he attended social events all over the world. Nellie's quality time came after the parties were over, when the couple would stroll alone together through the empty streets of some of the world's greatest cities. To this day, there are many places Nellie Connally has seen only in the dark.

Her memory of their first meeting seems right out of a Texas romance novel. In 1937 Idanell Brill was a star on the University of Texas campus, with more than her share of suitors. She wasn't beautiful in the conventional sense, but she was petite and lively and unafraid—sexy, in other words. "I was walking to the student union building, and this young man was coming my way," she told me, her voice softening at the memory. "God, I never saw anything as good-lookin' as that in my life. Tall, slim, black hair. We were separated by about twenty-five feet. When we got opposite each other, we just looked at each other and that was it. Poor guy, he didn't know his bachelor days were over." Soon enough, however, the terms of their relationship were established. "All I know is, I was the star, but the roles very quickly became reversed," she told a reporter several years ago.

The Sweetheart of the University had fallen in love with the ambitious president of the student body, a young man raised in poverty in South Texas who wanted to make damn sure he never had to return to it. (Connally's father, a heavy drinker, had scraped out a living as a farmer, a bus driver, a butcher, and a barber in an attempt to support seven children.) Nellie came from a family that was better off but not wealthy. Her father, a hunter and fisherman, worked alongside his father at the family leather shop, one famous for making holsters for the Texas Rangers. While John Connally's childhood was deprived—his happiest Christmas was the year he and his four brothers received one football as their only gift—Nellie's was rich, in spirit at least. Her mother in particular was a lively, strong-willed woman who never let disappointment slow her down and imparted that lesson to her children. When Nellie says, "I only look forward, never back," it is her mother talking, but the truth is that in her own life, she has had to do both.

Like so many relationships of that time, Nellie and John Connally each found in the other what he or she lacked—or could not express. He had the drive; she had the stability. He was formal and occasionally severe; she was unpretentious and irreverent, her compassion making up for his arrogance but without illusions. Several years before John Connally's death, Herskowitz was at the family ranch when an old college classmate teased Connally about the wide swath he had cut as a student.

"That was a whole different John Connally," the governor insisted.

"Oh, no, it isn't," Nellie argued, grinning. "He's just the same. Vain, arrogant, and pompous—the three things every woman wants in a man."

IN LATE AUGUST, Nellie and I drove to the LBJ ranch for an annual event, the laying of a wreath on LBJ's grave on his birthday. The ranch was a four-hour drive across Central Texas from Houston, and to make it on time, we had to leave at around five in the morning. Nellie came downstairs briskly, dressed sharply in a pin-striped, waist-cinching Armani suit and, planting herself in the back seat, groused good-humoredly about the tight seat belt and the design of the car's headrest, which blocked her view of the road. She reminisced steadily as we headed west, while the sun came up and mist lifted off the hills beyond Columbus. No one would have known that she was ambivalent about making the trip, torn between reading the final galleys of her book and her loyalty to the crowd that was her life for so many years.

As we approached the sprawling, oak-shaded ranch house, Nellie grew more animated. She hadn't been there in years, and every landmark—LBJ's birthplace, the cemetery, the road (now closed) that used to bring visitors across the Pedernales—seemed to remove a year or two until, by the time she leaped from the car, she was as giddy as a teenage girl.

It was an unseasonably cool morning, and until Nellie made her entrance, everyone had been milling about respectfully, sipping coffee from speckled tin ranch cups. LBJ's daughters, Luci and Lynda Bird, were there with their children, along with some old LBJ hands—Larry Temple, Julian Read, Ben Barnes—and the widows of others—George Christian's wife, Jo Anne, Walt Rostow's wife, Elspeth, and finally, Lady Bird herself, now ninety, who, due to a debilitating stroke, was rolled out in a wheelchair.

Nellie amped up the scene. She flitted and fluttered through the crowd, hugging, kissing, and squeezing almost everyone on the lawn. She craned her neck as she threw her arms around Barnes, nodded sympathetically as she listened to Luci and Lynda, bent over Lady Bird to kiss her hello. Little exclamations of joy and surprise followed her wherever she went. At the graveside, she sat among the widows, but while they were silent and stoic, she snuggled next to the former first lady while she listened, beaming, to a soloist who delivered an a cappella rendition of "America the Beautiful." When he finished, Nellie shook her fists in victory. She was back in her old role, pulling the group together and giving it life, as had been her job from her earliest days with the Johnson crowd.

Nellie and John were married in 1940. By then her husband had already caught Congressman Lyndon Johnson's eye, and the protégé was working late into the night in Washington, D.C., answering constituent mail and plotting political strategy. (Johnson was supposed to be the best man at the couple's wedding but never made it to the ceremony.)

Nellie didn't quite know what to make of Johnson at first. "I was not really political," she explained. "I just knew that this was a powerful man and he was going to be somebody." She did notice that he couldn't relax and that he was extremely coarse; he ate off her plate after finishing what was on his. She took it upon herself to lighten his dark moods with little ditties and tried to be his receptionist, briefly, but left sometime after he threw a book at her when she accidentally cut off a big donor. "It took me a while to love Lyndon Johnson," she admitted.

While Connally worked for Johnson, Nellie cooked dinner, kept house, and tried to create a life for herself. At one point, she considered joining a theater group in Falls Church, Virginia, but her young husband wouldn't hear of it. "Let me ask you something," Nellie told me, quoting John. "What if there's a special dinner and you were in rehearsal?" When she said she'd go to the rehearsal, Connally shook his head. "I don't think you'd better hook up with them," he told her, and she didn't. "Little did I know he would put me on a stage much bigger than Falls Church," she said. "I had to act, and I had to be real good."

When the war started and both husbands joined the military, Nellie shared an apartment with Lady Bird, who ran Johnson's congressional office in his absence. Again, Nellie took on the role of cheerleader, filming skits in which she cast Lady Bird as a femme fatale and sending Lyndon cheery notes. "I really threw one last PM," she wrote him. "I had six girlies out for a good drink, dinner, and a wild poker game. After drinks, I quit worrying about how my dinner would taste, because I could have fed them steamed grass and mud pies for all they cared."

When the war ended, John and Nellie moved to Fort Worth; John traveled frequently to Austin and Washington as a lobbyist for Sid Richardson, the legendary Texas oilman and uncle of the Bass brothers. Nellie was, by then, the mother of four children, an enthusiastic if at times eccentric parent. On trips, she dried diapers by rolling them up in the car window and letting them flutter in the breeze; at home she allowed the children to have a dog even though she was deathly afraid of all animals, large and small. The family began living on a grander scale, taking their cues from Fort Worth's old wealth, the Carters, Moncriefs, and Fortsons. "They just had so much that we didn't have," she told me. "I learned from watching them."

Their lives seemed nearly flawless until March 1957, when the Connallys' eldest daughter, who was sixteen, started dating eighteen-year-old Bobby Hale, the son of a former Texas Christian University football star. As John Connally recounted in his autobiography, Kathleen, or KK, was a bright, headstrong girl who had suddenly grown rebellious. "Nellie and I were both perplexed and agitated," Connally wrote. "We could hardly talk about anything else. We knew her behavior was irrational." John and Nellie came to suspect that Kathleen was pregnant; as Kathleen continued to deny that fact, the Connallys' home became a battleground. Finally, in frustration, John Connally slapped his daughter, an act he would regret for the rest of his life. The next morning, he left for another business trip to Washington, and that night Kathleen loaded her clothes into the family station wagon while Nellie, he wrote, "pleaded and cajoled and raged. She drove off with her mother begging her to stay."

After several agonizing days of silence, the Connallys got a letter explaining that the couple had eloped; Kathleen was living in a squalid boardinghouse in Tallahassee with her new husband. It was March 1958. John made one dispiriting visit to Florida; within a few weeks, he got the call in which he learned that Kathleen had committed suicide.

Lyndon and Lady Bird came to the funeral. It was, Lady Bird later wrote, "As painful a time as I can ever remember. John was just like a granite cliff, and Nellie was her sweet, warm, loving self. There was a whole lot of us out at their house. Love brought us all. We yearned to make it less painful, and there was no way to do it."

John Connally made public mention of Kathleen's death only once in his life, in his book. He wrote the chapter swiftly, late at night, and punctuated the recounting of his daughter's death with a promise: "This is the first time I have ever discussed it in any detail, and it will also be the last."

Nellie does not speak of Kathleen either, nor did she choose to write about her death in her book. "We lost her and I never got over it and I never will. There's hardly a day that goes by that I don't think of Kathleen," she told me. "I will never get over thinking there is something I could have done to help her." But at the time, she had three more children to raise. "I did the best with what I had and moved on," Nellie said on the drive back to Houston. Then, for just an instant, she allowed herself to look extraordinarily tired.

FOR SIX YEARS spanning my childhood and early adolescence, John Connally was my governor. I was nine when the Kennedys and the Connallys drove by my elementary school in San Antonio, just a day before the assassination, and John Connally was a Zelig-like figure in most of the American history I witnessed as a young adult. These facts may explain why I was taken aback by my first visit to Nellie's condominium. It is almost impossible to think of a home in the Four Leaf Towers as reflective of diminished circumstances, but if you grew up, as I did, on John Connally stories, you probably would have thought that too.

The place is pretty and well appointed but a little overcrowded with Connally memorabilia. The reason for this is not that Nellie has intentionally built a shrine to her husband but that, because of the bankruptcy, this is all she has left. They'd planned to retire to their Picosa ranch, she told me. He would commute (with his own plane and pilot) from South Texas to Houston, where he would run the new Sam Houston pari-mutuel horse-racing track while Nellie waited back at the ranch. Maybe that's why Nellie's condo had seemed so small: because the Connallys had lived so large.

The time between the assassination and John Connally's bankruptcy spans almost 25 years, during which he managed to pack in several careers—corporate lawyer and rainmaker, secretary of the Treasury, presidential candidate, real estate developer, and racetrack promoter—and never seemed to falter, at least from his perspective. "Connally wasn't given to great periods of introspection as to whether he was a great fellow," noted Houston's former mayor Bob Lanier, who was not only a political associate of Connally's but also a River Oaks neighbor. "Johnson had great self-doubt; Connally was very self-assured."

He moved easily from one world to another, from business to politics and from Democrat to Republican—perhaps too easily. When he resigned as Richard Nixon's Treasury secretary, in 1972, to head a group called Democrats for Nixon, Johnson supposedly said, "I should have spent more time with that boy. His problem is that he likes those oak-paneled rooms too much." Three months after LBJ's death, in January 1973, Connally switched to the Republican party. Liz Carpenter, Lady Bird's press secretary, weighed in with "It's a good thing John Connally wasn't at the Alamo. He'd be organizing Texans for Santa Anna now."

Even so, to Connally it seemed like the right thing to do: The Democratic party, he said, had been captured by Northern liberals. When Vice President Spiro Agnew resigned under a cloud of bribery accusations, Nixon, dazzled by Connally, wanted to appoint him to fill the vacancy. ("They didn't have many friends," Nellie told me. "So we tried to be their friends.") But powerful senators in both parties blocked the appointment, and soon Connally was facing his own bribery accusations over a contribution he had received from milk producers while he was Treasury secretary. He was acquitted but fatally wounded politically; when he ran for the Republican nomination in 1980, he spent $12 million and won exactly one delegate. "I reminded everybody of Lyndon," he told a reporter glumly.

He tried real estate, partnered with his old protégé, Ben Barnes, but when oil and real estate prices crashed in the mid-eighties, so did they. Then there was Connally's daring rescue, with his close friend oilman Oscar Wyatt, of several American hostages held by Saddam Hussein in 1990. These were the kind of events Nellie

Connally was referring to when she told me, "We had our ups and downs."

AT THE HEIGHT of the Barnes-Connally partnership, Nellie and John had amassed enough money to compete with the flashiest eighties moguls, including their friend Donald Trump. The Connallys had homes in Houston and Santa Fe, as well as a 3,900-square-foot penthouse in a condo on South Padre Island. (At some point, they sold their house in Jamaica, the one they'd purchased in the seventies as a possible Caribbean White House.) But their most important acquisition was the Picosa. Connally bought the spread near Floresville while he was governor, and as his fortunes improved, so did the Picosa's. It was their showplace: He turned the land a rich, loamy green by importing coastal Bermuda grass. He and Nellie covered the walls with the finest Western art and imported stair railings from an old London embassy. They built an extra floor to accommodate an antique banister. They furnished the dining room with a massive table and carved, high-backed Spanish chairs, two cushions of which Nellie needlepointed with their initials. The bricks in the fireplace came from the old Texas Capitol building; a floor of swirling black and white marble came from an old English mansion. ("When we went shopping, he was as bad as any woman," Nellie confessed.) Eventually, the ranch would include a main house, a guesthouse, a swimming pool, a tennis court, a skeet-shooting range, a landing strip, and an enormous rose garden behind the house. But by 1987, John Connally had debts of $93.3 million and assets of only $13 million. He had had such confidence in his business acumen that he had personally guaranteed his investors' money, and now he had to pay it back. Nellie does not count the bankruptcy as one of the "three bad days" she told me she'd had in her life—those being Kathleen's death, the assassination, and John's death—but it was, nevertheless, "a sad time." Reporters could not help but frame the four-day auction of the Connallys' possessions as a referendum on the Texas myth. Publicly, the couple promised to make a comeback, but privately, they were devastated. "We would lie in bed at night, wide awake, not talking to each other, our minds racing about what was happening to us," Nellie told me. "We knew we couldn't start over again in our seventies."

They presided over the liquidation, Nellie said, "even though it was like cutting off our arms and legs." But the dignity and humor with which they conducted themselves during the proceedings helped to resurrect Connally's reputation and to cement Nellie's. He would take the mike from the auctioneer and regale the audience with the history of an item; she would fluff the pillows on sofas on their way to the auction block. Their closest friends and biggest fans bought the few items they treasured most—Nellie's wedding silver, for instance—and, after a decent interval, returned them to the couple. But everything else was gone.

To get through it, she relied on friends and the unexpected kindness of strangers. One woman offered to send $50 to pay any of the Connallys' smaller bills. Another woman called for advice. She was living in a small town where she felt shunned because she wasn't making any money. What should she do, she asked Nellie.

"How old are you?" Nellie asked her.

The woman said she was thirty.

"Oh," said Nellie, who was then 69, "if I could just be thirty again. What's the matter with you? Get yourself to a new town, get yourself a job, and start living."

UNFORTUNATELY, circumstances precluded Nellie from following her own advice. She was lying in bed one night in 1988, almost asleep, with her hands on her chest. "My little finger felt something," she told me. "I sat straight up in bed. I knew exactly what it was." For several weeks, she told no one—she was on the committee for the one-hundredth anniversary of the Texas Capitol and didn't want to put a damper on the party. "I couldn't bear to tell all those people, and I didn't want 'em all saying, 'Poor Nellie, poor Nellie,'" she told me. She went to the party, suffered an anxious weekend afterward—"Saturday I thought about a lot of things and Sunday I went to the hospital"—and had a mastectomy after doctors found she had breast cancer. Her husband was sitting across the room, dejected, when she came out of the anesthetic. "Nellie," he asked, "do you think the stress of our bankruptcy caused your cancer?"

She was groggy from the drugs but still knew an opportunity when she heard one. "John," she said, "if stress causes cancer, I should have had this fifty years ago, because I have been under stress since I met you."

After her recovery, John worked their way back to financial comfort. He had retired from Vinson and Elkins law firm (where he had also worked as a name partner upon retiring as governor) in 1985. His old friends Oscar Wyatt and Charles Hurwitz put him on the board of their respective companies, Coastal and Maxxam. (He also modeled for Hathaway shirts, wearing an eye patch, an inside joke evoking the company's earlier ads that featured a similarly dressed pitchman.) Connally threw himself into the creation of the new racetrack, which was backed by Hurwitz, and in his off-hours planned a fund-raiser for the Juvenile Diabetes Foundation, with Nellie as the honoree. Barbara Walters and Donald and Ivana Trump showed up to honor her, and Richard Nixon played "Happy Birthday" on the piano. It may have been the first time in their lives that Nellie was the star of the evening instead of her husband; to the Connallys' friends, the night seemed to signal a new start for both of them.

But then, in May 1992, John began having trouble breathing. He got so sick that Nellie had to call 911. "Well, Nellie," he told her, "you saved my life once more." No one was particularly worried at first, because no one could believe that anything as minor as a lung infection could slow John Connally down. He may have felt differently. "If anything happens to me, sell the Picosa," he told Nellie. "It's free and clear."

When he did not respond to treatment, Nellie asked her friends to pray and even brought Billy Graham to see him in the hospital. A few days later, she called the evangelist to deliver the sermon at the state funeral, in Austin. No one there, least of all Nellie Connally, quite knew how she was going to survive without her husband.

John Connally, who had lived like a billionaire, left an estate reported to be worth only $500,000. Within two years, Nellie was calling her children down to the ranch. "Take what you want," she told them. "This is your heritage." The children flipped coins over the belongings; the ranch went to some wealthy caterers from San Antonio. Nellie returned only once. "It's not mine anymore," she told me. "It's beautiful, but I have no desire to go back."

WHEN JOHN CONNALLY began working on his autobiography in the early nineties, some thought was given to the idea that Nellie might do the same. An agent shopped a proposal around New York publishing houses, but no one, it seemed, was interested in the recollections of the wife of a former Texas governor, even if she'd been married to John Connally and even if she'd witnessed the assassination. Nellie's notes, pushed to the back of a file drawer in 1963, remained just where she had left them.

Then, one day in 1996, she was searching through some files when she came across some papers torn from a legal pad. "What in the world is this stuff?" Nellie asked herself. She pulled the pages from the file folder and looked closer: It was the notes she had written after the assassination. "This is good," she told herself as she reread them. "I did this and this is good." Her husband never saw those notes—she hadn't thought they were important enough to read to him. And, as she told me, "We would have fought over every paragraph."

But now Nellie felt differently. "I just thought somebody ought to hear them," she explained. And so she began reading them to small groups; initially she read without stopping or ever looking up from the page. She first read the notes to the Official Ladies Club, a group of political wives, in Austin. Then she gave another reading in Dallas. The response convinced her that, as a shy, 44-year-old political wife, she had created something of lasting value. ("Forget the magic bullet, the grassy knoll, triangulation, the Cubans, the mob, the CIA, the Warren Commission, and Oliver Stone," Alan Peppard wrote in the *Dallas Morning News* in 1997. "No amount of analysis of the JFK assassination can prepare you for the emotional sledgehammer that comes from hearing the former first lady, Nellie Connally, quietly read her personal notes describing the scene in the back of the limousine in Dallas on November 22, 1963.")

Then, a year ago, Larry King asked Nellie to come on his talk show to recall that day in November 1963. She was nervous, but, as usual, the story came alive with her telling. An agent named Bill Adler happened to be watching—he had represented both John Connally and Herskowitz for Connally's autobiography—and it struck him that the time was now right for Nellie's story. There were many people who had been born after the assassination, and her version of events would seem fresh. "It was like doing a book with Lincoln's wife, who was with him when he was shot," he told me enthusiastically. "No other assassination books coming out this fall will have a firsthand account." Even if Nellie wasn't the wife of the president at the time, Adler was right about the renewed enthusiasm for the assassination: He sold the book to a new publishing house, Rugged Land, on the basis of an outline.

It took Nellie and Herskowitz only a few months to write the book, but doing so resurrected old hurts. The awkwardness that always existed between Jackie Kennedy and Nellie had soured before the former's death. In William Manchester's *Death of a President,* Jackie had insisted that Nellie and John were screaming in the car, something Nellie always denied. Nellie had asserted in her speeches that Jackie could have been trying to get out of the car when she crawled across the trunk that day—"The car at that time was not a good place to be," Nellie told me—while Jackie claimed she had been trying to retrieve her husband's brain. These actions may explain why the executors of Jackie's estate refused Nellie's request to use in the book a note Jackie had sent her after JFK's death and Connally's recovery. Likewise, Nellie sent Caroline Schlossberg a note; she wanted to meet with JFK's daughter before she died. She longed to tell Caroline about her father, how happy he had been in Dallas that day, how promising the world had looked then. She never got a response.

Nellie's young publishers, in contrast, could be a little too enthusiastic about sharing her memories. She had to nix a Texas book tour, for instance, that followed the same itinerary as the one in 1963. Nellie also refused to let them describe her in the book as "tony."

ON MY LAST VISIT to see her, Nellie wanted me to meet her children. Dutifully, they all collected in her apartment one day in early September, cheerful adults in their fifties who wore the features of both parents equally. On that day, Nellie was happier than I'd ever seen her. She fussed over her kids, bantered with them, fed them cheese dip mixed with chili. When the joking died down, they praised her strength to me, but she demurred. "I am strong because of your father," she insisted. Her kids, products of another generation, argued the point. "You're not who you are because of him," her eldest son, John Connally III, countered. "You're who you are because of you." Nellie listened closely, her eyes darting quizzically from one child to the next, but she seemed unconvinced.

Then, once again, the talk turned to the assassination, and once again, the family of John Connally tried to make sense of the events of that November day. They argued over what happened when, over who did what. When had Nellie told them the president was dead? When had the children learned their father was all right? Why had the eldest child, John, been able to go to Dallas when the younger ones had been left at home? (The answer: because he hadn't asked permission; he'd just gone.) Everyone had a slightly different version of events, and finally, Nellie had had enough. She shook her head and hugged herself, as if warding off a chill. Then she allowed herself one moment of wishful thinking. "Well," she said, "I'm glad that deal is over."

*November 2003*

## CAN YOU TAKE A HINT?

*There's a reason why Heloise's household-advice column is more popular than ever.*

JAN JARBOE RUSSELL

**As a journalist, sometimes you find the story, but more often the story you most need to write finds you. This was the case in the fall of 1988 when I set out to profile Heloise, the high priestess of housework. At the time, I had two children under the age of five, a demanding job at *Texas Monthly*, and a husband who did not do dishes, much less laundry. During our first interview, I confessed to Heloise that as a feminist I wasn't sure how to manage the politics of housework. "Do you have a valet?" she demanded. No, I said, sheepishly. "Do you have a cook, a maid, a full-time babysitter, or a husband who just loves to do housework?" No, no, no, and hell no, I told her. "Then," said Heloise, "you need Heloise." To my astonishment, she was right. In the midst of my research for the Heloise profile, I completely reorganized my entire house, including closets and my refrigerator. To this day, my fridge stays organized by most of Heloise's rules: leftovers on the bottom shelf, dairy products on the top shelf, cottage cheese and yogurt upside down so they'll stay fresh longer. I do not, however, stash my nail polish in the fridge behind the leftovers to keep the polish from getting gooey. That particular hint was more than I could take.**

BEING HELOISE, the maven of the mundane, the high priestess of housework, the Solomon of the insignificant, is not a job, it's a way of life. On an airplane, flying from her home in San Antonio to St. Louis, where for a hefty fee she will lecture on kitchen hints at the Tinker Show, Heloise is approached by a starstruck flight attendant with a question. Not for herself, mind you, but for a colleague who accidentally washed a pair of white shorts with a red shirt. What should the poor woman do? "Well," says Heloise, settling back into her roomy first-class seat, "she has three choices. She can wash the shorts with color remover—they sell it near the dyes in the grocery store—or she can bleach the shorts and then re-dye them white. Or she can accept the fact that she now has a new pair of pink shorts." This leads to a rollicking conversation, ranging from the complexities of spot removal ("I rub out ink stains with hair spray," says Heloise) to how to get the smell of vomit out of the airplane lavatory ("Throw some used coffee grounds on it," advises Heloise. "Coffee kills the smell of anything"). When the pilot hears that Heloise is holding forth in first class he sends back a hint of his own: For hanging pictures, use a leveling rod to make sure they're straight. "Ahhaaa!" says Heloise, as she reaches for the tiny Dictaphone inside her purse. She makes a verbal note of the pilot's suggestion. Yet another hint from Heloise has been born.

The first time I met Heloise, back in San Antonio, she came to her front door wearing floppy yellow shoes with a glittery white-paper carnation garnishing each of her big toes, a pair of Levi's, and a white cotton shirt tied coquettishly at the waist. She was 37, with a magnificent mane of gray hair that was pulled off her long face, revealing a pair of merry brown eyes. Sleek and straight, Heloise intentionally shines. From the sparkle of her triangle diamond earrings and diamond-and-sapphire bracelet, it was clear that Heloise means to be a star wherever she goes, including her own front door. The dazzling effect was marred somewhat by the vegetable oil that was sprayed on her hands. "Scuuuuuuze me," said Heloise, shaking her hands furiously. "I'm Pam-ing my hands." I looked puzzled, so Heloise explained. "You can buy an oil to put on wet nails to help them dry faster, but I always reach for the vegetable spray in the can. It's handy and so much cheaper." This is a woman whose entire life is a succession of personal or household hints.

"Heloise" is only one of her six names. Her full legal name is Poncé Kiah Marchelle Heloise Cruse Evans. Her husband and friends call her Poncé (pronounced "Pawn-see"), but everyone else calls her Heloise. Even her American Express gold card has only one name: Heloise. Heloise was not her name at birth. She added it as a young woman when she inherited the "Hints From Heloise" column started by her mother in the fifties. The original Heloise had launched the column from another world, a world where women stayed home and measured their professional skills by the sheen on their kitchen floor. The chatty newspaper column, which serves as a running bulletin board, did not die with the first Heloise or with the fifties family. Heloise is more relevant than ever. In an age of feminism, careers, and economic pressures, women now go out to their jobs and *then* come home and do the majority of the housework. Today one of Heloise's most important modern functions is to absolve working women of the heavy load of domestic guilt.

In St. Louis a single mother walks up with a distraught look on her face. The mother has a job and can't seem to get a hot meal on the table more than three nights a week. Does Heloise think it's terrible that she takes her children to McDonald's? "I never cook more than three nights a week either." Total strangers come up to her and make their confessions. "I have the domestic capability of a toad," says a maître d' from an upscale restaurant. Two decades after the arrival of the women's movement, housework is still the skeleton in the closet in women's lives.

Not for Heloise. To her, housework is a cause. "I have a dream," she says, feigning piety, "that one day the wife of the man with a chronic ring around the collar will turn to him and say, 'Why don't you wash your filthy neck, you slob?'" Once, in the early eighties, she and Gloria Steinem happened to be on the same television show in Philadelphia. The producers of the show, mistakenly fearing an unpleasant clash of ideologies, brought Heloise through one door and Steinem out another. The producers need not have worried. Heloise has a very broad view of her constituency, and she is not above proselytizing. "Do you have a valet?" she demanded of me. No, I replied. "Do you have a cook, a maid, a full-time babysitter, or a husband who just loves to do housework?" No, no, no, and hell no, I confessed. "Then," said Poncé, with a look of certain victory on her face, "you need Heloise." Guilty women everywhere will be relieved to know that the most famous homemaker in the world hates to clean house. "There are a few people in the world who really love housework," she says. "Those people are sick."

## HELOISE'S LABORATORY

Heloise lives on a three-acre plot in Hill Country Village, a new-rich subdivision north of San Antonio. Here, in a four-bedroom, seven-bathroom rock house with such grandiose toys as a couple of hot-air balloons, an Explorer van, a pool, and an eleven-year-old chocolate-colored Porsche, Heloise directs her home-and-hearth empire. Her house is really a laboratory; it is here that Heloise tests the hints that appear in five hundred newspapers in twenty countries. She shares her house with her husband, David Evans, a plumbing contractor; her thirteen-year-old stepson, Russell; and three birds and three dogs.

"This is the office," says Heloise, sweeping her arm back, indicating a large room. Four secretaries are seated at their desks, sorting mail. Each week two thousand to three thousand letters arrive at Heloise's home. The secretaries mine the mail, looking for domestic gold. "How do you keep raisins soft after you open the box?" calls out one secretary. The answer to that question is so simple there's no need to go to the card catalog that covers one whole wall of the room. "Easy," answers another secretary. "You store the raisins in resealable plastic bags; otherwise they get like rocks." Such is the daily banter of the office. The atmosphere is homey and down to earth. It may be the only office in the world where each of the five computer terminals has a cozy to keep the dust off the keyboard. "I just love this hint. You can use the cozy to wipe off the screen before you turn it on," says Heloise. Instead of purchasing a table for a computer printer, Heloise stacked three boxes and covered them with leopard-skin wrapping paper. "I've been meaning to buy a printer stand, but these boxes have been here a year, and I like the way it looks," she says.

The command center of her operation is the kitchen table. Behind her are several small shelves with a security system that beeps whenever someone enters or leaves the house, a weather station for David's balloon trips, and a telephone with six lines. Another telephone is near the sink. All day long Poncé and David answer the telephone, attending to their separate businesses.

The house is three times larger than most of the others on the block, so large that it has six separate air-conditioning zones. All of it is carpeted, except a small square in Poncé's bathroom where she keeps her scales. "If your scales are on carpet, they aren't accurate," she explains. Poncé is the first to admit she selected cheap carpeting; none of it cost more than $7 a square yard. "We put the money into high-quality pads, because if we get tired of the carpet, we want to be able to change it," she says. The kitchen carpet is dirty brown—"so that you can't see the spots."

She has two stoves ("I wanted eight burners"), and her refrigerator is a marvel of efficiency. "Leftovers go on the bottom shelf, so that I always know where to find them. To the left of the leftovers, I store cold cuts," she said, pointing with her French-manicured index finger. It was here, behind the leftovers, that Heloise discovered that storing her expensive nail polish in the refrigerator makes it last longer and keeps it from getting gooey. Next to the polish is a plastic bag filled with damp clothes ready for ironing. "If it's back there, Russell and David know not to eat it," she says with a laugh. The center shelf is dominated by a turntable, on which Poncé stores mustard, mayo, and other condiments. "I put dairy products on the top shelf and place cottage cheese and yogurt upside down so they'll stay fresh longer."

Her typical at-home day begins around nine, when she goes into her office to pick up the letters that have already been sorted. If the letter requires an answer, one of the secretaries will have drafted a reply and Heloise rewrites it to make it more chatty. Often she refers to readers as "friends" and congratulates them on their "terrific" ideas for making gravy lumpless or mending a hem more easily. If a reader complains that a previously printed hint doesn't work, she sometimes telephones and tries to find out what went wrong. For instance, a woman from Tennessee wrote to say that Heloise's hint for cleaning a dishwasher—pour in a tablespoon of powdered orange drink or some other form of citric acid and let it run through a cycle empty—had produced brown spots in the woman's dishwasher. "I called her and said, 'I bet you get water from a well, don't you?' Sure enough, she did. The only way to clean those kinds of rust spots is by hand," she said.

Asking Heloise how she knows when she hears a great hint is like asking a theologian to explain the existence of God. "I just know," she insists. There is a metaphysical quality to her work that has to do with making the ordinary universal. When Poncé's mother first suggested using nylon net for scouring pans, she had no idea that almost thirty years later women would still be making what they call Heloise scrubbies—little pom-poms of nylon net—for hundreds of mundane household chores. To this day, her mother's recipe for killing roaches—a little dab of sugar and a lot of powdered boric acid—is a murderous standby. Poncé's list of absolute necessities includes prewash spray and vegetable-oil spray.

The endless pursuit of the Great Hint can sometimes lead Poncé to a kind of domestic spinout. Her concern for efficiency sometimes makes her do wacky and inefficient things. She often walks around her house with yellow notes stuck to her blouse, each a reminder of something important that she has to do. If she gets really busy and sidetracked from her daily itinerary, she sometimes calls her answering machine and leaves a message: "Pick up the laundry," she tells herself, or "Make doctor's appointment."

She is aware of her obsessive tendency, of course, because she sees it in her readers. Some of the hints are discarded right away because they lack the broad applicability that Heloise seeks. A woman from Dayton, Ohio, once wrote to tell Heloise that she saves time by praying while she dusts or vacuums. "I had been praying while sitting on the john," wrote the woman. "Now I sit on the john and shred newspapers for the cat box." Another reader with five children told Heloise she saves time by sitting on the john backward and writing thank-you notes. "All I could think of," Poncé said, "was that her children were going to grow up thinking they had a normal mother."

Recycling—a guiding principle of the hints—is also a guiding principle of the business. "The basic building block is the column," explains Poncé. Everything else—the TV appearances (she's a regular on *Hour Magazine*), the magazine articles (she writes for *Good Housekeeping*), the books (she has written three), the speeches (she gets paid up to $5,000)—comes from the column. The irony is that very little that appears in her column comes from Heloise—it's all recycled from readers. Yet from the column alone she earns roughly $100,000 a year. She won't say how much she makes altogether. "Let's just say it's six figures," she says.

Essentially, Heloise's job is to sell the hints, and she does that very well, always with an eye toward the future. Recently she signed a contract with Prodigy, a $500 million computer venture between Sears and IBM. Each day subscribers to Prodigy can ask Heloise a question about household problems—from their computers to hers in San Antonio. They are guaranteed an answer within 72 hours. "Right now we're getting only about ten questions a day," says Poncé. "But who knows? In another forty years this may be the primary way people know about Heloise."

## THE FIRST HELOISE

In 1958, when Poncé was seven years old, her mother, Eloise Bowles Cruse, and her father, Mike, then a major in the Air Force, went to a cocktail party in Hawaii. At the time, the Cruses lived an insulated life in a new suburb near Pearl Harbor. Mike flew jet planes, and Eloise was a housewife and mother of two children—Poncé and an older adopted son, Louis. Eloise spent her free time volunteering in military hospitals, playing bridge at the officers' club, and adhering to the military's strict social-caste system headed by women she called the Mrs. Generals.

During the course of the cocktail party, Eloise mentioned in a crowd that she would like to start a newspaper column in which housewives could exchange hints. The idea for the column had been born around her own kitchen table, where four or five of her friends gathered a couple of times a week to talk about ways of running their households more efficiently. Mike, a native of Rosebud, Texas, and Eloise, of Fort Worth, were typical of the kind of military couples who were living on the island. Eloise wanted a home like the one her own mother had provided, but her mother was thousands of miles away and unable to offer advice on how to remove banana stains from little Poncé's white cotton shirts. For practical and moral support, Eloise relied on the members of her morning coffee klatch. When she first voiced her idea at the party, a colonel who had two degrees in journalism laughed and bet her $10 she couldn't get a newspaper job. He then said the words that inspired Eloise to take action: "You're nothing but a housewife," the colonel jeered.

The next day Eloise, five feet two inches tall and 102 pounds, marched into the offices of the *Honolulu Advertiser,* armed with engraved calling cards and wearing a suit with matching shoes, gloves, and hat. She demanded to see the editor, who wasn't in the office. Undaunted, she returned the next day, this time with her hair sprayed silver to convey a look of wisdom, and persuaded the editor to try her column, then called "Readers' Exchange," on a thirty-day, no-pay basis. Mike didn't want her to earn more than $599 that first year anyway. Someone had told him that if she did, he couldn't claim her as a dependent. Her first column appeared in February 1959. She worked on a card table in her bedroom, teaching herself how to type by hunting and pecking her way through stacks of mail from readers she was already beginning to think of as "honeybuns" and "sugar bees."

At first, her husband was skeptical. "I was concerned about her going to work—she had two children to raise and a house to keep, but after the column took off, I told her to go for it," recalls Cruse, who is now retired from the military and still comes to Poncé's house three times a week to help edit the column. From the beginning, the column swept over the islands like a tsunami. When Eloise offered a free pamphlet about how to do laundry, she was besieged by more than 100,000 requests, the largest single mail delivery to any individual in Hawaii's history. It was also in Hawaii that Eloise printed her first tip for using nylon net—an elderly woman suggested using the net from worn-out petticoats to scour skillets.

In 1960 Eloise changed the name of the column from "Readers' Exchange" to "Hints From Heloise." She liked the alliteration and added an H to her own name. From then on, she was known only as Heloise. On her own, she sold the column to newspapers in Dallas, Houston, and Oklahoma City. In the fall of 1961 King Features Syndicate, a division of the Hearst Corporation, offered her a contract, and by the following year, she had readers in several hundred cities and was, in the truest sense, a household name. That year Heloise was distributed to more newspapers than any other columnist in King's stable; today the column is still number one with King.

Frank Bennack, the president and chief executive officer of Hearst (or Mr. God, as Poncé refers to him), says no columnist ever knew her readers better than Heloise. "To Heloise, housewives were our unsung heroes. She often said someone ought to build a monument to housewives. The reason she was so successful is that she completely identified with them," Bennack says.

Poncé has a clear memory of the day she realized her mother was a celebrity. Poncé was nine years old, and a steamship company had given their family four tickets to the mainland, but instead of using them, her mother asked if she could run a contest in her column and give the tickets as a prize. "I can remember walking in from school and there were bags and bags of mail in our house. Somehow, I knew our life was never going to be the same again," Poncé recalls.

Not that their life had ever been particularly normal. As Poncé puts it, "Mother was always Mother." By that, she means her mother was a flesh-and-blood eccentric. Even the story of Eloise's birth is charged with coincidence and mystery. Eloise's own mother, Amelia Bowles, who had a twin sister named Ophelia, gave birth to twin girls on her eighteenth birthday, May 4, 1919. She named her daughters Eloise and Louise. To this day, the happenstance of an identical twin giving birth to identical twins on her birthday is a treasured family story. Eloise's father, Charles, was a car mechanic who owned a garage near the old Justin boot factory in Fort Worth. Like a lot of young women who came of age in the early thirties, Eloise was a slave to glamour. She took private lessons to learn how to smoke, and from the time she became Heloise, she often tinted her hair with theatrical spray to match whatever outfit she might be wearing. If she was wearing a blue suit, she thought nothing of coloring her hair blue. Or orange. Or green. Or purple. "The funny thing is, it never looked gaudy on Mother," says Poncé. "Whatever she wore suited her perfectly."

When she was 27, Eloise, already a wartime widow, met Mike Cruse, then a captain stationed in Fort Worth, on a blind date. It must have been a case of opposites attracting. Mike was tall and soft-spoken, with a pilot's impressive countenance and attention to detail, and Eloise was wild and flamboyant. Three weeks later they were married. "She was a different bird than most military wives," Mike says.

Mike adopted Eloise's son, Louis, who is now an aeronautical and mechanical engineer living in Scottsdale, Arizona, and soon the entire family was off to China. Before leaving the States, Eloise had the good sense to open a charge account with Sears and Roebuck, so that she could order appliances, clothes, and household goods through the mail. Not only was she resourceful, but she also had flair. In Nanking the Cruses shared a large house with another couple from Texas. One day Mike and the other officer came home from work and found two Texas flags draped on either side of their front gates. Shortly after, Mike ran into the general. "Mike," said the general sternly, "I understand your wife has opened up a Texas embassy in China." The Texas flags were promptly lowered.

## MOTHER-DAUGHTER CONFLICT

Even in the womb, Poncé and her mother had a melodramatic relationship. Eloise had five miscarriages before giving birth to Poncé, after 32 hours in labor, on April 15, 1951, in Waco. Perhaps the reason she gave Poncé so many names ("Poncé," the baby's paternal grandmother's nickname, "Kiah" for Hezekiah, a biblical name popular on her father's side, and "Marchelle" for her father, whose given name is Marshall) was the many miscarriages and the unlikelihood of additional siblings.

Because of the difficult delivery, Poncé was severely cross-eyed. She had six operations to correct her vision and now appears completely normal. Nonetheless, Poncé has lousy depth perception; she sees with only one eye at a time. Her only memory of the surgeries is waking up in military hospitals and hearing nurses rustling sheets or clanging trays. "It was pretty scary," she admits. Her hearing is extraordinary, which is lucky; husband David has a hearing loss. "I can't see too well and he can't hear, but together we make a pretty good team," says Poncé with a laugh.

In the midst of her childhood operations, her mother made a deal with God. If God would cure Poncé's sight, she would give more than a 10 percent tithe to the blind each year. To this day, 15 percent of the income from the trusts Heloise established goes to buy Braille typewriters for blind students. Each typewriter is inscribed with the same message: "Sent with love, Heloise."

When Poncé was nine, she started helping her mother stuff envelopes and sort through letters. Even though she was being groomed to take her mother's place, she doesn't remember consciously considering becoming Heloise. She saw up close what the stress of deadlines and contract negotiations did to her mother, who was strong of will but weak of body. She remembers her mother once appearing on Mike Douglas's television show in Philadelphia. "She was so nervous that she went in the bathroom and threw up right before the show," Poncé says. Every time an executive from Hearst or King Features called, Heloise would freeze with fear. Success had come quickly, and she never seemed completely comfortable with it.

In 1966, when Poncé was fifteen, the family moved to San Antonio, where they rented two adjacent apartments on the edge of Alamo Heights, the tiny enclave that serves as the nerve center for all of South Texas snobbery. Her father retired early from the military so that he could help manage Heloise's business affairs. Poncé's mother could not have cared less about the social hothouse that is Alamo Heights. By then, all of her time was given over to the column. The family lived in one apartment, crowded with red and black furniture from China, and Heloise set up her office in the other. To get from her home to office without having to walk outside, Heloise had a hole cut in her bedroom closet, and she went back and forth through the clothes, like Alice stumbling through the looking glass.

The move was difficult for Poncé. In her previous high school new students moved in and out with ease. But Alamo Heights is one of those places filled with families who have memory streams longer than one hundred years. Newcomers, especially military children, are at the bottom of the social heap. Poncé made a place for herself with the out-crowd. Instead of shopping at fashionable stores such as Frost Brothers, Poncé bought her clothes at discount houses, such as Solo Serve and the Fashion Barn. (Even now, she cannot bring herself to pay full price for clothes and hunts for bargains like a relentless gumshoe.) The in-crowd drove their own cars to school; Poncé took the public bus. Her sophomore year in high school Poncé and three girlfriends formed the We Hate Heights Club and threw a party for everyone who wasn't invited to the stuffy dances the rich kids held at the private St. Anthony Club. Being snubbed at Alamo Heights proved to be a blessing; it forced upon her the affinity for the masses that is crucial to the column.

Aside from the problems at school, there were problems at home. In 1968 Heloise and Mike Cruse, long plagued by personality differences, were divorced. Poncé learned the divorce was final when she read about it in the newspaper. She still doesn't like to talk about it. "I don't think the column had much to do with it—they just grew apart," Poncé says. In 1970 Heloise married A. L. Reese, a Houston businessman, but was divorced again within six months. "It was a crazy, flash-in-the-pan sort of thing," explains Poncé.

There were always two sides to Heloise—the fun-loving, flamboyant side and the side that needed a lot of hand-holding. One of Heloise's friends was Texas humorist Cactus Pryor, who recalls her as the "most completely open woman I've ever known in my life." If Heloise saw a woman on the street whose dress she admired, she would buy it off her back and switch dresses in a restroom. If she danced with a man who wore dentures and had bad breath, she thought nothing of suggesting that he soak his false teeth in a bleach-based solution. The first time Cactus met Heloise was at a Headliners Club roast in Austin, where she told him she liked only bald men. "I immediately pulled off my toupee, and it was love at first unveiling," Pryor recalls. Later he saw the insecure side of Heloise as well. He was hired to help her produce a radio show, but Heloise couldn't memorize the script. Moreover, she couldn't read it without fumbling and uttering a string of profanities. To make her feel more at ease, they tried to do the show in her apartment and ended up taping it in a closet to muffle outside sounds. "I guess we spoke ten thousand words on tape—nine thousand of them were profane," Pryor says.

By the time Poncé was a mathematics major at Southwest Texas State University in San Marcos, the conflict that most mothers and daughters face when the daughter is an adolescent had escalated into professional warfare. During summers and semester breaks Poncé worked in her mother's office as an hourly wage employee. Theirs was the classic rivalry between the parent who founded a business and the child who saw obvious ways to make it better. Poncé wanted to buy modern office equipment and do a better job of indexing hints. Her mother was comfortable running the office from card tables. Poncé wanted the column to bow to modernity and include hints on women fixing their cars or fathers caring for their children. Heloise never made the feminist leap. "There were times that we detested one another," Poncé says.

Unlike her mother, Poncé was completely at ease appearing on television, making speeches, and disagreeing with executives about editorial policy or compensation. The gap between Poncé and Heloise was more than generational; it seemed to be constitutional. Perhaps because she had grown up watching her mother physically suffer from the stresses of her job, there seems to be an invisible hula hoop surrounding Poncé. She knows who she is and what her limitations are; anyone who tries to intrude upon her time or energy bumps up against the hoop. A book editor who tries to push her into an early deadline gets a polite but firm "That's impossible, Roger." A TV producer in Seattle who calls on Monday and wants Poncé on the show on Friday gets an imitation of *Saturday Night Live*'s Church Lady. "Isn't that special?" squeals Poncé, before telling the producer, "No deal."

Like fathers and sons who quarrel over the operation of a family business, the blowups between Heloise and Poncé were often so severe that they sought the counsel of a trusted outsider. It fell to T. Kellis Dibrell, the family lawyer, to negotiate temporary truces. "Part of it was professional, and part of it was what was going on at the time. Poncé was riding motorcycles and doing other things Heloise didn't approve of, and Poncé told her mother, quite correctly, that her personal life was her own business," Dibrell recalls.

One day Dibrell was sitting in his office in San Antonio when Heloise marched in with her entire staff. She lined up all the women in front of Dibrell's desk and faced her lawyer. "I've brought all these people down here to tell you I'm firing Poncé," Heloise roared. The complaint that day had to do with Poncé being late to work. Dibrell listened and then looked Heloise in the eye and said, "You are not going to fire Poncé. I don't care what she has done. You can't replace your daughter. So take your army and march right out of here." Heloise did just that. Dibrell had hit upon the central fact: Heloise couldn't replace her daughter. Slowly, the founder started letting go of control of the business.

After graduating from college, Poncé considered teaching high school math. She even went so far as to sign a teaching contract but at the last minute decided she would continue to work in her mother's office. "I really did like the work, and Mother wanted me to help out," she says. Part of the reason Heloise wanted Poncé in the office was that by the mid-seventies Heloise was often ill with stomach and respiratory ailments. In 1975 Poncé and Heloise agreed that Poncé would begin writing her own hints in the column under the byline "Heloise II," in addition to running the office. Over time, the arguments subsided. Poncé remembers taking her mother to a doctor one day and Heloise telling the doctor proudly, "This is my grown daughter. She's making it on her own. She doesn't need to get married."

In the winter of 1977 Heloise, then only 58, contracted pneumonia. She never recovered. She died of a heart ailment on December 28, 1977. It was on the night Heloise died that Poncé first made the decision to assume her mother's name and her work. "The people from the syndicate called and said, 'What do you want to do?' and I realized I didn't want to muck up Heloise," Poncé recalls. The next morning King Features put out a press release announcing that Poncé would continue her mother's work. For the next three years, however, she wrote the column under the "Heloise II" byline. When she began receiving letters from readers who clearly knew the column was being written by her, not her mother, Poncé dropped the junior.

Considering the professional issues that confronted her, Poncé was relieved that she didn't have to plan her mother's funeral. Efficient unto the afterlife, Heloise had arranged the entire event. She was buried in the red Japanese wedding robe that she usually wore on New Year's Eve. A song she had written herself, titled "There Are No Phones to Heaven" (the chorus goes: "Talk to your loved ones while there's time / 'Cause after all, there are no phones to heaven"), was sung. Two years before she died, she had purchased her own tombstone, which simply says, "Heloise, Every Housewife's Friend," and the number "30," the way journalists of her era noted the end of a story. There was one moment of general uneasiness when Heloise's twin sister, Louise, showed up at the church. It was as though Heloise had come to her own funeral.

## MR. HELOISE

Who would Heloise marry? Who would marry Heloise? Judging from her devotion to glamour, you would expect Poncé Cruse to be married to a churn-and-burn stockbroker or a jet-setting corporate executive. In fact, she has been married for seven years to David Evans, a plumbing contractor and hot-air balloonist.

"People took bets at our wedding that we wouldn't last three years," Poncé admits. "David and I just laugh about it." David, the supreme tinkerer, is the perfect husband for Heloise. Tinkering is their common denominator. Both work odd hours, often on similar problems. David helps Poncé test hints, especially when the hints have to do with the kitchen or the bathroom. "I'm one of those people who can fix anything," he told me. "I'm not bragging, but it's true. If Poncé doesn't have time to see if something really works, I do it for her." She routinely quotes David in her speeches ("David says to remember that a garbage disposal is just an appliance, not a black hole capable of withstanding any amount of gunk").

Before she and David married, they designed the house they now live in. The basic design principle of the house is similar to the principle that governs their marriage: separate but equal. They have separate bathrooms (his has a urinal and a steam bath), and they have decorated separate living areas to reflect their individual tastes (the den, dominated by a wet bar and a big-screen television, is papered with hot-air-balloon posters; the formal living area is crammed with the oriental furniture that belonged to Poncé's mother). Poncé owns the house, and they keep their finances totally separate: David pays his personal bills, and Poncé pays hers. They even have separate sinks in the kitchen. Poncé's is the standard 34 inches from the floor; David's is 7 inches higher and is in the kitchen's center island. Poncé loves her two-sink kitchen. "If you have only one sink, it never fails that you're standing there, with your husband at your elbow. You're busy and he's bugging you because he wants something below the sink," she says. Such problems do not exist in Heloise's household.

On a recent weekday morning, David stands by the kitchen island, leaning over his sink. He is dressed in red shorts and a baggy short-sleeve shirt, the same shorts and shirt I've seen him in the past three mornings. David has no thyroid and is, by his own estimation, about forty pounds overweight. He grew up in San Antonio in a family of craftsmen—steam fitters, carpenters, and plumbers. His father still owns a plumbing business. Since he was ten, David has worked with his father. One of the reasons Poncé liked David was that he understood what it was like to work for a parent and supported her in the conflicts with her mother.

Poncé and David met in 1977, when Poncé and another man she was dating went to a party at David's bachelor apartment. "I was curious about him because he had baby bottles drying in his sink," she recalls. David had recently been divorced, and his son, Russell, stayed with him on weekends. After the party, David asked Poncé's date if he could ask her out. "We had picnics and went hot-air ballooning, and eventually I fell for him," she says. They were married on Friday the thirteenth in February 1981.

They have no children together for now—by choice. The woman who tells the world how to keep children's socks from getting mixed up ("Buy the same color socks") has not yet figured out how to manage work, marriage, and babies. In the final analysis, maybe the only way to be guilt-free is to earn more than $100,000 a year, stay childless, and have household help—Poncé has a maid who comes in twice a week to do the major cleaning. "Some women manage jobs and children, but I personally couldn't do it. I saw how hard it was on Mother, and I remember what it was like to be a kid. I wouldn't want to do that to myself or a child," she says.

When Russell came to live with them last December, Poncé and David laid down clear rules about not interrupting her while she's working. Poncé is trying to rear Russell to assume his share of the housework. He makes his bunk bed every morning and has a long list of chores, including washing the dogs and cleaning out the bird cages. "He thinks I'm the wicked stepmother, but someday his wife is going to love me," she says.

On the day of her wedding Poncé's father gave her the second piece of advice he had ever given her. (The first time he had given her advice was when she took over her mother's column. "Meet your deadlines," he told her.) Right before the two of them walked down the aisle, the old military father said, "Whatever you do, never let him be introduced as Mr. Heloise."

## LIGHTS, CAMERA, ACTION

Heloise and I are standing in a gigantic exhibit hall in St. Louis, surrounded by three hundred booths manned by clean-faced young factory representatives demonstrating riding lawn mowers, bathroom sinks, the latest in light fixtures, and every kind of cleaning gadget you could possibly imagine. This is the Tinker Show, an event that over the course of one weekend will attract 50,000 people. In her purse Heloise is carrying the small bottles of shampoo and hair conditioner that she picked up from last night's hotel room. "One of my favorite hints," she tells me, "is that people who travel should take all the soap and shampoo from nice hotels and give them to their local battered women's shelter."

In this crowd of tinkerers Heloise cannot move two inches forward or backward without being stopped by someone who wants an autograph. She signs most of them: "Hugs, Heloise." Most of the encounters involve absolution to all those guilty, guilty women. "I can't get my house to smell fresh," one of them says. "No problem," says Heloise. "Just a few sticks of cinnamon in a pan of water on the back burner of your stove." Another presses close and confesses, "My housework just gets the best of me." A consoling look crosses Heloise's face. "Everyone needs a vacation, especially working women," she says. "Some days it's better to let the housework go and be nice to yourself."

Heloise's 45-minute speech to an audience of four hundred is an even mixture of hints and zany anecdotes from readers. "How many people here store mustard in the refrigerator?" asks Heloise. Almost every hand in the audience goes up. "Did you know you don't need to do that? There's enough vinegar in mustard to keep it fresh in the cabinet. But if doing it like your mother did makes you feel better, by all means, do it." (Which is what Heloise herself does.)

Heloise tells the crowd she tries not to edit letters from readers, because she wants to keep the column conversational. Sometimes, however, discretion demands changes. "I got one hint from a reader who wanted to suggest ways of cleaning baby bottle paraphernalia. Her letter said, 'Dear Heloise: When I boil my nipples . . .'" Fade-out to laughter. "I got a similar letter from another reader who said,

'Dear Heloise: The other day I was in the kitchen flouring my liver . . .'" Some of the people in the audience take notes when she suggests that a good way to keep wet garbage from smelling up the house is to store it in sealable plastic bags and put it in the freezer. "Of course, you need to label it garbage; otherwise you'll use it for soup starter," she advises.

Heloise has learned to be careful about giving clear instructions. Once, she suggested in the column that a good way to clean seed hulls from the bottom of a bird cage is to simply vacuum the cage. Soon after the column appeared, Heloise got a letter from a grief-stricken reader that said, "Dear Heloise: I tried your hint about the bird cage. Unfortunately, you didn't tell me to remove the bird from the cage, and my bird got sucked up in the vacuum." Her mother had her own domestic waterloo. Years ago the first Heloise wrote a column at Thanksgiving about how to prepare turkey and dressing. She suggested putting a cup of liquid into the cavity of the bird to keep it moist. An angry reader wrote back: "Dear Heloise: I tried your recipe and my turkey was fine, but the cup I put inside the bird melted." From then on, all of Heloise's recipes stated clearly, "pour," not "put."

Midway through the speech Heloise takes a poll. "How many of you," she asks, with a schoolteacher's proper manner, "hang toilet paper out and over the roller, and how many of you hang it back and around?" Half the room screams, "Over!" and the other half screams, "Back!" I sit in the middle of the crowd, watching in utter astonishment as each side tries to out-scream the other in this great debate dividing America. Afterward I ask Heloise which way she hangs the toilet paper. "Both ways," she says, with the immutable coolness that will allow her to be Heloise for the next forty or fifty years. "I try not to get obsessed about these things."

*November 1988*

# WHAT DOES KAY WANT?

*She's the most popular vote-getter in Texas history, she has a U.S. Senate seat, a Republican leadership position, and at 59, the children she has always longed for. Yet she can't forget the bitter disappointments of the past. What does she really want? Exactly what she has always wanted. Everything—except psychobabble.*

SKIP HOLLANDSWORTH

I rarely write about politics, but I was simply determined to write about Kay Bailey Hutchison. She had this curious past—a University of Texas cheerleader turned University of Texas law student—and she had an equally curious rise to fame, which included a bizarre criminal indictment that she eventually beat in court, which in turn made her even more famous. Then, at an age when many women were becoming grandmothers, she became a first-time mother—and she did that at the very same time she was ascending to the position of senior U.S. senator from Texas. I went into the story asking a few simple questions. What drove Kay Bailey? What did she want out of life? And what did she want to do with her career? As I was about to learn, those were the questions that were the most difficult to answer.

IT WAS THE MONDAY MORNING American Airlines flight from Dallas–Fort Worth to Washington, D.C., and the business crowd in the coach section was packed six to a row, everyone reading papers or typing on laptops. Suddenly, out of first class came a toddler wobbling down the aisle, a pink sippy cup in one hand, a little doll in the other. She was cute, really cute, with sandy hair falling in her light blue eyes. She started swaying left, then right. "Oh, hell," you could see the businesspeople thinking, "she's going to crash into me and knock the coffee off my tray." A couple of men on the aisle shifted their bodies toward the center seats, their eyes focused on the intruder, waiting for the inevitable.

Then a nice pair of black pumps came into their field of vision. The men on the plane couldn't help but notice a nice pair of legs attached to that pair of pumps. Their gazes continued upward, and they saw a dark purple St. John Knits skirt with a matching blazer and silk blouse, very expensive. They saw a pearl necklace and matching pearl earrings. They saw a woman's face, surrounded by perfectly placed, highlighted blond hair. And right about then is when their mouths dropped wide open.

"Careful, honey," said 59-year-old U.S. senator Kay Bailey Hutchison to her twenty-month-old daughter, Bailey. She gave the other passengers an apologetic smile as the child recovered her balance and continued her march to the rear of the plane, at which point she turned and headed back to the front. Bailey dropped her sippy cup and then emitted a noise from her bottom that sounded much like a small lawn mower trying to get started. "Oops," said the distinguished senior senator from Texas.

Kay Bailey Hutchison has now been in the public spotlight for thirty years. In terms of votes received, she is by far the most popular politician in Texas history. No one else—not George W. Bush, not Ann Richards, not Phil Gramm, not Lyndon Johnson—has ever gotten more than four million votes in an election, which she did in winning reelection to the Senate in 2000. She is also the vice chairman of the Senate Republican Conference, which comprises all the GOP senators, and that arguably makes her the most influential woman in the new Republican-controlled Senate.

Yet there is one reason, and one reason only, why she is today the source of such enormous curiosity among many Texans. A year and a half ago, she and her husband, Ray, a prominent Dallas bond attorney who is seventy years old, announced that they had adopted a girl, whom they named Kathryn Bailey. A few months later they announced that they were adopting a second child, a baby boy they named Houston, who is three months younger than Bailey.

The Hutchisons had been so secretive about adopting the two children that many of their friends did not know what they had done until published accounts appeared in the newspapers. Even their closest friends, who received telephone calls from the couple just before the news broke, were astonished. Many of these people had grandchildren older than the Hutchisons' new children. "We joked that Kay and Ray were going to be having their cars taken away from them just as their kids would be getting their drivers' licenses," one of her former Pi Beta Phi sorority sisters from the University of Texas told me.

Almost everyone who read or heard about the adoptions was puzzled. "Please tell me—what was Kay thinking?" asked a wealthy Dallas woman I know, whose husband contributes to Kay's campaign fund every time she runs for office. "I can't figure it out." Why, indeed, would a woman who must debate the issues of the day with 99 other senators, sit on various committees, meet with representatives of special-interest groups, and deal with 20 million constituents back home, suddenly decide after more than twenty years of childless marriage that the time had come to raise two young children? A woman, it should be noted, who is going to turn sixty years old in July?

"Oh, no," Kay lamented when I raised the issue during lunch at the City Cafe in Dallas. She aimed her pretty blue eyes at me as if they were rifles. "Here you go with the psychobabble questions."

She ought to be used to it by now. Kay has had to deal with what she calls psychobabble ever since she became the first Republican woman to serve in the Texas House, in 1973. Women who enter politics learn quickly that their personality and mannerisms come under far more intense public analysis than those of male politicians. Was anyone, for instance, ever interested in learning about the inner life of the bombastic Phil Gramm during his eighteen years in the Senate? But people have been putting Kay on the Freudian couch for a long time, in large part because she seems to embrace so many contradictory qualities. She cultivates the image of her state's foremost female stereotype—the blond former University of Texas coed, sorority girl, and cheerleader—yet one does not have to spend much time watching her at work to recognize the intense, driven perfectionist that lies behind the image. Although she does indeed look, as *Newsweek* once wrote, like Senator Barbie Doll, the impeccably dressed girl next door with the perfect smile and the teased honeyed hair on top of her head, she is also regarded as one of the toughest and most demanding bosses in the Senate.

Although she projects a fundamental niceness wherever she goes, she is renowned among her staffers for her fierce stare, which she will level on those who in some way disappoint her—a stare, says her former chief of staff Mark Franz, "that can feel like a sword being driven through you."

And so her motives, ambitions, personal life, fashion taste, and even her hairstyle have been studied and restudied. Political insiders love to sift through the details of her past—which include great triumphs, great disappointments, and a controversial felony indictment over ethics violations that ended with her exoneration—to try to figure out what makes her tick. They ask questions about her that would never be asked about men, who, in the double standard of politics, are allowed to put their ambitions and egos on public display, while women are expected to shield theirs: Is she a devoted public servant motivated by a love for her state to relentlessly push herself and those who work for her to get things accomplished? Or is she, to use a word that Kay herself employed to characterize what her critics say about her, a "shrew" with a wicked temper, driven by a burning need to take on men and beat them at their own game?

The surprise announcements of the adoptions have only added to the psychological mystery about who Kay is and what she wants out of life. A few cynics have wondered aloud if the kids were a political ploy to give Kay an even more favorable image among voters in case she someday runs for governor. That hardly seems worth the effort involved in raising two children, considering that some polls show Kay's approval ratings are nearly ten points higher than any other Republican officeholder's in Texas.

What's more, since the announcements of the adoptions, the new Senator Mom has done nothing to exploit her motherhood. Just the opposite: According to aides, she has turned down more than one hundred media requests for interviews and photographs of herself with the children, including the *New York Times Magazine* and CBS's *48 Hours*. It was the kind of publicity that most politicians could only dream of. No, she said. Her family life was a private matter.

"I never want to make my children the subject of a story," Kay told me in a firm tone during our lunch, reiterating that she would not allow her children to be photographed for this article. "I cannot tell you how thrilled I am that we do have children, and I cannot begin to tell you what a joy they are to have in our lives, but I don't want them the object of publicity, ever."

She did agree to pass on a few details about the adoptions—the first time she has ever spoken publicly about how they came to pass. She told me that she and Ray, whom she met in the seventies when he too was a state legislator, had always been intent on having a family and that they had tried unsuccessfully for many years to have children of their own. She was so hungry for children, she said, that she was still trying to get pregnant as late as 1993, when she was fifty years old. But at about that time, the seat for the U.S. Senate became open with Lloyd Bentsen's resignation to become secretary of the Treasury, and she devoted her attention to getting elected. "And we didn't think about it for a while," she said. Then, just a few years ago, she began talking to Ray about adoption.

Their decision to adopt was certain to raise eyebrows. Many adoption advocates say that the small pool of children available for adoption should be going to younger parents. Yet she and Ray began getting their names to licensed adoption agencies. Perhaps because of their prominence, and certainly because they were willing to pay the $20,000 to $30,000 fee, the Hutchisons, after two years of waiting, received a call about a little girl who was from another state. Then, later that year, when they were only a few days from having their adoption of Bailey legally certified by a court, they got a call from another agency, asking if they would like a little boy.

They said yes—and just like that, they were brand-new parents twice over. Kay began changing diapers and lugging around a satchel filled with sippy cups and teething rings to go along with her satchel full of briefing papers. In her immaculate Washington office, decorated with grand sofas and noble wingback chairs, a gilded mirror, and an oil painting of William Barret Travis, she placed a bright green Graco playpen next to her battleship-size desk. Instead of getting work done on planes—she used to be renowned on those Dallas-to-Washington flights for putting her head down over her papers and never looking up until the airplane pulled up to the gate—she worried about whether Bailey or Houston would spill milk or jelly on her designer clothes.

"You have to admit," I said, "that a lot of people are curious whether you can handle both lives—the life of a senator and the life of a new mom."

The senator sighed, put down her fork, and gave me a look, already sensing that I wanted to head into that "psychobabble" territory. "You know, hasn't everyone read a lot of those stories about women who can work and raise a family at the same time?" she asked. "Is it really that interesting anymore? Many mothers have been in my position, you know."

But, of course, no other mother with toddlers has been in this position: in the U.S. Senate at age 59. A month after our lunch, she let me travel with her from Dallas to Washington so that I could watch her work, and during the three days I was with her, she was in frenetic action from early morning until late in the evening. On the first Monday I was with her, for instance, she: (1) walked three miles around her Dallas neighborhood at about five-thirty in the morning, (2) woke her children, gave them breakfast, dressed Bailey and took her to the airport (Houston stayed home with the nanny), (3) walked Bailey up and down the aisles on the flight to Washington, (4) jumped with Bailey into a staffer's car at Ronald Reagan National Airport and cooed at her child while talking on a cell phone, (5) dropped Bailey off at her Washington home, where her babysitter waited, then headed to the Russell Senate Office Building, (6) literally ran up two flights of stairs to her second-floor office, where she talked for a few minutes to staff members, (7) strode quickly from her office to the main Capitol building, at least a quarter of a mile walk, passing up the subway reserved for senators because she likes to get in aerobic exercise whenever she can, (8) participated with other Republican Senate leaders in a meeting about the upcoming Homeland Security Bill, (9) strode quickly back to her office, again passing up the subway, (10) conducted more meetings in her office and made phone calls, (11) spent a few minutes playing with Bailey, who had been brought up to the office by the babysitter, (12) met with various legislative aides, a group of intense policy wonks who spend their days in an office across the hall reading the fine print of bills and watching C-SPAN, (13) and finally, at about seven, went to dinner with Bailey and select members of her staff at Tortilla Coast, a Tex-Mex restaurant on Capitol Hill.

That dinner was the first moment I had had a chance to talk to her since the flight that morning. I brought up her constantly pressing schedule, and she was about to answer, but then, as if on cue, she was distracted by her chief of staff, who was speaking in stern tones into his cell phone. He was talking about an anonymous senator who was trying to hold up one of Kay's bills, which was scheduled for a vote that evening. Suddenly, she leaped up and headed to the car to return to the Senate chamber, followed by staffers. She stopped only to give a quick good-bye kiss to Bailey, who was taken home by her administrative assistant. At the Capitol, she disappeared into the Senate cloakroom, working with aides to make sure there would be no more parliamentary "holds" put on her bill. She waited on the Senate floor until her bill was passed by unanimous consent and then gave a ten-minute speech about its provisions, which would impose tighter security requirements for cargo shipped on passenger flights to prevent another terrorist attack.

By that time of night, I was the only visitor sitting in the gallery. Across from me, the press gallery was empty. There was no other senator on the floor to listen; they had all gone home for the evening. Kay could have just as easily handed her speech to a clerk, who would have had it inserted into the *Congressional Record* and made it appear as if she had given a speech. But by giving the speech, she ensured that the bill's purpose would receive more prominent placement in the *Record*. "There is no point in carefully screening every piece of luggage if the cargo placed aboard the same flight is not inspected at all," she declared, punctuating her remark with a clenched fist, which she swung from left to right. I looked at my watch. It was 9:45.

None other than Tennessee senator Bill Frist, the new majority leader, told me that Kay's work ethic is legendary in the Senate. "I'm considered a workaholic, and it's nothing compared to what she does," he said. Her nickname around the Senate is the Needle, a phrase coined by deposed majority leader Trent Lott a few years ago during a tax-cut fight, when she kept needling him and other Senate leaders to eliminate the marriage-tax penalty, the part of the tax code that resulted in two-wage-earner couples having to pay higher taxes if they were married.

Her husband, Ray, cheerfully described his wife as "one of the great nitpickers." This attention ranges from her hair—she has an almost mystical ability to know when one strand is out of place—to the activities of her staff. Whenever she has a free moment, she is typing notes to her staffers on her BlackBerry, a handheld Internet messaging device. One day when I was following her around in Washington, she stood with the other Senate Republican leaders at a press conference in which a ceremonial phone call was made to President Bush to inform him that the Homeland Security Bill was finally going to pass. The news media and several photographers had gathered for the occasion. As the phone number was being dialed and flashbulbs were going off everywhere, Kay, standing right behind the speakerphone, took a moment to glance down at the BlackBerry in her hand to see if she had any new messages.

Kay is such a perfectionist that she will sometimes go to astonishing lengths to make sure she gets tiny things right. This past summer, she was asked to throw out the ceremonial first pitch for a baseball game between the Texas Rangers and the Houston Astros. She cornered Jim Bunning, a Hall of Fame pitcher for the Philadelphia Phillies and the Detroit Tigers who is now a senator from Kentucky, and asked him to teach her to pitch. In a hallway outside the august Senate chambers, they threw a baseball back and forth, Bunning showing her where to put her fingers on the seams and how to follow through. When she returned to Dallas for the summer recess, she had a staffer come to her Dallas home and practice throwing with her in the front yard. On the night of the game, she walked out on the field and fired a perfect strike. Fans began chanting, "Sign her up! Sign her up!" Bunning happened to be throwing the first pitch for a Reds game that summer, but he missed the strike zone high and outside. "I told Jim that the next time he needed pitching tips to call me," Kay recalled with a sly grin.

What is perhaps most impressive about her nonstop schedule is that she is one of the few commuting senators. When Congress is in session, she comes back to Texas every weekend, no exceptions, and usually one day of that weekend she makes a public appearance somewhere in the state. During his senatorial years, Phil Gramm rarely made public appearances when he came home. A lot of Texans never laid eyes on him except when they watched television. Kay, on the other hand, attends an almost ridiculous number of ribbon cuttings and chamber of commerce dinners. "She doesn't have a normal hobby like golf or tennis," said former chief of staff Franz, who is now a Washington lobbyist. "She works. But she works because she likes it. On a down day, she likes to get into a small, cramped airplane, travel around the state to little towns, meet constituents, and talk issues."

"Kay is simply a prodigious worker, and she expects everyone she hires to be just as prodigious a worker as she is," said Pat Oxford, one of her closest friends since college, who is the managing partner at the Bracewell and Patterson law firm in Houston and has been her state chairman during her past two senatorial campaigns. "And she will confront you on a regular basis if you are not working prodigiously. She is not one to say to me, 'Pat, you must not feel good today, because you didn't get this done.' She'll say, 'Pat, we talked about this issue yesterday at four P.M., and you said you would have it done at nine A.M., and I need it right now.'"

It is this passion for her work that has generated so much of the psychobabble. Anyone who has tried to keep up with her during her race-walks around the Capitol cannot help but ask the question "What makes Kay run?" Is she running for something—like president? Is she running from something—like disappointment? Or is she running because she constantly feels the need, even now, to prove herself? Kay once admitted that her mother used to tell her, "Stop working so hard." Growing up in La Marque, between Houston and Galveston, she was not a particularly accomplished student academically—"I made B's," she said—but she was very much like her father, an insurance agent and homebuilder who worked seven days a week and then came home and made phone calls. She was in a myriad of activities and clubs and won a bundle of school honors and elections, including Miss La Marque High School. Think of the Reese Witherspoon character in the movie *Election,* whose blond hair and beauty-pageant smile hid a dogged determination. That was Kay Bailey in the early sixties.

At the University of Texas, she was ahead of her time in seeking to have it all—social life (Pi Beta Phi sorority), highly visible position (cheerleader), and career path (law school student, one of only 5 women in a class of 269). But two things happened to her in law school that would have a profound impact on her life. She got married to a young man who was in medical school in Galveston. In that era, of course, just about every sorority girl thought she should get married as soon as she graduated from college. But her marriage lasted less than a year. The divorce had to have been a humiliating experience for a young woman who had always had everything working in her favor. "After that experience, I did realize, more than ever, that I'd better be able to know how to make my own way through life," Kay told me. Another disappointment came when she graduated from law school, in 1967, and no established Texas law firm would hire her. The managing partners of the firms told her and other female graduates that they didn't want to invest time or money in young women lawyers because they were afraid the women would get married, get pregnant, and quit.

"Surely," I said to her one day when we were having lunch in the private dining room reserved for senators, "there must have come a moment when you looked at all those men running the big law firms and said, 'Those sons of bitches.'"

"No," she said. "What I thought was, 'This is a man's world, and if I'm going to be successful, then I'm going to have to be better prepared than a man—always.' And I still think that. A woman can't be just okay to make a difference. She has to be great."

She got a job as an assistant at a one-man firm in Galveston, and then one day she drove past television station KPRC, in Houston. On an impulse, she stopped the car, walked in, and told news director Ray Miller that she thought she'd make a good television reporter. Miller, who had been thinking about hiring the station's first woman reporter, gave her some basic training, then sent her to Austin to cover the Legislature. She wasn't a political person—"I hadn't spent much time thinking about government," she said—but like almost every other member of the Austin press corps who has covered the Legislature, she thought to herself, "I can do better than these guys." In 1972 she ran for a Houston legislative seat. Her Republican primary opponent's campaign slogan was "A family man who wants to represent your family"—a veiled reference to Kay as a 29-year-old single woman. He also declared that the upstart candidate was not qualified because she hadn't joined the Young Republicans during her years at the University of Texas. "I didn't even know UT had Young Republicans," she recalled. She won after knocking on doors throughout her district.

Her major piece of legislation during her two terms in the House was a bill (co-sponsored with Democrat Sarah Weddington, of Austin, a law school classmate) preventing district attorneys from bringing up the sexual histories of rape victims during the rape trials, unless their histories were directly related to the case. She left the Legislature in 1976, when President Gerald Ford named her to the National Transportation Safety Board; while in Washington she had a few dates with a Washington bachelor named Alan Greenspan. But in 1978 she moved to Dallas to marry Hutchison, with whom she had served in the Legislature. He was running for governor but lost the Republican primary to Bill Clements, who went on to become the first GOP governor of Texas since Reconstruction.

In 1982 Kay tried to resume her political career. She ran for a Dallas congressional seat but encountered some old prejudices about women and some new ones about whether she was conservative enough. She says that one of her male Republican opponents pointedly asked voters in an ad, "Who's tough enough to stand up to Tip O'Neill?"—the clear implication being that a woman was not. During the runoff campaign against Steve Bartlett, an anonymous letter was sent to Republican voters suggesting that she had wrecked Ray Hutchison's first marriage. "Back then, you beat a woman in an election by degrading her," Kay told me, her eyes narrowing at the memory. When she gave her concession speech on election night, she cried—the only time she has ever broken down in public.

It appeared that her political career was over. She bought a candy manufacturing plant and a decorative showroom and settled into a new career as a businesswoman. But when Ann Richards ran for governor in 1990, the state treasurer's office was open, and Kay decided to try politics for the third time. She won easily, and in 1993, when Lloyd Bentsen resigned as U.S. senator to serve as secretary of the Treasury, she went after the seat in a special election. The Democrats threw everything at her. Gloria Steinem called her a "female impersonator." Cybill Shepherd pronounced that she was "no good for women or children." Columnist Molly Ivins, drawing on how Kay epitomized the power-suited Dallas career woman, called her the Breck Girl, a line that stuck. But there was no way she was going to lose; the suburbs had mushroomed with Republican voters. Soccer moms especially saw in her a friendly, feminine, conservative face who took traditional Republican positions for lower taxes and less government spending but at the same time wanted more mass transit and arts funding. She rolled up 67 percent of the vote against Richards's appointee, Bob Krueger, and it wasn't long before pundits began talking about her as a possibility for a future national ticket.

And then, as had happened before, with her divorce, her law career, and her congressional race, she once again faced a life-changing event that threatened to snatch her dreams away from her. In the spring of 1993 Travis County district attorney Ronnie Earle investigated her for committing ethical infractions when she was the state treasurer. In September she was indicted for official misconduct and tampering with government records and physical evidence. Earle contended that she had used public employees to conduct campaign business and had altered phone records kept on state computers. *The Almanac of American Politics* later called the affair a "rotten prosecution," and the charges, if true, should have been treated as misdemeanors and forgotten. But the prospect of a high-profile felony trial for a sitting U.S. senator created an uproar around the state. Furious Republicans claimed Earle and other Democratic officials were conspiring to get her out of the way so their party could reclaim the Senate seat. But the most damaging publicity for Kay came from her own employees at the treasury and had nothing to do with the charges against her. Sharon Connally Ammann, the daughter of former governor John Connally, claimed in a deposition that her boss had once hit her with a notebook when she couldn't find a telephone number. Another employee said she had witnessed Kay pinch another aide who didn't get something out of his briefcase fast enough. The tales painted a portrait of her as manipulative and dictatorial. But she was vindicated when Earle declined to proceed with the trial, and the judge directed the jury to reach a verdict of not guilty.

Kay went on to win a full six-year term in 1994 by a landslide. But the episode tarnished her just as she was starting her Senate career. She was forced to give one interview after another declaring that she had passed a polygraph backing her contention that she had never physically abused an employee. When I brought up the decade-old episode in one of our conversations, her face fell and she shut her eyes. It was still the source of enormous pain. "I just cannot believe you want to write about that again," she told me.

Looking back on that time, her friend Pat Oxford recalled, "It nearly buckled Kay's knees. I saw a lot of tears back then, a lot of grief. The whole patina of the thing—hiring criminal lawyers, getting a defense lined up, fighting off those Sharon Connally comments—changed her. In the past, she was perhaps a little more ladylike in politics. But after the indictment, she became more aggressive and far more wary. She wouldn't let the other guy throw the first blow."

As part of that wariness, she became much more cautious around reporters who arrived to write profiles of her—and seldom liked what they wrote. ("They always turn out to be so wrong," she told me.) Although she could be a charming storyteller who rattled off anecdotes from her family history (her great-great grandfather was a signer of the Texas Declaration of Independence), she was determinedly reserved when interviewers asked her to talk about herself, always thinking about how her words might look in print and always trying to push the conversation toward her work. And with her BlackBerry firmly in hand, she made sure that neither she nor her staff was ever caught unprepared regarding a matter of public policy. No one was going to get the chance to publicly humiliate her again. "I'm very intense when it comes to work," she told me. "I don't lose control, and I never raise my voice, but I'm very hard to work for because I push you. I feel my job is to pull more out of you, to make you better than just okay. I'm just as hard on myself, you know."

For all her exhaustive work, however, Kay is not yet a senator who has defined herself nationally with a particular piece of legislation or an issue, the way Gramm did repeatedly—from budget cuts and banking reform to opposition to the Clinton health-care plan. She is considered one of the most active senators in writing legislation aimed at improving the lives of women—sponsoring or cosponsoring bills to allow homemakers to deduct $2,500 a year for an IRA, to make "cyberstalking" a federal crime, to increase mammogram standards, and to eliminate the marriage-tax penalty—but that doesn't get you a lot of points in the male-dominated Senate. She did receive belated praise for pushing for legislation to improve airport security before the attacks on the World Trade Center and the Pentagon, at a time when no one else was thinking about such matters.

One reason that she may not have become a national figure is that she had to tend to Texas's interests and needs without any help from Gramm. She has fought for Texas's military bases, historic sites, and oil industry, and more highway and mass-transit funding. "If there's a federal bill out there that might adversely affect Texas," says Republican state representative Dianne Delisi, of Temple, "there's a saying among Democrats as well as Republicans around the Legislature: 'Call Kay.' She has always been the go-to person in Washington for almost any Texas issue. And she doesn't need a staffer to give her a briefing beforehand about what the issue is."

But Gramm was a Senate heavyweight, while Senator Barbie Doll has had to struggle to be taken seriously. The *Congressional Quarterly* wrote in 2000 that she is sometimes dismissed as a senator who is "more fluff than substance." That perception, if it was ever widely held, seems to be changing. Majority leader Frist chuckled at the criticism when I talked to him, pointing out that she had, on her own, without any committee chairmanship, pushed her way to the forefront of the debate on defense and national security. Republican senator John Warner, of Virginia, told me that Kay would be highlighted more on domestic issues during this coming session because the Republicans will need a female face to counteract Nancy Pelosi, the new Democratic minority leader of the House of Representatives. Perhaps one of the problems for Kay—one that Phil Gramm never had—is that the Senate, despite now having fourteen female senators, remains a boys' club.

"The Senate can be a lonely place for a woman," Kay told me. "But Washington in general is a lonely place. The women senators meet socially for dinner once a month, but other than that, everyone lives autonomous lives. There's no real life here. I still think back on those days in the Legislature, where we got together at someone's apartment and played bridge at night."

Maybe loneliness was one of the reasons the idea of children came back to Kay. No matter how much work she did every day as a senator, she still felt that childless void in her life. A couple of her close friends told me that Kay reevaluated her life after the death of her mother, Kathryn Bailey, in 1998, five years after the death of her father. Kay worshiped her mother. She was a woman, Kay once told me, "who spent her life chauffeuring me around, telling me I could become whatever I wanted to be, which few mothers were telling their daughters back in the fifties." When she died, said one of Kay's friends, "Kay looked around and said, 'We need to keep this family going.' And Kay being Kay, she decided to do something about it." I asked her if she had to give the speech of her life to persuade Ray, who has children in their forties from his first marriage, of the advantages of becoming a father one more time at age seventy. Although she kept insisting to me that she was going "to keep our private lives private"—she said she didn't want her children to grow up and have to read some "psychobabble" about their adoptions—she did want to make it clear that Ray was just as ecstatic about having children as she was. When I went to see him at his Dallas office, he pulled out half a dozen photos of the kids from his briefcase and roared with laughter as he talked about the way Houston liked to wrestle with him on the floor.

For people who have known this very political, very career-driven couple, the transformation has been remarkable. They have been seen taking Bailey and Houston to a Dallas park, to a Fourth of July fireworks celebration, and to Dallas's Valley View Mall, where the kids climbed on small rubber sculptures designed for children. At Republican gatherings, Kay finds herself besieged by women who want to hear what she has to say about the children, not Iraq. And at night, instead of turning to Robert Caro's recent book on Lyndon Johnson's Senate years, she is reading *Beauty and the Beast* to her children. "The Caro book is one I'm dying to read, and I haven't gotten past page two," she said, giggling like a young mother.

It was moments like this that made me wonder whether her attitude about her career was changing. As driven as she is by politics, she exhibited a delight regarding her children I never saw when she was discussing her Senate achievements. She is obviously not fond of life in Washington, and she has never hesitated to tell her friends that she wants to raise her children in Texas and send them to schools there. The question is, How does she get back home and stay in politics? She has never made a secret of her desire to be governor, and she considered running against Rick Perry in the 2002 Republican primary, but she told me she passed up the chance when Gramm announced his retirement: "I knew I couldn't walk away from the Senate at the same time as Phil and leave Texas with two freshman senators." (GOP insiders say Perry adroitly got the backing of big-money GOP contributors early in 2001 to keep her from launching a major challenge to him.) If Perry has a good run as governor and decides to run for reelection in 2006, her next good chance to be governor would not come until 2010, when she would be 67 years old. When I asked her during a flight if she would still consider a run in that year, she said, "It's hard to say what's going to happen."

"Well," I said, "have you thought about life outside politics?"

There was a long pause. She seemed, once again, to be weighing her answer, deciding how it would look in print. Finally, she said with a soft, almost wistful voice, "I have thought about what it would be like to have free time again. And as the children get older, I do want to be there to take them to *The Nutcracker* and to soccer games, to stand on the sidelines and cheer."

But then she began to talk about all the things she still wanted to do for Texas. It was amazing to listen to her; she talked nonstop about projects ranging from a national heritage site for Buffalo Bayou in Houston and national monument status for the Waco Mammoth Site to more mass-transit funding for the cities. "I know this is what all politicians say," she said, "but I love this state. I will do *anything* for this state." The airplane was landing, and the senator, as always, checked her BlackBerry. A message had arrived from one of her staffers about an impending piece of business. Before she got off the plane, she had pulled out her cell phone and was telling a staffer about five or six things that she wanted done. "We need to get on this now, right now," she said. She grabbed her satchels and walked briskly out of the plane, where an assistant was waiting to take her to a meeting. Within moments, she was getting into a car and making another phone call. She grabbed some papers from a satchel and put them on her lap. She barely had time to wave goodbye to me before she was gone.

*February 2003*

## THE PRICE OF BEING MOLLY

*Once upon a time, Molly Ivins was an outsider—a crusading political columnist with a sharp wit. Now she's an insider, and what's happening to her life isn't always funny.*

MIMI SWARTZ

**When I was growing up in the sixties, Molly Ivins was a real role model for me—a hilarious voice of reason in the wilderness that was Texas political life then. It was formative to see a woman so fearless and so funny—I saw that I could do that too. Hence, doing the story was a real pleasure for me, to see that Molly was as funny and sharp up close as she was in print. I have one powerful memory that stays with me to this day: of shadowing her during the 1992 Republican Convention—the one Pat Buchanan made so rancorous, a precursor of what was to come. For the event Molly wore a wonderful turquoise top in a light, flowing print, so that she looked like a big blue butterfly, flitting happily above the dire proceedings.**

MOLLY IVINS, Texas's most famous resident journalist, pulls on a cigarette, shoves an errant strand of strawberry blond hair out of her eyes, stares down the mountains of notes and messages blanketing the surface of her rolltop desk, blinks twice through her glasses, stabs the Play button on her answering machine, and states her goal for the day and, perhaps, the rest of her life. "What we try to avoid," she says in a smoky voice that snags each and every syllable, "is that help-I'm-drowning feeling."

What Ivins is drowning in, of course, is her own success. Her best-selling book, *Molly Ivins Can't Say That, Can She?*, has propelled her out of her modest regional stature as a political columnist and the last remaining voice of old-time Texas liberalism into nationwide stardom. Suddenly she finds herself getting that A-list everyone-wants-you rush that comes with being (a) the nation's favorite professional Texan, (b) a political pundit-humorist appearing on national newscasts, including *60 Minutes* and *Nightline,* (c) a widely read author and two-time Pulitzer nominee, and (d) a 48-year-old woman reaping fame and fortune for the first time. But if something is getting lost along the way—such as the definitive book about Texas politics that she has always wanted to write—well, Ivins may be the only one who cares. She is, like so many Texas liberals of the old school, not entirely comfortable with attention and acclaim.

Ivins copes by cloaking her fairly formidable six-foot frame in the informality for which she has become infamous: bare feet, bare face, purple cotton shorts with a matching purple T-shirt. She is never without her most critical accessory, a smoldering Marlboro Light. She snatches serenity in measured steps, padding through her sunlit home in politically correct South Austin, tracing a path from the work-littered dining room table to the sunny kitchen, where she lights another cigarette off the burner, puffs, and then heads back to the desk to check, once more, the appointment book that is already filling up with writing assignments and speaking engagements, coast to coast, through much of next year and beyond. Mostly, Ivins keeps at it, trying to ignore the anxious internal whisper that at times suggests she does not deserve it all, that hisses that she is in grave danger of becoming one of those self-aggrandizing, self-important souls she has spent more than two decades satirizing. "I saw a shrink because I thought I suffered from fear of success," Ivins confides grimly, "but I found out I suffered from fear of becoming an asshole."

So, in essence, everyone wants Molly—except, perhaps, Molly. The unexpected blockbuster status of *Molly Ivins Can't Say That, Can She?*—a collection of columns satirizing George Bush, Ronald Reagan, and the Texas Legislature, among others—raises those nagging fears that her impact as a journalist has been eclipsed by her impact as an entertainer. But what can you do when the national media keep calling?

In her column for the *Fort Worth Star-Telegram,* which appears three days a week and is syndicated in 96 newspapers, Ivins explains politics and brings government to life. She may not be the country's most trenchant analyst or its most dazzling reporter, but her unrelenting enthusiasm for human foolishness invites readers to take on the political process. "The most amazing, amusing and fascinating of games once again bursts upon us in all its insanity," Ivins wrote at the beginning of the 1982 Texas legislative session. "The stakes they play for in politics are paper and money. The chips they play with are your life."

She has, as the jacket of her book declares, "a sharp eye and a sharper pen." She writes about stupidity in politics, and she never runs short of material. Her targets have ranged from pretentious yuppies ("In the New Age none of the vegetables are their regular color. It's all red lettuce, yellow bell peppers, golden beets") to the president of the United States ("Calling George Bush shallow is like calling a dwarf short") and Ross Perot ("all hawk and no spit"). Yet she retains a tolerance for human weakness that sometimes borders on admiration. What other female journalist would have jokingly defended girl-crazy congressman Charlie Wilson of Lufkin by writing, "His standing order on secretaries is, 'You can teach 'em to type, but you can't teach 'em to grow tits'"? And they love her—the politicians, the yuppies, the so-called conservative East Coast media elite. They can't get enough. To meet the ever-growing demand for her work, Ivins begins with her column. Then she does short pieces for her favorite lefty journals—the *Progressive*, the *Nation*, and *Mother Jones*—and longer ones for mass-market publications such as *McCall's* and *Playboy*. On top of that, she gets calls at least twice a day from radio shows, begging for her salty opinions. Ivins is also a frequent contributor to the *MacNeil/Lehrer News Hour*, National Public Radio's *All Things Considered*, and any other news show that suddenly finds itself in need of an authority on Texas. Finally, there are speeches; everyone from the American Civil Liberties Union to Republican clubwomen, it seems, wants to hear Ivins hold forth. "Do I want to speak to a bunch of women at the River Oaks Country Club?" Ivins asks herself, as she squints at her datebook. "No," she answers, moving on to the next request.

And so it goes, day in and day out, as Molly schedules herself into mainstream America. You'd think she'd be happy. She's famous. She's almost rich. Texas finally has a governor from her side of the political spectrum, her old friend Ann Richards. The place that has supplanted Scholz Garten as the new Austin lefty hangout, La Zona Rosa, is even semi-air-conditioned. But in fact, Ivins is wary. Get her on the subject of success, and the West Texas marbles-in-the-mouth accent falls away, the one-liners dry up like a played-out well. "I have always been a left-winger and an outsider. I loved being that. I was perfectly cheerful with that role," Ivins says. "Then suddenly you're one of the talking heads on *Nightline,* and you think you must have sold out."

Ivins takes another long drag on her cigarette, enveloping herself in that ever-present cloud of smoke. Behind it, the expression on her broad, open face is one part perplexed, one part mournful. No wisecrack, no punch line, follows. Because the truth is, for Molly Ivins, fame hasn't been all that funny.

"I SPEND MOST of my life feeling like I've been shot out of a cannon," Molly Ivins says, her long hair whipping wildly in the wind as a Yellow Cab hurtles across Houston toward her next destination. It is the third day of the Republican National Convention. Ivins, armed with three packs of Marlboro Lights, is dressed in a flowing turquoise ensemble and scuffed running shoes. She looks like a big butterfly in a big hurry.

Her schedule would exhaust weaker mortals. Today Ivins not only must write her syndicated column but also has to gather information for assignments from the *Nation* and *Newsweek.* She will also fulfill her obligations as a pundit, hitting the talk show circuit, and of course, find material for her next column. It is a media star's day, evenly divided between work and promotion.

Not a second goes to waste. By the time Ivins finishes breakfast at the Ritz-Carlton with the media elites from *Newsweek,* she has settled on a topic for her column: lying. "It used to be politicians were afraid to do it because they'd look dumb if they got caught," Ivins remarks in the cab. In particular, she is amazed by the Bush camp's distortion of Bill Clinton's tax record and Hillary Clinton's legal opinions. Dashing to the *Star-Telegram*'s makeshift office in the Astrohall, Ivins fortifies herself with coffee and cigarettes and starts her column. It is still unfinished when she grabs her purse, her notebook, and another cab for the ride to lunch at Brennan's.

Barreling up Main Street, Ivins puts these free minutes to use. Inspired by Patrick Buchanan's confoundingly divisive speech of the night before, which called for a house-to-house battle against decaying values, she tries out a line. "We missed the Renaissance, the Reformation," Ivins declares, her unmade-up face brightening and her voice rising. "Now let's have our own religious wars in this country!" Like comics and politicians, she is always either collecting lines or trying them out. Often, it's hard to separate the real Molly from her shtick, conversation from rehearsal.

At the elegant, crowded restaurant, Ivins is feted by friends and ogled by the patrons. She floats her religious wars bit over the meal and is rewarded with another quip for her column. When a friend cracks, "Why should the Bosnians have all the fun?" Ivins swiftly appropriates it.

After lunch, Ivins races downtown to the Hyatt Regency, where she appears on NPR's *Talk of the Nation*. The host is a balding, bearded man named Robert Siegel; the topic is humor at the convention. Ivins shares guest duties with *New York Times* reporters Maureen Dowd and Frank Rich and comedian Al Franken, who is participating by phone. Ivins's role, naturally, is to be the professional Texan.

"You are our native Texan here," Siegel begins, "so I assume Houston strikes you as a reasonably normal place." Ivins, who has made her name by making Texas a very abnormal place, knows what to do. Her syllables soften as she explains why convention delegates aren't out jogging ("Republicans do *not* exercise in the public parks") and jokes about Phil Gramm's political alter ego, Dickie Flatt.

Siegel remarks that in Gramm's keynote speech he had referred to "my mama" instead of just "mama," which Siegel understood to be improper Southern usage. "It's just 'mama,'" Ivins concurs. "I wonder if the Republicans have to close up the mama gap."

Maureen Dowd wants to know why so many Houston events have been decorated with baby elephant shrubbery: "Why do they have this topiary fetish?" Siegel wants to know about Lubbock: "What is it about Lubbock, by the way?" Finally, it is time for the inevitable question: On Ivins's Top Ten List of Things Journalists Ask About Texas, this is number one. Dowd, at least, poses it ruefully: "Is George Bush a Texan?"

Ivins hunches toward the microphone and, like a sandwich chef at Sonny Bryan's, starts to slather her words together. "Damn near everyone who died at the Alamo was from out of state," Ivins admits, only it sounds like "Damnnear everwon whodahd atthalamo wuzfrum outtastyte." Then she gives her stock response: "Real Texans do not use the word 'summer' as a verb. Real Texans do not wear those navy blue slacks with little green whales all over them. And no real Texan has ever referred to trouble as 'deep'"—long pause—"'doo-doo.'"

Ivins does the show on automatic pilot, using lines she has used so many times before, validating the tired notions outsiders cling to about Texas. Not until she gets back in the cab does she let the professional Texan facade drop. "Bush hasn't lived here for twenty-six years," she says wearily. "The connection has become a little attenuated."

Such is the price of being Molly Ivins—too much time spent on mindless pursuits and endless promotions. Her heroes are journalists like William Brann, the nineteenth-century Waco editor known as the Iconoclast, who was assassinated for his acerbic writings. But Ivins's own great work remains unwritten. The year before last, she took leave from her columnist's job at the *Dallas Times Herald* to write what she christened The Big Book. It was conceived as a way to explain the effects of governmental actions on ordinary people—what happens, say, when a bill passes from the Texas Legislature into real life—and it would be told in Ivins's sharp, irreverent style. But devoid of her daily deadline, Ivins foundered. Eventually she returned to the *Times Herald*, sporting a T-shirt that warned, "Don't Ask About the Book."

But the *Herald* proved to be no retreat. After lingering for years, the 112-year-old paper finally expired, and Ivins found herself on the unemployment line, accepting, as she says now, invitations from "everyone from the Marfa masons who wanted me to speak."

At the same time, the project Ivins had christened The Little Book—otherwise known as *Molly Ivins Can't Say That, Can She?*—was taking on a life of its own: It hit the *New York Times* best-seller list and dug in for 27 weeks. In other words, The Little

Book was turning into A Very Big Book. Unfortunately, payment for The Little Book was contingent on delivery of some portion of The Big Book; hence Ivins found herself broke and out of work, even as she was making those requisite appearances on Leno and Letterman, denying rumors that she would replace Andy Rooney on *60 Minutes*, and advising actress Judith Ivey on playing a Molly-inspired character on *Designing Women*.

The serious work would have to wait. The new job with the *Star-Telegram* and a renegotiated book deal—Ivins is now committed to doing a second collection of her pieces while she works on The Big Book—have erased her money problems. But fame and financial security have once again interrupted the ambitious project that might satisfy those inner demons and prove that Ivins is, indeed, the definitive voice of Texas.

Back at the Astrodome, Ivins is wowing Jeremy Paxman of the British Broadcasting Company. She declares that "in the absence of a flying pig," the Republican nominee will be George Bush. She talks up Hillary Clinton, trots out Pat Buchanan's speech ("Religious warfare, what an idea!"), and analyzes Bush's chance for re-election. "Frankly," she says, "I think he's dead meat." This cracks up the Brits in the control room. "She's very good, this woman," they say to each other. "She's fahntahstic!"

Ivins gallops back to the Astrohall to finish her column, then grabs another cab to meet with some editors at *People*, who are also charmed with her religious warfare line. Later, at the *Star-Telegram* pressroom, she downs a brownie for dinner and catches Marilyn Quayle's speech on TV. When the camera pans on the Quayles' daughter, Corinne, Ivins deadpans, "Is she the one who has to have the baby?"

Then it's off to another TV show—for ABC News, with humorist P. J. O'Rourke. As Ivins makes her way through the convention crowd, it is clear that everyone knows her. A security guard screams, "Molly Ivins, mah favorite columnist!" Other journalists, who have either worked with her or written about her, come up for a quick embrace: *Los Angeles Times* editor Shelby Coffey, the former editor of the *Times Herald*; Alexander Cockburn of the *Nation*; Calvin Trillin of the *New Yorker*; and Murray Kempton of *Newsday* ("I liked you when you were semi-successful!").

The only event of the evening that completely commands Ivins's attention is Barbara Bush's speech. For this, she takes a seat in the press box adjacent to the stage. To her left she can see the first lady on the podium; straight ahead she can see the surging crowd and an enormous TV screen aglow with shimmering white hair. Ivins straightens her spine as the steely Mrs. Bush dons her grandmotherly mask. She rolls her eyes when Midland is described as "a small, decent community." But when Mrs. Bush hushes the floor with her symphony of selflessness and sacrifice, Ivins is galvanized. "However you define family, that's how we define family values," the first lady tells the crowd. "For us, it's putting your arms around each other and being there." At the end of the speech, Ivins's grin is as wide as a West Texas sky—and not because this unmarried, unruly liberal has bought a ticket on the family values train. "This is really an effective piece of political theater," she declares. "Just ace."

With eleven o'clock approaching, Ivins hustles off to one more appointment. On the way, syndicated columnist Cal Thomas snags her arm. "Molly," he asks smugly, "what Texas colloquialism do you have tonight?"

"Dead meat," Ivins mutters and pushes past him, making her way to another show.

IN A NAIL SALON in Northwest Austin, Molly Ivins is getting the second manicure of her life. The first one was for the Republican Convention, and now, as she prepares to ride a campaign bus with Bill Clinton and Al Gore, she is treating herself again. The salon is located in a small converted home; the front room is full of girlish things, like makeup and sweatshirts decorated with ribbons and bows, and the back room is crowded with a baby swing and toys. A cheerful toddler appears and disappears. It is not an atmosphere one would normally associate with Ivins, who has come late to the world of femininity and domesticity. Part of Ivins's shtick is her declaration, sometimes accompanied by batting lashes and rolling eyes, that she always felt excluded from "the norms of southern womanhood." Indeed, she has lived most of her adult life as a nomad and a rebel, directed by her notebook, unfettered by convention. She did not plan her life this way. "In all my fantasies I always assumed I would get married and have six children along the way with the greatest of ease," she says, splaying her nails so that the barely pink polish catches the light. At her twenty-fifth college reunion in the spring of 1991, Ivins confessed to her classmates that she was astonished at how they had planned their lives and met their goals. "I don't think I've decided much in my life," Ivins says now, bewilderment creeping into her voice. "Don't you think life just happens?"

When Ivins talks about her childhood, her voice drops to a whisper and she becomes more terse than normal. The "sweethearts" and "darlin's"—the Southern girl's social grease—disappear from her lexicon. As with the stories she tells on others, Ivins has been known to embellish the story she tells on herself, though she tends to leave out the jokes: The biography she fashions for readers and viewers can create the impression that she is a product of a tiny East Texas town, especially when the information is delivered in her best down-home patois. She also says that she was shaped by the racism of her era. A much-recounted memory is of being told that the water fountains designated for black people were dirty, while she could see even as a young child that the fountains for whites were the ones choked with chewing gum and litter.

While true enough, the stories Ivins has shaped for herself obscure a somewhat more complicated history. The East Texas of her childhood is actually the better neighborhoods of Houston, where her family moved from California after she was born. Her parents were from Illinois. Her mother was from a prominent family; her father, a proud and ambitious oil company executive, was not. "A classically upwardly mobile family," Ivins says dully. The Ivins home was prosperous—they moved to River Oaks when Molly was in the seventh grade—but it was also highly regimented and deeply conservative. Friends recall Molly's father, James E., as a commanding figure who was hard of hearing as the result of a World War II injury. "He was kind of a Captain Ahab type," an old friend remembers. "He yelled a lot, and you had to yell around him."

Ivins, a bright student and a voracious reader, struggled to be heard in more ways than one. In the fifties and early sixties Houston was a segregated town, and the same hypocrisy Ivins saw on the street she also perceived at home. The family dinner table became the scene of screaming matches over civil rights between Ivins and her father, then general counsel for Tenneco. (Her older sister and younger brother, as well as her mother, were less political.) Ivins rarely won. "He was not the kind of guy you would identify with Molly," says Roy Bode, an editor who worked with Ivins at the *Times Herald*. "He was the kind of guy you would identify as one of Molly's targets." Though father and daughter eventually called a mealtime truce, Ivins was marked. "I've always had trouble with male authority figures," Ivins says, "because my father was such a martinet."

Like many shrewd children, Ivins found other people who encouraged her worldview: a firebrand teacher at St. John's, Houston's most exclusive private school, who nurtured her writing talent and her budding liberal views; her best friend's parents, social activists who subscribed to the *Texas Observer*, which was then literary and left-wing, the only publication of its kind for thousands of miles.

Another factor also moved Ivins from the mainstream: She was six feet tall by the sixth grade. At St. John's she tried basketball without success and took up smoking, hoping it would stunt her growth. Her best friends were also bright but eccentric. "We weren't cute; we weren't in a sorority mold," recalls one. "The only thing we had in common was that we just didn't fit anywhere." Dates were rarer than liberals, a fact Ivins took to heart. "If you're a woman who's never been picked, you're able to take a different approach," says the same friend. "You don't have to be ladylike and prim."

So at a time when many women, particularly in Ivins's social strata, planned to stay close to home and join the Junior League, the tall girl from Texas set her sights on a career as a foreign correspondent. She studied philosophy and language at Smith College in Massachusetts, doing a little fine-tuning on her personality as well. "You try going to Smith from Texas after November 1963," she says. "Being a Texan was not a treat. I learned to speak with no accent very quickly." She took a year at the Institute for Political Science in Paris but soon after found herself back in Houston, reporting on sewers for the *Chronicle*. Ivins persevered, however, and won the Perle Mesta Franco-American Friendship Foundation Scholarship to the Columbia School of Journalism. She got her master's degree, living on Campbell's split pea soup with ham, and in the late sixties she got a job at the *Minneapolis Tribune*. She moved from the police beat to one she calls "movements for social changes"—blacks, women, student radicals—but her heart was elsewhere. Ivins answered an ad in Ronnie Dugger's *Texas Observer,* flew down to Austin for an interview, and was hired almost instantly. "Home," she would come to say, "is where you understand the sons of bitches."

"What people saw in the *Observer* was another way," says Kaye Northcott, who was editor in 1970, when Ivins was hired to be co-editor. Often, the person who pointed the way was Molly Ivins. She had been teaching herself how to be an *Observer* writer—opinionated, funny, unabashedly left-wing—since her adolescence; now she turned her talents on a state that was as backward, poor, and ignorant as any Third World country. The first day Ivins set foot in the statehouse, she saw one legislator dig another in the ribs and announce, "Hey, boy, yew should see whut Ah found mahself last night! An she don't talk, neither." Ivins was hooked, not just on politics but on the theater of politics, and her great gift was that she could convey these comic but crucial scenes to her readers.

While other newspapers were mired in the House-Bill-x-passed-by-x-votes form of political reporting, Ivins was crisscrossing the state, packing a typewriter and one wrinkled, defeated dress, sleeping on air mattresses in the homes of *Observer* subscribers, reporting on the foibles of public servants. She brought home national issues of the day—racism, sex discrimination, abortion, busing, pollution. Almost always, her weapon was humor. On a case of rural air pollution, she stated, "Even hardy folk who enjoy the sharp, natural odor of a fresh cow pie find feedlots overpowering." She described Governor Dolph Briscoe as having "all the charisma of bread pudding." *Dallas Morning News* stories contained "the most meat-headed, shallow, unctuous, sanctimonious, vapid, ludicrous, knee-jerk prose ever printed in all seriousness by a major metropolitan daily." In a sense, she had become the foreign correspondent she had dreamed of becoming, reporting back to the civilized world on the farcical barbarians who were making the laws. Ivins was also restaging her family dinner-table drama—only this time, she would be heard. Using the *Observer* as her forum, Ivins promoted her "dripping-fangs liberalism." She was for labor and against racism, for big government and against big corporations. She believed criminals could be rehabilitated and that gun control should be legislated. Above all, she believed in the sanctity of the First Amendment. If Daddy didn't like it, lots of other folks did.

Ivins was having a great time. "Being a liberal meant having more fun than anybody else," she says. Texas's kamikaze-like left held no power—"it was better to be right than win" is the way the left thought of itself—but these liberals were the state's embattled intellectuals. For many, the futility of their enterprise fueled their sense of humor. Money didn't matter; what counted were politics and beer, books and ideas, pranks and stories. Those were the days when a legendary crowd gathered at Scholz Garten, and under the stars and the live oak branches would flow twelve-beer arguments on the nature of man.

The *Observer* office, in an old house at Seventh and Nueces, was a rat's nest of old newspapers, empty beer bottles, and overflowing ashtrays, but the people it attracted became the family Ivins should have had: Ann Richards and her husband, Dave, who practiced law from the first-floor office; writers like Gary Cartwright and Bud Shrake; good-time politicos like Don Kennard and Bob Armstrong; and humorist John Henry Faulk. Faulk, a garrulous activist and folklorist who had been blacklisted in the fifties, was a particular inspiration, teaching Ivins that she could be both a committed liberal and an entertainer. On the river trips and camp-outs, at the sing-alongs and great debates, the shy, self-deprecating writer perfected a new persona: thick-talking, quick-thinking, hard-drinking Molly Ivins. In Austin she could be an outsider, but she also belonged; for the first time in her life, she fit.

But only briefly. The *New York Times* had taken note of her work, asked her to write some op-ed pieces, and in 1976, hired her away. Friends believed she was bound for stardom. But the *Times* of that period was quite different from the paper it is now. In the mid- to late seventies it had few women reporters, few feature sections, and very little lively writing. For Ivins, that meant trouble.

She covered many of the big stories of the era and tried to imbue them with as much of her voice as the paper would allow. She covered the Son of Sam killings, Elvis's funeral, and the state's fiscal crisis. "Governor Carey proposed an $11.345 billion New York State budget today that calls for major cuts in welfare and Medicaid, along with a revised formula that would reduce local school aid to many districts" was a lead of one front-page story that ran under Ivins's byline. In 1977 she was made Rocky Mountain bureau chief. From her home in Denver, she covered nine states, writing about, among other things, Mormons, Indian tribal courts, grasshopper plagues, ski bums, and the joys of Butte, Montana.

Her work was fresh and funny, but she was unhappy. "It's hard to leave Texas behind," Ivins says. "I carried it right with me." She tried to style herself as the eccentric outsider—affecting her tall Texan act, wearing a buffalo-hide coat to cover the legislature in Albany, greeting everyone with "Hidy!" and taking her dog, Shit, to the newsroom—but it backfired. The *Times* did not want Molly to be Molly; they expected Molly to become, well, the *Times*. The copy desk regularly translated Ivinsisms to *Times*isms—converting "beer gut" to "protuberant abdomen," for example—and the paper's executives didn't go for her laid-back Austin look. After her probationary period ended, Ivins was criticized not for her reporting but for dressing badly, laughing too loudly, and walking around the newsroom in bare feet. "That did bring back a whole lot of feelings," Ivins says now. "'I'm too big, I'm too loud, I'll never fit in'—the way Texans are perceived in the East. I was just miserable."

The situation deteriorated, and Ivins became more rebellious. After describing a ritual chicken slaughter as a "gang pluck," she was called to the office of Abe Rosenthal, the paper's legendary Napoleonic editor, and was demoted to number two on the city hall beat back in Manhattan. The painful episode exposed a conflict in Ivins's nature: She wanted to be an outsider, but she also wanted to be a player. Expelled from the loop, she was sitting right back at her father's dinner table all over again.

The *Times Herald* came to her rescue. In 1982 Dallas was still booming, and a real newspaper war was flourishing. The *Herald* had become a flashy paper of rogue columnists—John Bloom dreamed up drive-in-movie critic Joe Bob Briggs there. Ivins was recruited with the promise that she could write what she wanted; instantly, she resumed her traditional role, skewering the city's white-male establishment. She called Ross Perot "a man with a mind half-an-inch wide" and Eddie Chiles "a loopy ignoramus." Mayor Starke Taylor she nicknamed Bubba, Governor Bill Clements the Lip. She satirized Dallas's passion for positive thinking: "The entire contents of one such rally," she wrote, "is contained in the children's book about the little train that thinks it can." She regularly took aim at the city's delirious devotion to conspicuous consumption: "The inequities in our society are becoming too glaring, too cruel, finally obscene. It is not just that the upper middle class hastens to switch to rice vinegar while children starve in Ethiopia—our fellow citizens are homeless in our streets."

Eventually the city fathers stopped getting the joke, especially when her leads began with "It's been ten years this month since Saul David Alinsky died" and "Happy May Day, comrades." The bust was settling in. Pressure was put on the paper's owner, the Times Mirror Corporation. It was felt, in the words of then editor Will Jarrett, that "Molly was not in love with Dallas and Dallas was not in love with her."

In what appeared to be a brilliant compromise, Ivins was dispatched to Austin to cover the Legislature once more. She was forty. She had learned from Saul Alinsky that a journalist should never want anything, but three years later, she bought a house—a real one, a nice one, with big windows and a garden. She began to plan—the idea for The Big Book was percolating—the *Herald* would be her base from which she could come and go. But then the *Herald* was gone, and as had happened with so many plans before, this one seemed to slip from her grasp.

Driving back over the river toward that home in South Austin, Ivins is thoughtful. At the convention she had bemoaned the lack of role models for women. "With Hillary Clinton on one side and Barbara Bush on the other, you wind up thinking there's something wrong with you," she had told a reporter, adding, "I don't think there's a woman in America who doesn't suffer doubt, confusion, and anxiety." Today Ivins drops the pundit's mask. She never married, she says, because the men she liked never asked. She is sorry that she never had a child. Her face, in the setting sun, is proud, but her voice is soft. For years she had something to prove to herself, and now maybe she doesn't. She turns into her driveway and pulls out her keys, and out of ten polished fingers, only one is chipped.

INSIDE THE CAVERNOUS Art Deco interior of the auditorium, Ivins is alone on a naked stage, behind a podium flanked by two small areca palms. She is dwarfed by the space. Something about the stripped-down scene—the hall blissfully unremodeled, the lone performer, the unreserved warmth of the crowd—gives this night at Lamar University–Port Arthur a timeless quality. Scenes like this one have played in Texas for decades: the sophisticate bringing to the smaller towns stories of the larger world.

As part of the university's distinguished lecture series, Ivins is talking presidential politics, but the subject has been folded into her basic speech, the one that reveals how and what she thinks. Aglow in a bright purple dress, rhinestone earrings, and the adulation of the audience, she begins by spinning those seductive insider's tales. She tells them what Perot sounds like when he calls to gripe about a column ("A Chihuahua," she says, mimicking his high-pitched bark expertly) and what it was like to watch Bush, at his most dorky, milk a cow on the campaign trail in 1984 ("Worst case of attempted milking by a presidential candidate I had ever seen"). She's polished without being intimidating, and she's got a seasoned comic's timing. Guarded and sometimes haughty offstage, Ivins has the star's gift of appearing open and intimate in front of a crowd.

When Ivins gets to Bill Clinton, the jokes taper off and her sermon begins. First she proffers an endorsement. "He likes to campaign and he likes to govern," she says. She follows with an endorsement of the political process in general ("I still really believe in all of it"), followed by a recitation of the Declaration of Independence. "These are ideas people are dying for," she tells the crowd. Turning somber, she warns, "We are in danger of taking our political legacy and flushing it away out of sheer inertia."

Money is ruining our political system, Ivins declares, her voice quickening with intensity. "Sixty to seventy percent of the money that puts people in office comes from organized special interests," she says. "This is legalized bribery." Ivins exhorts the crowd to take back their government and to regain control over an "economy hijacked by ideological zealots in the 1980s." The after-dinner speech has become a call to arms, Ivins style. "It's actually great fun to be a freedom fighter," she tells the audience.

If it seems odd for a journalist to be endorsing candidates and freedom fighting, it pays to remember that Molly Ivins has never styled herself as an ordinary journalist. Her beat, as she sees it, is injustice, and objectivity is, to her, of only limited value. As her speech—and her column—reveals, Ivins knows what she thinks and knows how to package her ideas. "What I really want to do is get people interested," she says. "They should be as absorbed by politics as they are by sports. The best way to get them interested is to be funny." The irony is that as Ivins's fame has grown, it has become harder to accomplish her goals.

The most obvious example of this is Ivins's professional Texan routine. "She's singing for her supper," says media critic Jon Katz, who hired Ivins at the *Herald* and remains a fan. True, Ivins can't control which questions she is asked. *Talk of the Nation* was just one example of many; on C-SPAN an interviewer once asked Ivins whether there is a building in Texas in the shape of the state, whether Jim Hogg had a daughter named Ura, why so many Texas men have two initials for a first name, how Texas could possibly elect a woman governor, and of course, whether George Bush is a Texan.

Ivins has perfected stock answers to such questions, but geographical gridlock has set in. Although she privately admits that Texas has changed enormously in the twenty-odd years she has been covering it—"There's a real decline in the number of outrageous crooks and outrageous characters"—she hasn't yet found a way to capture the place that is Texas now. The old Texas was a sorry joke for all thinking people, easy to parody. It was racist, poor, uneducated, and proud of it. The new Texas—multiethnic, two-party, more sophisticated, more ambivalent about its own myths—still has its problems but often deserves better, or fresher, material than Ivins offers. Her coverage of Dallas's foibles was livelier, for instance, than her coverage of the Legislature is now. Perhaps the most disheartening example is the first essay in her book, which she calls "an attempt to explain Texas to non-Texans." It was written in 1972: "The reason folks here eat grits is because they ain't got no taste. . . . Art is painting of bluebonnets and broncos, done on velvet. Music is mariachis, blues and country. . . . Texans do not talk like other Americans. They drawl, twang, or sound like the Frito Bandito, only not jolly. *Shit* is a three syllable word with a y in it." It isn't that contemporary Texans can't laugh at themselves; it's simply getting harder to see themselves in Ivins's jokes.

Celebrity status has also converted Ivins from a reporter to an armchair columnist. Perhaps because she has spread herself so thin, she does little original reporting, choosing instead to draw her opinions from the reporting of others. (Colleagues note that she rarely appears on the House floor, and they were surprised to see her take a seat on the Clinton-Gore bus.) Whenever she actually goes somewhere—such as the political conventions—the freshness quotient of her column soars.

The other drawback to armchair reporting is the opportunity for error. Little mistakes creep into the column with unfortunate regularity—Ivins wrote that the largest newspaper in Arkansas nicknamed Clinton "Slick Willie," but it didn't—as do an unfortunate number of corrections. (One August column contained two.) Ivins has also made her share of television bloopers, as when she declared on NBC that Jesse Jackson won the Texas primary during the 1988 presidential campaign (he didn't) or when she told Jay Leno on the *Tonight* show that Texas House Speaker Gib Lewis had resigned (he hadn't).

Finally, as Ivins's fame as a liberal has grown, her worldview has not; she's loyal to a fault to her side of the political spectrum. While other journalists of the left, notably at the *New Republic* and the *Washington Monthly,* have taken a second look at entitlements, regulations, and the limits of government in times of diminishing resources and conflicting needs, her bogeymen have remained constant. Corporations, bankers, and Republicans are still the villains in her columns. The *Morning News* is still "a right-wing newspaper." Lloyd Bentsen gets no credit for his dogged work on health-services policy, while Ann Richards is rarely criticized. (It's doubtful that a conservative politician would have received the kindness that Ivins bestowed on Lena Guerrero—an "excellent" railroad commissioner—in her column.) These days, Ivins is revealing less and preaching more. When pressed, she will admit that the left has been no more successful in tackling social problems than the right, but she lives for conflict, not complexity. "There's something fun about being on the front lines," she says of the Texas she sees. "It's much easier in a place where the good guys wear white hats and the bad guys wear black hats and there are fewer shades of gray." For Ivins, the fun is all in the fight; it is the fight, after all, that tells her who she is.

Back onstage, Ivins's speech is drawing to a close. She has grown nostalgic. She tells a favorite funny story about John Henry Faulk battling censorship in South Austin, then warns again that we could lose our freedoms if we don't fight to preserve them. She closes by quoting another old political warrior on his memories of battle: "'Tell them how much fun it was.'" Her smile is blissful, her voice rich with passion and something like joy.

"You get out there and freedom fight," she says to the expectant faces in the dark, "and you're gonna have a glorious time."

IT IS FRIDAY EVENING at La Zona Rosa. Instead of Scholz's worn wooden floors, beer signs, and an oak-shaded patio, this place is stage-set funky, with corrugated tin walls, ceiling fans, folk art, and south-of-the-border hues. Good new music plays on the sound system, and the tables are filled with politicos, artistes, and a pair of young lesbians with matching bleach jobs, necking aggressively. Few people seem to be thinking about changing Texas, much less about the nature of man.

But along one wall, Molly Ivins holds court with a group of friends. They are mostly middle-aged guys, quick with a quip and loud with their laughter. As the shadows grow and the waitress pours refills, the table grows damp with water rings and dusty with cigarette ash, and the conversation rises and falls like the waves of a warm and friendly sea. Concessions have been made to the passing of time and youth, as the group complains about aches and pains, Austin traffic, and the efficiency of their liquid diets—the kind of talk that probably didn't figure much in conversations at Scholz's. But soon they're diving into James Baker's role as Bush campaign guru ("How long is this guy bein' paid by the taxpayers?" Ivins demands. "Is this an ethical question that would puzzle Gib Lewis?"); the Republicans in general ("It's getting wiggy out there—did Barbara say she couldn't imagine why anybody would sleep with George?"); and maneuvering in the ongoing morass that is congressional and legislative redistricting. "How fast does it move and what is the time frame?" Ivins asks of one plan. When a friend hints that a liberal victory may come to pass, Ivins clutches a fist, raises it, and laughs, and you believe for a moment that, for her, this is almost enough.

A few more Capitol groupies arrive, as do a couple of reporters, including Kaye Northcott, now with the *Star-Telegram*. Bob Slagle, the wizened, gum-chewing state Democratic party chairman, takes a seat at the opposite end of the table from Ivins, and she looks slightly abashed. "Shit," Ivins grumbles. "I been crappin' on him for years." But as the voices grow louder and the smoke thickens, the good-natured ribbing at the table continues. Someone even teases Ivins about being introduced as a "talk show maven." A rowdy consultant with unruly hair brings a baby in a carrier, plunks her down near Slagle, and then grabs a seat near Ivins to smoke. Ivins graces the baby with one long appraising look and then rejoins the guys.

The conversation floats to the left, as she complains she can't find the right bumper sticker for her new pickup truck. "I liked one that says 'Visualize World Peace,'" Ivins says, "but I think I want one that says 'Visualize Armed Revolution.'" Someone brings up Martin Wiginton, a much-beloved Austin lefty who died and chose to be buried in a pauper's grave. It's suggested that they take up a collection for a headstone inscription. Everyone eagerly agrees.

In the seconds that follow, you can sense a world slipping away, that ordered one where right and wrong were separate and distinct, where the battle lines were drawn and the boundaries clear, where wars were waged against enemies from without, not within. It was a world far, far from best-seller lists and talk show appearances; it was a world where it was easier to see what really mattered. For Molly Ivins, that world is gone. She has learned to claim her place in this one even as she mourns, like the most faithful lover, the loss of the old.

"I've made Kaye co-executor of my will," Ivins confides. Then she pauses just a beat; the line has come to her, and a look of the devil lights her eyes. "I said, 'Kaye, if there's anything wrong with my head, pull the plug. Scatter my ashes in the Hill Country. Give my money to the ACLU.'"

*November 1992*

# LADY BIRD LOOKS BACK

*In her own words, a Texas icon reflects on the lessons of a lifetime.*

JAN JARBOE RUSSELL

When I first interviewed Lady Bird Johnson on a cold and rainy day in November 1994, Mrs. Johnson was 81 years old. The interview was *Texas Monthly*'s way of celebrating Mrs. Johnson's long, remarkable life. She met me at 9:00 A.M. in the kitchen of her house in Northwest Austin. Standing at the stove, dressed in a pleated navy skirt and cotton print blouse, Lady Bird leaned on a steel cane and asked the first question. "Do you take your coffee black or with sugah?" she said, rolling the *r* as only well-bred women from East Texas do. I felt the past rise up between us. Soon we were exploring the many rooms of Lady Bird's vast memory: her childhood in Karnack, her marriage to Lyndon, the major events of the Cold War era, his efforts to end poverty, her efforts to spread beauty like wildflowers. "If we can get people to see the beauty of the native flora of their own corner of the world with caring eyes," she said, "then I'll be real happy."

IF TEXAS HAD A QUEEN, Lady Bird Johnson would be it. But this is a state that loves wealth yet despises aristocrats, so she will have to settle for the lifetime title of first lady. It suits her. She looks plain, even common; she has rooted herself firmly in nature through her love of wildflowers, and she stands for the simple pleasures of daily existence.

"Do you take your coffee black or with sugah?" she asked, replacing her r with a long Southern h. She was standing in the kitchen of her home, which is on a high hillside in Northwest Austin, and as she poured the coffee with one hand, she leaned on her steel cane with the other. Everything about her—from her pleated navy skirt, sensible cotton print shirt, and flat black lace-up shoes to the fresh sunflowers on her table—seemed a comfortable fit.

For 21 years Lady Bird has lived on her own, without her famous husband. Her stature was once derived from Lyndon Johnson's position, but make no mistake: Today it comes from the force of her personality. Throughout their highly public marriage, Lady Bird benefited from the comparison with LBJ. He was ham-handed, gruff, often offensive; she was gentle, polite, always easy company. He was prone to excess and violent mood swings, and a careless pursuer of women; she was balanced, calm, and committed to the awesome responsibility of keeping him under control. In the hard times he gave us controversy over Vietnam; she gave us the Eden-like serenity of gardens.

Over the years, she became the embodiment of much of what we think about Texas women of her generation. To begin with, there's her hair: rolled, teased, waved at the front, and sprayed into place. Go to any garden club in Texas on any day of the year, and you'll find a room full of Lady Bird wannabes. Nellie Connally, John's wife, copied her hairstyle. So did Janey Briscoe, Dolph's wife. Ann Richards adapted it slightly, turning it into a silver helmet suitable for war. Then there's Lady Bird's manner: nice but unwavering, and always a little suspicious that a conversation is about to turn into criticism of Lyndon. Whenever I look at a photograph of her, I see a template of my mother and my grandmother, women who sacrificed their own wants and desires for their families and therefore would not allow anyone to say an unkind word.

By now, of course, many biographers have spoken ill of Lyndon Johnson, calling him everything from an adulterer to a thief. It's not surprising, then, that Lady Bird has been reluctant to speak publicly. It has been several years since she gave an in-depth interview to the media, and this particular interview was first requested more than three years ago.

She moved into her high-ceilinged living room, its walls filled with pictures of flowers and scenes from nature, and looked out her window for deer among the scrubby woods below. "I'm in constant battle with the deer out here," she said. "I feel sorry for the poor deer. The land is so built up now there's nothing for them to eat. They're starving, but they still make me mad!"

This is the way Mrs. Johnson naturally talks: of the outdoors, the deer, the weather, the way heavenly light ought to fall on the land near sundown, and a good deal about getting the colors just right for a meadow of wildflowers she's thinking about planting. She will be 82 years old on December 22, and this year's birthday signals the onset of yet another phase of her relationship with the earth. This spring she will open the new location of the National Wildflower Research Center on a 42-acre site southwest of Austin.

Our interview took place over an eight-hour period at her house in Austin, during lunch at an Austin restaurant, and on the grounds of the new wildflower center. Once she started talking, she seemed happy, even eager, to reminisce about her life.

"Let's talk a while to history," I said to Lady Bird as I placed a tape recorder between us before the interview began.

"Oh, yes," she said, staring into her coffee cup reflectively, "let's do."

*What are the biggest changes you've seen in Texas?*

When we began in public service in 1937, Texas was a rural, agricultural state. The biggest voting bloc was the farmers and ranchers. Things really changed when Lyndon helped FDR get the Rural Electrification Act through the House in 1936. Until then, farmers and their wives had no electricity. Once they got dams, they got electricity and then farm-to-market roads. Then both men and women had a way to get to the city to work. It really opened up the state.

Fifty-eight years later, Texas is an urban, technological state. Some days I hardly recognize it. I'm not really sure that Lyndon could be elected today in Texas. For one thing, he was never really comfortable with television. Lyndon liked owning TV stations, but as far as using it as a tool of explanation, persuasion, a transfer of himself and his beliefs and desires into the public mind, he didn't ever really make friends with television. He was a son of the courthouse steps. He loved going to the county seat on a Saturday afternoon and mingling with the old farmers with their drooping moustaches. They would chew tobacco and sit, looking very intently at you, as if they were peering into your mind to get whatever you were talking about.

*What has happened since President Johnson died that would have made him angry or troubled?*

In many ways I guess you could say Lyndon was lucky he died when he did. He couldn't have borne to see the presidency denigrated in the minds of the people the way it has been since Watergate. I don't mean to add to the many bad things that have been said about President Nixon. I just mean the public reaction to the office since Watergate has continued to decline. That would have troubled Lyndon.

Then, of course, Lyndon died before John Connally became a Republican. That would have been hard for him to take, but he died in an era when party discipline meant something. To Lyndon, party discipline was everything. I don't think he would have ever become a Republican himself, but he would have been sorely pushed if Nelson Rockefeller had been nominated because he liked him so much as a person and as a public servant.

Also, I just don't think he would have believed that we had come to the point in our country when people were talking openly about the failure of the public school system. He couldn't have swallowed that, because the public school system is one of the landmarks of America. We are perhaps the only country that has succeeded in offering an education to every child. Lyndon passed more than sixty bills about education as president—everything from Head Start to adult education—and he would never have given up the ideal of public schools.

*LBJ was the first president in modern history to find himself hated as a person as well as for his policies. But since then every president, including President Clinton, has evoked the same kind of visceral hatred that Johnson did over Vietnam. What do you think triggered his unpopularity?*

I think the reason that so many people got angry at Lyndon was because he stuffed so many changes down the nation's throat. Don't imagine that the Vietnam War was the hardest thing for him to take. Oh, no, it was not! The upheaval over civil rights was harder on him, I think, because it was our own people—the people we grew up with—who were waving the placards and glaring.

I remember some of Lyndon's best advisers came to him when he was about to launch full-scale civil rights through the Congress. They told him, "You better not do this. You're very popular right now, and you're going to lose it all over civil rights."

And I remember Lyndon told them, "What's political capital for then, if you don't use it?"

***What would he think of the changes his legislative agenda has brought about?***

Lyndon took great satisfaction in getting the Voting Rights Act through Congress. However, he seemed to know intuitively that the bill would make us more of a two-party nation. I remember that he walked into the family quarters of the White House, and there were a few people there ready to do a postmortem on the bill. There were always a few close friends who gathered around at the end of a long fight just to talk things over.

"Well," Lyndon told them, "I think I just may have handed the solid Democratic South to the Republican party."

AS LADY BIRD TALKED, we were seated on the back porch of her two-level home. She wore white-rimmed dark glasses to shade her eyes from the sun. In the distance stood the Capitol and the University of Texas tower. It was pleasant just to listen to the sound of her voice: Its rhythm is velvety, lilting, definitely Southern, but with hardly a twang at all. By the sound of it, she could be from Charleston or Atlanta. "That was a won-n-n-duh-ful day," she said, recalling one of many days past. "I've had so many won-n-n-duh-ful days."

I showed her a copy of a letter she wrote to Lyndon when he worked as an administrative aide to Congressman Dick Kleberg. It was written one month after their first date, over breakfast in the Driskill Hotel in Austin, and one month before they were married in San Antonio. Lyndon had asked her to marry him on that first date, and by the time she wrote the letter, the "wine of youth," as Lady Bird described it to me, was clearly flowing.

*Dearest Beloved,*
*Your letter Saturday morning just came. I think it's funny nobody has noticed that I look different. I feel different.*
*Lyndon, please tell me as soon as you can what the deal is. I'm afraid it's politics. Oh, I know I haven't any business—not any proprietary interest—but I would hate for you to go into politics. Don't let me get things any more muddled for you than they are, though, dearest! . . . [her ellipses]*
*Bird.*

***Did you change your mind about politics?***

Oh, yes, I did. I remember the first public utterance of mine was about politics. I guess it was in the first congressional race in 1937, when Lyndon and I were just starting out in public service.

I was sitting at a banquet when somebody leaned over and said, "You might be called on to say just a word or two." So I wrote something down on the back of an envelope. It was very simple, about two sentences long, about how politics could be a wonderful life for a man and his wife. And so it did turn out for me, but I cannot say that's true these days.

***Many biographers have had unpleasant things to say about your husband's private life. Some have suggested that he may have been a manic-depressive. Do you think that's true?***

I think the world is too strung up about psychology today and too intrusive into the private thoughts of public figures. When people ask me these sort of things, I just say, "Look to your own lives. Look to yourself, everybody. Fix yourselves, and keep your problems to yourself." The public should weigh what their public servants are doing, not their private, innermost feelings. We need to ask, "Are these policies working for America, or are they doing harm?" I think we are getting into a state of wanting to know so much about the intimacy of everyone's lives that we don't judge people by what they do for the country.

Lyndon was certainly a man of high emotions and strong feelings, of strong joys and strong pains. Life with him was an adventure, always exciting! He was awfully happy about his victories and awfully crushed about his defeats, but I never saw him too crushed to keep working.

***How did you feel about his accepting the vice-presidential nomination after he lost a chance at the presidency?***

I cannot say that I really wanted Lyndon to accept the vice presidency in 1960. It all happened so fast, and I was uncertain that it was the wisest course, but his role as majority leader of the Senate had played out. He'd done all he could do. I guess you could say that the orange had been sucked dry.

Lyndon knew that it would not be the same job in a new administration. He had served with a Republican president and a sizable Democratic majority and a very powerful Democratic Speaker in the House. Those were political characteristics that allowed Lyndon to work and get a lot of things done. It would be a very different atmosphere to have a Democratic president and a Democratic majority. The White House would be setting legislative policies, not the majority leader.

On the other hand, he realized the vice presidency had no real power and wouldn't be as important a job either. But the way I viewed it, at least as vice president he'd still [preside over] the Senate, and it could be the capstone of his career there.

***Do you think Lee Harvey Oswald killed President Kennedy?***

I have no doubt that the findings of the Warren Commission are correct. I guess the two oddest committees Lyndon ever had to put together were the one to decide what to do about Senator Joseph McCarthy and the one he appointed to look into the assassination.

Lyndon was very concerned about the possibility of a conspiracy when it first happened. The reason he wanted to get on that plane in Dallas and get airborne as soon as possible and get sworn in as president had to do with his fears about a conspiracy, but he certainly wasn't going to get the plane in the air until the president's body and Mrs. Kennedy were aboard.

He appointed the best people he could find to look into the matter, and they researched it until they sucked all the information dry. After the report came out, we just all wanted to get on with the business of the nation.

*When did things start to return to normal after the assassination?*

We didn't move into the White House until December 7. The main thing I remember was how black it all was. The White House was full of beautiful chandeliers, but they were all swabbed in black net. Everywhere I looked, the house was draped in black.

It has long been the custom in our country to mourn the president for a month, and so on December 22—which happened to be my birthday—Lyndon saw to it that the black net came off. We put up Christmas decorations, and I walked the well-lit halls for the first time with a sense that life was going to go on, that we as a country were going to begin again.

*What was your relationship like with Jackie Kennedy?*

There was a distance of age between Mrs. Kennedy and me, and frankly she belonged in a different society frame than I do. However, I liked her, and I think she liked me. In private, she had humor and a laughing side. But I felt—and I think a great many people felt—that she came across as a little girl you wanted to help. On the other hand, I always recognized there was steel beneath that exceedingly youthful exterior.

After the assassination, Lyndon and I treated her exactly as she asked to be treated. She sent word to us that the house held too many sad memories [for her ever to visit there]. She wanted her privacy, and we gave it to her, although I was real proud of Lyndon for writing to her and to her children. She knew he would have done anything he could to ease her grief.

On the last summer of her life, I had lunch with her on Martha's Vineyard. Her home had her unmistakable imprint, and oh, how she loved it. I guess one of the sad, sad things about her death was that she had finally attained what she had wanted and that was not to be a public figure.

*Which former first ladies are you closest to, and how do you think the role of first lady has changed over the years?*

Perhaps the fondest relationship I've had is with Betty Ford. She and I knew each other when our husbands were leaders in Congress. Both of us were members of the 81st Club [an organization for congressional wives], and we shared a lot of memories.

But all the first ladies have been nice to me. I've also had a warm, admiring relationship with Barbara Bush. I am closer to her than I am to Hillary Clinton because Barbara and I both come from Texas, we're closer to the same age, and we've shared so much of history.

My relationship with the Clintons is totally from a distance. I think that Hillary Clinton is proving that the role of first lady has marched with the times. I saw my role as giving Lyndon a little island of peace, a comfortable setting in which to work. It's a big, important role, and I don't think that role should be denigrated. On the other hand, Mrs. Clinton is a product of the cultural and social change of the last good many decades. I listen to her public speeches and I think she is a strong, intelligent woman who handles herself well. I tip my hat to both of the Clintons. As I used to say when things were at their worst in Lyndon's presidency, the greatest courage is just to get out of bed in the morning and get back to work.

***You defined yourself as a helpmate and extension of Johnson. Is that right?***

Yes, absolutely, and I don't think I was limited by that. I was able to continue to learn new things.

Personally, I regret that women these days don't stay home with their children until the children are at least in school. I realize I have no right to express myself on this point because I'm not raising children in this day and age and I'm not undergoing the same economic pressures that young people today have to face. However, I think young mothers today are missing one of life's greatest opportunities: to help babies grow up and train them well. I had a lot of help rearing my two daughters, and goodness knows I'm glad for every bit that I had. But these days people live so much longer than they used to, and women can have a career after their children are in school or even after they are in high school.

***Do you have any advice for the first woman president?***

Someday I think we will have a woman president, but since I'm almost 82, it's not going to be in my time. She will have to overcome a natural, inborn cultural prejudice that the man is the leader of the family and therefore should be the leader of the nation. I hope for her sake that she is healthy, both spiritually and physically, and that she has a husband who is very understanding and supportive. I also hope she has a lot of smart daughters to help her out. A president needs somebody to help carry the emotional load that wives and families have traditionally carried.

MANY TIMES in our conversation, Lady Bird talked about how time has passed her by. She sounded cheerful but also resigned. Once I asked her about Johnson's Great Society programs and whether a new kind of approach to social welfare was in order for the upcoming millennium, an approach based on something other than a handout. "Oh, my," she said. "I'm going to leave such problems to another generation."

Lady Bird is from a different time and place. I wanted to know what she remembered about her own upbringing. She was born Claudia Alta Taylor in Karnack on December 22, 1912, and nicknamed at age two by a black nurse who pronounced the child "purty as a lady bird." Both of her parents—Thomas Jefferson Taylor and Minnie Lee Patillo—came from Alabama. Her father, called Cap'n or Boss by his mostly black workers, was the richest man in Harrison County. Her mother died when Lady Bird was only five, and in her solitude, she made a connection with nature. In most of the early photographs of Lady Bird, she is standing among trees or near rivers. Her love of nature gave her a life of her own, which is probably how she survived the turbulence of the sixties and private hard times as well.

*What was your life like after your mother died?*

When I was six, my Aunt Effie came from Alabama to help Daddy raise us. She was my mother's sister. As we said in those days, she was a maiden sister, a spinster. She was the sweetest person generally, but she had no idea of discipline, no idea of how to choose the right clothes or how to put a girl in the right society. She did, however, love beauty and nature, and she spent hours explaining how lovely the fields and meadows could be. She taught me how to listen to the wind in the pine trees and to the way birds sing.

My life consisted of roaming the hills, creeks, and woods, and playing with two little black girls who were my own age. Occasionally, in an effort to do what she presumed she ought to do, Aunt Effie would import the daughters of some friends for me to play with. The girls and I would sit around looking at each other. I can't say it was a great success.

I was a child of nature. I went wherever I wanted to go, and if I got lost, I'd come across some black person, most likely, and they would recognize me. "Which way is it back to the Brick House?" I'd ask. And they'd show me the way home.

***I've heard it said that you took as much pride in the passage of the Civil Rights Act as Lyndon did, because you grew up in such a segregated society. How were your attitudes about race formed?***

I came from a part of Texas—deep East Texas—that was heavily populated by blacks, and it was the hardest place in Texas for civil rights changes to be made. The part of the world I grew up in was just like the Old South transplanted. It was cotton culture—plain, simple, hard country, just like Alabama, Louisiana, and Mississippi.

I remember once when I was a little girl that a group of white men cornered a black man in the middle of the night and accused him of some crime. The poor man was so terrified that he just took off running. When he did, the white men shot him in the back. It happened near Karnack. I heard about it the next morning, and I was just a little girl, but I remember thinking to myself, "This isn't right. Somebody ought to change this." Lyndon did.

***In* The Path to Power, *Robert Caro describes you as a wallflower. Were you a wallflower?***

I never thought of myself that way, but I did wear saddle shoes when the other girls were wearing silk stockings and lipstick. I was always scared to death when some boy sat down by me and began to talk.

But this was the period when I was eleven to thirteen and going to school in Karnack, and thirteen to fifteen when I went to high school in Marshall. I did not have any beaus then, but when I got to Austin in the spring after my seventeenth birthday, I just blossomed. From the time I was seventeen until I left the university, I had all the beaus I could handle. I had a lot of fun. Crazy, wild, city fun. I think I fell in love every April.

LIKE MOST PEOPLE, Lady Bird has built her life in retirement around memories. If her house caught on fire, she told me, there are only two items that she would grab before running outside. Both are black and white photographs that hang on the wall beside her bed: one of their daughter Lynda, after the birth of her daughter, Lucinda; and one of LBJ and their daughter Luci, after the birth of Luci's daughter, Lynn. Lady Bird's bedroom is painted in soothing shades of pink and green. "I love all kinds of pink!" she told me as she walked through the room. A TV tray, with breakfast dishes still on it, stood near her bed. In the middle of the floor was a white towel on which she had done her morning exercises. Walking into a solarium dominated by an enormous hot tub, she exclaimed, "Here is my bow to total self-indulgence!"

*Were you prepared for LBJ's death?*

Lyndon always told me, "You know, I'm not going to live to be an old man." That would make me mad, but I knew it was true.

Lyndon had his first massive heart attack in July 1955. He had a second massive one in April 1972, when we were visiting Lynda and Chuck [Robb, Lynda's husband] on our way up to see Mrs. Eisenhower. At the time, Dr. Willis Hurst, one of our marvelous friends and Lyndon's doctor, took me aside and told me, "I want you to know that with as many blocked-up arteries as he has, he will die suddenly, and it won't matter if the five best cardiologists in the United States are in the room. It just won't matter." For the next six months, there were repeated angina attacks. Lyndon described them as hurting almost as much as kidney stones.

So we lived the last bit to the fullest. On the last Christmas of his life he sat at his desk at the ranch and signed book after book [of his memoirs]. I said, "Lyndon, that's more books than you can possibly give away this Christmas." And he looked up at me and sort of smiled slowly and sadly and said, "The library can use them sometime."

We had a happy Christmas together. He got to know four of his seven grandchildren. I have some funny pictures of him riding with some of the grandchildren on the lawn mower around the airplane terminal at the ranch. All the grandkids called him Boppa. I remember Lyndon dressed up like Santa Claus and one of the grandchildren climbed on his lap and looked at him and said, "This isn't Santa Claus. It's Boppa!"

***What did you do when you were on your own, without LBJ?***

The biggest thing that ever happened to me on my own was being a regent at UT for six years. I remember when Governor Preston Smith called in late 1970 and asked me to be on the board. I felt greatly honored, but I told him I couldn't accept. Lyndon was pretty sick at the time, and I told Governor Smith that I did not want to be away from him a lot.

Lyndon was lying in bed resting. When I hung up the telephone, he said, "Come in here. I think I know what you were talking about, but tell me." So I told him.

He said, "How did you feel when I would try to convince some really capable citizen to take a government job, a Cabinet post, or head an agency, anything in the service of his country, and he said no because his family didn't want to move to Washington or because he was climbing the ladder in his company?"

I had strong feelings about that. Lyndon knew that. I always wanted him to get the best people.

So Lyndon told me to get back on the telephone and tell Preston Smith I'd be glad to do it, if he hadn't already appointed someone else. So, after my usual protestations, I did.

***You had a fund-raiser for Chuck Robb at the ranch and went to Virginia to campaign for him in his Senate race. What do you think of his opponent, Oliver North?***

Chuck's race in Virginia was about as bad a campaign as I've ever seen. We're in an ugly, contentious mood in America. I hope it will pass. These days I just turn my TV dial looking for something that's not about O. J. Simpson. Maybe I look at politics through the veil of time, but when Lyndon and I were in it, there was a basic feeling of camaraderie. You traded philosophies. You talked about your part of the country. You talked about what you had to have. But you didn't hate people who had different philosophies, and you didn't oppose just to oppose.

I don't think Lynda will wind up being marred by all this, in the sense of becoming bitter or angry. Lynda is one of the smartest people I know, and she has strong spiritual roots that she doesn't wear on her sleeve. In politics, you see the best of people and sometimes you see the worst. Sometimes people that were your dearest friends may not be able to support you because of business considerations. It's easy to be bitter or angry, but I don't believe Lynda will fall victim.

I've never met Oliver North, and I'm not in the judgment business, but let me just say that I want to be represented by someone solid, stable, someone I believe to be looking out for the best interests of the country. I think what he had to say during the campaign [about President Clinton not being his commander in chief] was a wild and loose thing to say. Clinton is his commander in chief. He may not be his choice, but he is his commander in chief for another two years and two months. He may not like it, but that's the way it is.

AS WE DROVE from her house to the wildflower research center, Lady Bird pointed out the hike and bike trail along Town Lake in Austin, one of the projects she helped raise money for when she returned to Texas in 1969. "What you want out of these kinds of places is use—joyous use," she said. "We have to get more and more places where people can get exercise and fresh air." These days, Lady Bird spends her days relaxing at the LBJ Ranch in Stonewall, attending events at the presidential library in Austin, and supervising construction and fund-raising for the wildflower center.

*Why have you devoted so much time to wildflowers?*

I don't like homogenized country. When Lyndon and I came back to Texas in 1969, I was dismayed that every place was starting to look like everyplace else. The meadows and hillsides were all being replaced by highway grids and shopping malls. I wanted to try to restore some of our native habitat. We in Texas are blessed with what we have. I just want Texas to keep on looking like Texas. It's a modest ambition, but it's mine.

***What do you think your legacy will be?***

I'm not interested in any legacy. The wildflower center is my love. I can't control the purity of the air or solve the problem of acid rain, but the wildflower center is an effort to fill a little niche in the whole environmental picture. If we can get people to see the beauty of the native flora of their own corner of the world with caring eyes, then I'll be real happy.

***Do you believe in heaven?***

Oh, yes, I do, but I don't presume to know what heaven will be like. But I do know that there is something hereafter, because all this has been too significant, too magnificent for there not to be something after. I have some friends who believe that the pearly gates are really gates and really pearly. Not for me. I prefer to leave it as a great mystery.

I like adventure. I've gone through my life liking adventure, and that's the way I like to think of heaven. It will be a once-in-a-lifetime, never-to-be-repeated, wonderful adventure.

NEAR THE END of our day together, we were walking on the grounds of the wildflower research center. Lady Bird tapped her way across a field, using her cane to find two particular yaupon bushes she had planted earlier. She knew exactly where the bushes should be, but she couldn't see them.

"My eyesight is deteriorating badly," she said. "I'm legally blind in one eye and see very little in the other. I've got a condition called macular degeneration, something that ten million of us in the country have. Even nature dwindles now."

The timbre of her voice was matter-of-fact, resolute. "Do you see any bushes in there that have any red berries on them?" Lady Bird asked me. I scanned the area, looking for the missing yaupons. "If they look gray to you, I'm going to slide in and butt my head against one of these rocks," she said. "If they're gray, they're defoliated, and that's a bad sign."

At that moment I spotted the yaupons. "I see the red berries," I told her.

She looked as relieved and contented as a farmer who had just been told her crops had been spared and she wouldn't have to sell the family farm.

"Oh, good," she said, staring at a patch of ground in the direction of the bushes. "Tell me what they look like."

*December 1994*

# O JANIS

***She loved her family, but she left them.***
***She hated Port Arthur, but she kept coming home.***
***What demons drove Janis Joplin to her death?***

ROBERT DRAPER

**Janis Joplin was both an avatar and a victim of the sixties, and reporting on her odyssey meant revisiting that wild and complicated era. Self-indulgent, self-destructive, certainly. But Janis's saga demonstrates that the sixties were also about self-expression, about daring to shun the gray-flannel prescription of postwar America. Texas had a very narrow idea back then of what a woman musician should be. Janis exploded that notion once and for all.**

JANIS CAME HOME to Port Arthur one last time in August 1970, seeking satisfaction: revenge, acknowledgment of her superiority, perhaps an apology or two from those who once called her a pig and a whore and threw pennies at her, perhaps simply acceptance at last, at last. It was her tenth high school reunion, and in those ten years the world had gone crazy. In that span of time, Janis had become a star, an icon of the counterculture, a wealthy woman, an alcoholic, and a heroin addict. Her whole world revolved at high speed. For that matter, even the world of Port Arthur had begun to spin. Some of the kids wore long hair. The schools had integrated. And when cars trolled along Procter Avenue with the windows down, you no longer heard the Coasters, Chuck Berry, and the sweet nothings of girl groups bubbling out of the radio speakers. Now you heard Janis Joplin.

But the essence of Port Arthur hadn't changed any more than

Janis herself had changed. It was still a small town where appearances counted, and she was still a thin-skinned rebel—"needing acceptance," as one of her close friends put it, "while at the same time rejecting the society from which she needed the acceptance." Janis was still of Texas, in her music and in her soul. No matter how frayed the bond, no matter how much she slashed away at it, no matter how much it tortured her, there it was. Unlike Janis, her tight circle of high school friends hadn't bothered to attend this gathering. Reunions weren't their trip; they didn't give a damn if Port Arthur accepted them or not. And not one of them had achieved the fame and fortune Janis Joplin had. Yet all of them had found a way to make peace with their pasts.

Janis had not, nor would she. She arrived at the Goodhue Hotel in full flourish, wearing purple and pink feathers and open-toed silver slippers and oversized sunglasses and fluorescent orange paint on her toenails and enough metal on her wrists and forearms to build a prison cell, accompanied by three long-haired guys of undetermined origin. Her peers spent the evening gawking at her or making catty comments out of her earshot. Several asked for autographs. At least one of them, who had never been close to the singer, assured Janis that she'd given the media the wrong impression about Port Arthur's treatment of her. "Janis, we liked you!" she insisted.

Janis did not respond. She had pledged to a reporter that she would attend the Thomas Jefferson High School reunion "just to jam it up their asses," to "see all those kids who are still working in gas stations and driving dry cleaning trucks while I'm making $50,000 a night." But now that she saw them and they saw her, what was there to say? What deep scars could suddenly disappear? What damage could possibly be undone? She spent the evening drinking, then returned to California, where she phoned a close friend, her publicist and eventual biographer, Myra Friedman. In a dejected voice she told Friedman, "Well, I guess you can't go home again, right?"

Less than seven weeks later, on October 4, 1970, 27-year-old Janis Joplin died of a heroin overdose. Her will stipulated that her body not be buried in Port Arthur—rather, that it be cremated and the ashes spread across the Pacific coastline of Marin County,

California. With Janis's last wish fulfilled, Port Arthur was forever denied a piece of its prodigal daughter's heart.

THE MOVEMENT to reunite Janis Joplin with her native state has been made possible only by redefining Janis Joplin. As the years passed, visitors from all over the world would drive through Port Arthur, searching for tributes to the city's most famous celebrity. Yet no sign, no building bore her name. Her childhood home had been torn down in 1980. Her family moved to Arizona. And those who remembered Janis did not always have nice things to say. For what had she said about Port Arthur? A town filled with bowling alleys, rednecks, and plumbers, leading "such tacky lives." Jimi Hendrix, Jim Morrison, and John Lennon may have appalled the establishment, but at least they didn't get personal about it. To some in Port Arthur, Janis Joplin symbolized the very worst of her generation. She was a spiteful, ungrateful ragamuffin who made a spectacle of herself, slept with everyone in sight, and ultimately drugged herself to death—though not before influencing thousands of gullible children toward the same doom. Small wonder that when another Joplin biographer, Ellis Amburn, strolled through Port Arthur a few years back and asked passersby why there wasn't a street named after Janis, "most people were outraged that I would even bring up the subject," he says.

Amburn would later term Port Arthur "a town without pity." But by the mid-eighties, fate had dealt the town a pitiless hand. Oil production had dried up. In 1984 Gulf laid off 1,600 workers in a single day. One year later, unemployment in Port Arthur stood at 25 percent. The city's downtown area looked as if it had been beaten and left for dead. All of this is not to say that civic leaders were completely receptive when, in 1987, the owner of a local barge and tugboat business and former classmate of Janis's named John Palmer offered to pay for a bust of the singer if the city would agree to unveil it during a fitting memorial ceremony. Recession or no, Port Arthur still wasn't inclined to honor drug users—especially drug users who publicly ridiculed Port Arthur.

But what was the use in fighting anymore? Janis was dead and Port Arthur had wounds to heal. It happened, then, that on January 19, 1988, a crowd of about five thousand people wedged themselves into the Port Arthur Civic Center and viewed the unveiling of the bust. They cried and sang along to "Me and Bobby McGee," the Kris Kristofferson song that Janis once sang like the sweetest heartache: "Freedom's just another word for nothing left to lose." One Port Arthuran after another lined up and told the dozens of reporters in attendance, "We love Janis." That, and "We forgive her."

Among those attending the event was Laura Joplin, Janis's younger sister. Two years earlier, their father, Seth Joplin, had angrily declared to *Houston Post* reporter Clifford Pugh, "The people in Port Arthur disliked Janis and did everything they could to hurt her." But Seth was now dead, and Laura found herself deeply moved by Port Arthur's desire to make peace with the past. Then and there, Laura Joplin determined to write her own biography, which would paint Janis in a different light: Janis as a beloved girl, even a normal girl, in a world that was not so troubled after all.

Thus began the recasting of Janis Joplin—and by extension, of the era that begat her. The bust of Janis now sits in a Port Arthur library, surrounded by odds and ends donated by the Joplin family. The impression these objects leave is that of a thoroughly conventional girl, one who sang in the church choir, painted religious motifs, wrote loving Mother's Day cards, and had her high school yearbook signed by dozens of pals. These tokens represent only a sliver of the woman. Yet it is the sliver that gives the city comfort. Port Arthur cannot find it within itself to immortalize what was immortal about Janis Joplin.

Those characteristics—the outrageous behavior, the excesses, the voice that wailed a hurt that could not be contrived, the need for love that no one could sate—are now dismissed by Port Arthurans as media hype. "I think she made up every single thing in that book," a local librarian told me in reference to Myra Friedman's critically acclaimed biography of Janis, *Buried Alive*, which has just been updated and re-released. The author unapologetically discusses "Janis as victim," primarily of her own pathologies, and paints a desolate portrait of Port Arthur: "The air is gummy with humidity, and it howls—heat, mediocrity, boredom." Soon, however, the most unpopular book in town will be Ellis Amburn's *Pearl: The Obsessions and Passions of Janis Joplin*. Amburn, who himself has bad memories of growing up in Texas, lays the Janis Joplin tragedy squarely at the feet of Port Arthur. "Though she survived into adulthood," he writes, "the emotional deformities sustained in youth prevented her from having a normal life."

Port Arthur, and the Joplin family, will hear nothing of this damaged account of Janis. "If you think of Janis as a wounded puppy, you've got the wrong image," says Laura Joplin, whose *Love, Janis* has just been published. The book is part of her family's organized effort to control Janis's life in a way that they could not when she was alive. They have sued a Seattle theater company over the right to base a play on Janis's life, denied Friedman permission to reprint letters from Janis that were included in the first edition of *Buried Alive,* and sent letters to Port Arthurans implicitly urging them not to cooperate with Amburn's book. Surprisingly, the family's version of Janis's life is both earnest and comprehensive. Yet its central mission—that of normalizing Janis—is apparent on almost every page. In *Love, Janis,* pages and pages are devoted to childhood scenes that cast the Joplin family in a dubiously Rockwellian glow. The pain of her high school years is attributed simply to adolescence, her oddball demeanor to the group she hung out with.

The book's distinguishing feature is that it contains 25 letters from Janis that have never before been published. The letters are to Janis's mother, and they reveal a young woman desperate to please her parents—desperate, in spite of her brave new world, to be the normal Port Arthur girl she could not possibly become. Unfortunately, Laura Joplin has used these letters to suggest that her sister was, in the end, just another young woman with a dog, a boyfriend, a nice apartment, a well-managed bank account, and a promising career. One of Janis's roommates in San Francisco and closest friends, Sunshine Nichols, recalls the singer mocking the letters even as she wrote them. "This is what just drives me insane about Laura basing her book on these letters," says Nichols today. "I mean, anybody who left home knows the letters you write your parents are lies."

In fact, the letters are exactly half the truth, the words of a woman torn in two.

JANIS JOPLIN GREW UP in Port Arthur in the late fifties, moved to Austin in the early sixties, and said good-bye to Texas in 1966. Her path to San Francisco had already been blazed by other young Texans who felt stifled by the culture of their native state. She caught up with them in a hurry: If there exists an icon of the counterculture, it is Janis Joplin. And yet psychically she remained trapped within the fault line that divided two cultures. Janis was a middle-class white girl who sang the blues. No one had any difficulty reconciling this: The ear didn't lie, and besides, Janis's blues were a matter of public knowledge, excruciatingly so. Perhaps in counterculture etiquette, it was bad form to show anything but indifference toward the world you left behind, but Janis Joplin was far too honest to conceal her agony. Practically up until her last breaths, she spoke of her native state with the kind of hostility anyone could recognize as the language of the spurned: "They laughed me out of class, out of town, and out of the state." She said it so often that today Port Arthurans and the Joplins have had to resort to the shaky claim that Janis's whole feud with Texas was just a well-rehearsed publicity hook that she and the media played for all it was worth—as if to suggest that the generation gap was nothing more than a PR ruse perpetrated by Timothy Leary and Spiro Agnew.

Yet it would be unfair to expect Port Arthur to make sense of the sixties when no one else has. The era dawned in the middle of a postwar daydream, when towns like Port Arthur were well-off and had no reason to anticipate anything but more of the same. By the time Janis Lyn Joplin entered Thomas Jefferson High School in 1957 at the precocious age of fourteen, Port Arthur had 57,000 residents, the majority of them beneficiaries of the oil boom. The boom meant that workers could afford a decent home, that their roads would be well tended and safe, and that their children's schools would be well financed.

There remained something disquieting about the oil-town culture, however, something that traveled through the air with the rest of the refinery fumes, something that was not readily exhaled. A kid could get a good education in Port Arthur. But as David Moriaty, one of Janis's schoolmates and longtime friends, says, "There was no social premium on being educated. In a normal small town, if you get educated, you become a banker or lawyer and attain a position of standing. In Port Arthur, the stillmen made fifty thousand dollars a year without much schooling." The middle-class life made possible by the port was accompanied by a churchgoing small-town moral code. But the port also brought in other elements. Brothels operated in plain view. Gambling joints openly advertised their activities. "When we were in high school," says Tary Owens, another friend and classmate of Janis's, "the city was on the one hand very straitlaced. But on the other hand, the town was absolutely wide open. I mean, the hypocrisy just glared."

"The blacks in town, at least 40 percent of the population, lived 'on the other side of the tracks,'" writes Laura Joplin. If oil-town prosperity reduced some of the financial inequality between the races, oil-town culture kept the blacks in their place. During Janis's last year of junior high, a frequent debate topic was "Will federal aid to education bring integration?" As Owens, who was on a debate team in Beaumont, recalls, "We weren't allowed to argue the pros and cons of integration—it was a given that integration was a horrible thing. The argument instead focused on whether you could get federal aid without having to integrate."

Still, by reading Jack Kerouac books, Janis and her friends got a taste of the black world; more importantly, they heard black music on the radio. By the late fifties, Elvis Presley had been drafted and Buddy Holly had died, and little was left that deserved the term "rock and roll." In contrast to the sickly sweet pop tunes that dominated white radio stations, the music of traditional folk and blues musicians such as Willie Mae Thornton, Odetta, and Leadbelly carried a raw honesty that was devastatingly seductive to Janis's crowd. Devastating, because that raw honesty served only to underscore the inconsistencies in Port Arthur's moral fabric.

Had Janis Joplin been able to overlook these inconsistencies, she might have passed her days in Port Arthur untormented. For there was much to recommend the girl. She was intensely bright, an excellent student, with a natural gift for painting, and her doughy features were not without their appeal. But the same acute sensitivity that made her a painter also made her resent the social obstacles to individuality. By her junior year in high school, they seemed to hit Janis all at once: Why did girls have to wear their clothes and hair just so? Why were the practices of drinking, cursing, and having sex forbidden and yet widespread throughout Port Arthur? And why could you listen to black music on the radio and yet not have black classmates in school?

"A key to her personality was that she could not abide hypocrisy," says David Moriaty. Janis spent her junior year hanging with the senior beatnik crowd, which included Moriaty, a jazz musician named Jim Langdon, and a music enthusiast named Grant Lyons, whom Janis would later credit with having introduced her to the music of Leadbelly and Bessie Smith—the music that inspired her to sing. She wore black turtlenecks and tights (the closest she could get to pants, which were forbidden by school authorities) or sometimes skirts, which she took pains to hem just above the knees. They passed the evenings driving restlessly through town, singing along to the songs on the radio—Janis and the boys, freethinkers plowing through nights that burned with the demon glow of the refinery lights.

If the boys were a little weird—and they were—then that could be forgiven. A guy was expected to go off the beam now and again. But when Janis fell into their company and took the night drives and drank beer and dyed her hair orange and hollered "F—k" in the high school hallways, that was something else again. Talk began to spread. She was weird. She was obscene. She was no longer a virgin. She was a whore! Boys who had never met Janis bragged openly that they had slept with her. Girls in the locker room cast furtive glances toward Janis's private parts to see if there existed some kind of visible evidence of her promiscuity. The barbs were aimed specifically at Janis, the female—despite Laura Joplin's assertion, in *Love, Janis,* that "the guys got as much flak as Janis did." (Tary Owens, who was interviewed for *Love, Janis,* distinctly recalls, "She bore the brunt of the abuse.") But for a time it was only low talk. "When she was in our group in high school, she was under our protection," says Moriaty. "But after we left, she got messed with. Her senior class essentially turned on her."

For all the differences between the Joplin biographers, they agree that Janis Joplin's life took a drastic turn for the worse in 1959. Her protectors had graduated. She had grown pudgy, and her acne festered to the point that her face had to be sanded. Classmates began to follow her down the hallways, calling her a pig, asking her for sex, goading her into saying the word "F—k." Rather than ignore them, she screamed back obscenities. Janis could not keep her mouth shut. She decried segregation in class and thus was declared a "nigger lover." She continued to wear her skirts short and to spend evenings with beatniks at the Sage Coffeehouse or slugging beer in Louisiana juke joints, ensuring her status as a cheap girl. It is possible that a part of her relished her position as a teenage outlaw. It is absolutely certain that she was not about to change for anyone. Yet it is equally certain that Janis suffered—not simply out of frustration over Port Arthur's unwillingness to concede that her way was the right way, as Laura Joplin theorizes, but also because she felt socially inadequate. Privately she would paint her nails and agonize over her figure. She felt downcast when no one asked her to the senior prom and experienced further dejection when the senior class's steering committee attempted to bar her from attending the school's Black and White Ball. Many years later, starry-eyed reporters would ask her what it was like to be Janis Joplin, only to hear the singer bemoan her failure to have a husband and children. Beneath the pleasures of celebrity, Janis Joplin—the Janis who was not asked to the prom, the one whose craving for acceptance was matched only by her refusal to behave acceptably—would not find satisfaction.

By the time Janis graduated in 1960, she had already been in and out of psychological counseling and had brought so much turmoil into the Joplin household that Laura fled to the church, where she prayed for God to bring peace to her family. Janis's parents, Seth and Dorothy, hardly fit the mold of strict disciplinarians, but it was obvious to them that Janis's behavior invited scorn. She enrolled at Lamar State College of Technology in Beaumont, where most Jefferson High graduates went if they went to college at all—meaning, as Laura Joplin notes, "the gossip mongers who had talked about Janis in high school had followed her to college." She spent most of her evenings across the state line. She stopped going to class. Not yet eighteen, Janis was already showing signs of alcoholism. She sought counseling. But at least she had music.

No one seems to be able to recall exactly when Janis discovered she could sing. They remember only that when Janis came to her friends offering proof of her talent, they listened to her voice and agreed: God, yes, she could sing. At parties she took to mimicking whatever was on the phonograph: Joan Baez, Jean Ritchie, Bessie Smith, Odetta, even Little Richard—she could do them all. As her confidence in her voice grew, her interest in painting declined.

Among the Joplin biographers, the popular explanation for Janis's giving up painting is that she met a fellow who could paint better than she could, and realizing that she could not be the very best, she put down her brush for good. That Janis did, in fact, have a competitive streak makes it hard to imagine that she would give up so readily on anything that meant so much to her. What seems more likely is that Janis recognized that singing suited her needs and temperament better. "I don't think she had the discipline for painting anymore," says Tary Owens. "And in singing there's immediate acceptance, and that's what she was after—love and acceptance."

IN THE SUMMER OF 1962, Janis Joplin enrolled at the University of Texas at Austin. The change would do her good, and Janis was ripe for change. She had spent the previous year in Venice, California, haunting the coffeehouses, hitching from one bar to the next, having sex with strangers. She brought back a World War II bomber jacket, which she wore inside out, along with a smug awareness of street life that gave her instant cachet with the Austin hipsters who congregated just west of campus at 2812 1/2 Nueces, at a building that came to be known as the Ghetto.

Built in the twenties, the Ghetto consisted of eight apartments, some fairly comfortable in size, some not much larger than a closet. The rooms rented for $35 to $65 a month, utilities included. Some of the occupants were young men who had just come out of the military on the GI Bill; others were musicians, artists, and political leftists. At times it was difficult to tell just who lived at the Ghetto, because a rotating cast of individuals tended to crash out there on the hammocks and chairs and sofas that had been dragged out into the yard to accommodate the evening festivities. There was always a party at the Ghetto, usually with musicians jamming—and usually, by 1962, featuring the powerful voice of Janis Joplin.

Though Austin as a city was light-years ahead of Port Arthur in its cultural eclecticism, the atmosphere at UT reflected the numbness of the country at large. The males wore their hair short and their clothes starched; to grow a beard was to foreclose any possibility of a job interview. The young women stuck to gray wool skirts, white bobby socks, penny loafers, white cotton blouses, and beehive hairdos. Recalls one of Janis's friends, "You could go on campus in between classes and see just hundreds of women who were dressed exactly like that."

The Ghetto crowd kept their own table at the Student Union's Chuck Wagon Cafeteria. Among them, none stood out as alarmingly as Janis, who wore jeans, a dirty blue work shirt, and no bra. "She Dares to Be Different!" declared a story about Janis in the *Daily Texan* (written by Pat Sharpe, now a senior editor at *Texas Monthly*), and indeed it was a dare that entailed certain risks. "There were only a handful of us oddballs there," says Powell St. John, who lived at the Ghetto and who was beaten up by fraternity boys for his beatnik appearance. "You had to kind of cluster together and keep your heads down."

But provoking frat boys was not all Janis's new gang had to fear. The repressive culture at the university had darker manifestations than tacit dress codes. There lingered an odor of McCarthyism in the early sixties, an attitude that freethinking should be not merely discouraged but treated as a serious threat. When a former high-ranking UT official retired three years ago, he left behind boxes of papers, including a list with the heading "Ghetto." A note at the top of the list says, "The following information was extracted from the records of the Office of the Dean of Student Life." It consists of 68 individuals, along with information such as their majors, their home addresses, and their disciplinary records at the university, and comments such as "one of the leaders of the Ghetto group," "secretary for the local chapter of the Young Peoples Socialist League," "believed to be using heavy drugs," "believed to be a homosexual," "suspected of sabotaging the air raid sirens in Austin," "believed to be very promiscuous," "believed to be a communist," "has had trouble with bad checks," "has psychiatric problems," and "pathological liar." Among those listed are *The Gay Place* author Billy Lee Brammer, cartoonist Gilbert Shelton, several current or former professors and government officials, Dave Moriaty, Tary Owens, Powell St. John, and Janis Joplin.

Recalls Travis Rivers, who attended UT before moving to San Francisco in the early sixties, "I used to say, 'The eyes of Texas are upon you—at all times.'"

But none of the Ghetto crowd was fully aware of the surveillance activities—least of all Janis, who smoked marijuana despite prevailing paranoia that meant, as Owens says, "You didn't tell your best friend you smoked pot." Janis felt utterly sure of herself. Among her crowd, which included several other women, she distinguished herself as a singer, and the locals flocked to watch her perform at Threadgill's, a converted gas station owned by yodeler Kenneth Threadgill where rednecks, beatniks, and English professors alike gathered to hear the bands play for the wage of two bucks and all the beer they could drink. People sat on tables and window ledges to hear the Waller Creek Boys, which consisted of St. John on harmonica, Lanny Wiggins on guitar, and Janis, singing and playing the autoharp. She still mimicked Odetta, Bessie Smith, and Leadbelly, but there was nothing borrowed about her wailing soprano and her bawdy, unrestrained presence.

Janis's reputation as a singer spread throughout Austin. Back on campus, however, her reputation remained primarily as that of a weirdo, far more so than the reputations of others who congregated at the Ghetto. "The rest of us kept a modicum of going to school or keeping a job," says Owens. "But she was totally in that lifestyle. Janis once said to me, 'Tary, I don't see how you can live in both worlds. I can't. I've got to be all the one way or all the other way.'"

She remained, then, the most obvious target for insults. At the close of 1962, Alpha Phi Omega sponsored its traditional Ugliest Man on Campus contest as part of a charity drive. Each fraternity paid $5 to nominate one of its own, who would then dress up in a mask and ragged attire with artificial blood and parade around in hopes that people would spend a dime to vote for him as Ugliest Man. Though no one seems to know how it began, apparently a write-in campaign developed to elect Janis Joplin as the Ugliest Man on Campus. And although she did not win, as is popularly believed (first place went to Lonnie "the Hunch" Farrell), it seems that she did receive votes. Thirty years later, a few people contend that this event was of no consequence to Janis or that she found it amusing or even that she threw her own name into the ring. ("I think that it was easily within the realm of possibility that Janis nominated herself as Ugly Man as a joke," says Laura Joplin.) But the overwhelming consensus among those friends of Janis's who attended UT that year is that she was humiliated by the contest. When interviewing Janis's mother for *Buried Alive,* Myra Friedman was told by Dorothy Joplin that Janis wrote an "anguished" letter home, detailing the contest's effect on her.

Less than a month after the Ugliest Man on Campus contest, Janis wrote a song and recorded it at a friend's house. The song is called "It's Sad to Be Alone," and Tary Owens retains a copy of the tape, featuring Janis on autoharp, singing in baleful, desolate tones.

A week later, Janis Joplin dropped out of school and hitchhiked to San Francisco. Her companions were her autoharp and Chet Helms, a long-haired, deeply spiritual young man who had already hitched to San Francisco the year before to escape the racism and right-wing morality he had encountered in his youth in Fort Worth and at school in Austin. To Janis, Helms seemed to be a worldly and romantic figure. To Helms, Janis was unlike any woman he'd ever met in Texas. Together they hitched to Fort Worth, where Helms's mother, a fundamentalist Christian, took one look at Janis in her jeans and pink sunglasses and blue work shirt unbuttoned halfway down and informed her son that they could not stay the night. Helms's brother drove them to the edge of town, past the Stockyards, and deposited them there.

Some fifty hours later, Helms and Janis were in San Francisco's North Beach. That night she played her first gig, at a folkie hangout called the Coffee and Confusion that had heard any number of wispy Kingston Trio–style singers but nothing like this woman from Texas. She brought the house down, prompting the owner to violate a long-standing house policy against passing the hat. Thereafter, Janis and her autoharp played at the Coffee Gallery, at the Catalyst and the Barn in Santa Cruz, and at St. Michael's Alley in Palo Alto. Word came back to the Ghetto: Janis had made it.

A YEAR AND A HALF LATER, in May 1965, Janis Joplin returned to Port Arthur, haggard, her weight down to 88 pounds, her arms punctured with needle tracks. In the City of Lights she had met all her inner demons, the holes in her soul she filled with all the sex and drugs her body could withstand. She spent equal time at the Amp Palace, a Grant Avenue cafe where amphetamine junkies hung out, and at the Anxious Asp, a lesbian bar. She was doing speed and heroin, bouncing from one sex partner to the next, fast revealing herself to be what her classmates at Jefferson High had accused her of being all along.

Her singing had won her notoriety, including attention from record companies. Yet her capacity to self-destruct had overwhelmed her ambitions. She injured her leg in a motor-scooter accident, got beaten up outside of the Anxious Asp following a confrontation with a few bikers. Physically and mentally she was going to pieces before her new friends' eyes. Most of them did drugs too, but what was happening to Janis was nothing to act casual about. Together they raised money to put Janis on a bus and send her back to Port Arthur.

Her lifestyle having edged her toward death, Janis now swung to the other extreme. She resolved to become a good Port Arthur girl. She bought dresses with long sleeves to cover the needle tracks. She fixed her hair in a bun and wore makeup. She enrolled at Lamar Tech. She threw a party at her parents' house—only this time, the party was for straight Port Arthurans, husbands and wives who did not booze it up.

Janis herself was about to become a wife. She had met a fellow in San Francisco who went by the name of John Pierre Smith, and though little was known about him, Seth Joplin consented when the young man traveled to Port Arthur to ask for Janis's hand in marriage. Thereafter, Janis picked out her china and her wedding gown. She would become the girl in her letters to her parents, demanding nothing but what the others had, dreaming only the simple dreams of the oil town.

But Janis's fiancé never returned to Port Arthur, and with that humiliation, her newly straightened life began to tilt. She found her classes at Lamar Tech dull and unchallenging. She took several opportunities to visit her friends in Austin. On Thanksgiving weekend in 1965, Janis performed at the Half Way House Club in Beaumont. Among those who saw the young woman with the bun and the freshly pressed dress was her old beatnik friend from Jefferson High Jim Langdon. Langdon was now writing an entertainment column for the *Austin American-Statesman*. He was not as stunned by her new look as by her startling evolution as a singer. Both in print and in person, Langdon encouraged Janis to play wherever they would let her play.

Janis returned to Austin, now with guitar in hand, performing at Threadgill's, the Eleventh Door on Red River, and the Methodist Student Center. Her old band mate Powell St. John sat in the audience one night and was awed. If Janis can stay straight, he thought, we'll have another Odetta.

If she stayed straight. No one was more aware of that provision than Janis. "California is behind me," she would say. But now she looked ahead, and the road through Texas simply went around and around. There remained few clubs in Texas, and there remained in Texas a hostility toward its freethinking sons and daughters. One by one they were leaving Texas: Steve Miller, Boz Scaggs, Mother Earth, the Sir Douglas Quintet, the Thirteenth Floor Elevators. And not just the musicians. Chet Helms was organizing musical events, Travis Rivers was opening the legendary Print Mint poster shop, and Wichita Falls native Bob Simmons was on his way to becoming one of the nation's seminal FM disc jockeys. But not in Texas. All of them had gone to San Francisco to blossom, and others still would follow, deserting Janis.

Sometime in 1966, Travis Rivers learned that Chet Helms had been auditioning vocalists for the band Helms was managing, Big Brother and the Holding Company. More than thirty women had tried out, but none was what the band was looking for. The band members had heard about Janis's talent, but they weren't sure if she was right either.

The issue didn't come to a head until Rivers and a friend named Mark borrowed a 1953 Chevy and drove to Austin. There, Rivers learned from friends that Janis had gotten off of drugs, was attending classes at Lamar Tech, and was making straight A's. It sounded to Rivers as if Janis had finally found happiness. "So I decided not to call her," he says.

Early one morning, Rivers was asleep at a friend's house in Austin when Janis showed up, fresh from a gig in Bryan. Rivers felt obliged to tell Janis about the Big Brother audition. Janis mulled it over. As she had to many of her other friends, she told Rivers that she felt stuck in Texas but fearful of San Francisco. She wanted to become famous, but she didn't want to fall back into her drug-dependent ways. Rivers could see that the dilemma had been eating at Janis for some time.

That night Janis and Rivers went to an Austin club and watched Boz Scaggs's former band play rock and roll. Janis imagined herself without her autoharp, without her guitar, rocking the house with a full band. Then she turned to Rivers. Her eyes were on fire. "That's what I want to do," she said. "Man, let's go!"

First they drove to Port Arthur. Rivers sat in the car outside the Joplin house while Janis explained her decision to her parents. When she returned to the car, she gave Rivers the impression that her parents had given their approval—which was hardly the case. From there they drove to Beaumont, to Lamar Tech. Janis met with her counselor, who advised her that she should find some balance between her straight life and her creative life. Then she went to the Lamar Tech registrar's office to report that she would be leaving the state and would like to retain the option to return for the fall semester.

Janis and Rivers drove back to Austin. They made a beeline to the house of Houston White, who would later found Austin's Vulcan Gas Company nightclub. Rivers used White's telephone to dial the number of Chet Helms, then passed the receiver to Janis. Without hesitation, she relayed her interest to Helms and also her concerns. Where would she live? How would she support herself? And what about all the drugs?

Helms loved Janis. He wasn't going to deceive her. Sure, drugs are still around, he told her. But the scene has changed. Things are less reckless, more relaxed. Speed and heroin are out; organic drugs are in. As for money, Janis would make plenty with Big Brother and the Holding Company. But until she did, Helms would put her up himself. And if things didn't work out, he would personally pay her way back in time for the fall semester.

Okay, said Janis. She was on her way.

Hastily she packed and contacted a few of her friends. Jim Langdon told her she was making a mistake: She should play things slowly, groom her skills in Texas for a while, establish herself as a solo artist or take up one of the many offers she had received to play for a Texas band. Powell St. John was excited for her, although, as he says today, "I was afraid it would kill her right away." Dave Moriaty and a few other Jefferson High friends were also horrified. "The first time she came back from San Francisco, she was so near to being dead that we figured the second time was gonna take," Moriaty says.

But everyone could see that Janis wasn't going on a whim. "She took it real seriously," Owens remembers. "It was a business proposition all the way."

AND SO IN JUNE 1966 she and Travis Rivers set out from Austin, driving U.S. 290 west, pushing on to El Paso and out of Texas; replacing a flat tire with another soon to be; getting stranded with another flat in Golden, New Mexico, and making love in an abandoned house and minding the town's general store while its proprietor drove to Albuquerque to fetch a replacement tire; meeting up with a gold prospector, lingering with the Indians at a reservation south of Taos, encountering a terrain of volcanic stone and nearby a lake as clear as glass, and making love again; Rivers contending with another flat in Flagstaff, Arizona, while Janis sat on the hood of the '53 Chevy, reading *Zelda;* and having $30 wired to them from someone in the Midwest, which fueled them at last to San Francisco.

And in two weeks Janis auditioned with Big Brother, learned the songs, and performed to an adoring crowd at the Avalon Ballroom. Then more of the same, only to bigger crowds and greater acclaim—astounding them at Monterey in 1967, flooring them in New York's Anderson Theatre and Fillmore East in 1968. Big-time management, a salary of $150,000, a debut album that sold more than a million copies as fast as they could be pressed. An explosive U.S. tour, the breakup of Big Brother, Woodstock, still more fame. Faster and faster, the record revolving at speeds never imagined in Port Arthur, Janis swinging round and round, bottle of Southern Comfort in hand, tracks on her arms again, her voice now a desperate growl, the blues plain for all to hear even after all the years and all the cheers, pig, whore, you can't go home again, you cannot stop . . .

And then an explosion and utter silence, and the sky cried ashes of Janis. Perhaps not all of them fell into the sea. Perhaps some never fell and somehow caught a rogue eastern wind and floated lazily toward home, where they now hover with the dreams and the fumes, seeking satisfaction.

*October 1992*

# THE MAKING OF BARBARA JORDAN

*I looked over Jordan and what did I see?*

WILLIAM BROYLES JR.

Barbara Jordan was the first African American woman on the cover of *Texas Monthly*. It was 1976, the year of the bicentennial of the United States. I was wondering, Who stands for America now? I couldn't think of anyone who better personified how far our country had come in the two hundred years since our slaveholding ancestors signed the Declaration of Independence than Barbara Jordan of Houston's Fifth Ward. She'd turned the state capitol upside down and was doing the same thing in Washington. That voice, that presence, that sense of humor, that cold-eyed political mind that made even LBJ stand up and salute—it was all part of a package of wonderful contradictions contained in one memorable human being. The last thing I wrote was the cover line: "I looked over Jordan and what did I see?" It came from an old gospel song my mother had sung to me since I was a boy and nicely combined her Texas with Barbara Jordan's, both of them memorable Texas women, part of that band of angels coming for to carry us all home.

AT NIGHT DOWLING STREET is one of the toughest streets in Houston. From its ramshackle bars and flophouses bursts a surging stream of sex and energy that can easily explode into violence. But during the day Dowling is one of the main thoroughfares of the Third Ward, the cultural and intellectual heart of black Houston. Black artist Edsel Cramer has lived at the corner of Dowling and Wheeler for 25 years. To this brick bungalow, nestled amid convenience stores and bars, Barbara Jordan came in the spring of 1973 to sit for a portrait. She was just beginning her first session as a member of the U.S. Congress, and her former colleagues in the Texas Senate, still flush with affection for her, had decided on the unprecedented step of commissioning her portrait to hang in the Texas State Capitol alongside portraits of Davy Crockett, Sam Houston, Lyndon Johnson, and Jefferson Davis. She made six visits to Cramer's studio, always arriving precisely on time and staying exactly two hours.

Cramer has spent years studying the faces of his subjects, searching out the planes and angles, the subtleties of bone structure and coloring, that define appearance and character. He did the same with Jordan, isolating the elements of her face and putting them back together on canvas. "Studying her up close you see exactly how intense she is," Cramer remembers. "There are fine lines etched around her eyes, the sort of lines that mean stress, hard work, and determination. Her head is like a bull's head; across her brow is a lump of bone that stands out like the forehead of a bull. That look of bull-like strength is part of her character. But the most impressive thing about her is she is simply so big—both in size and personality. I just couldn't paint normal scale no matter how hard I tried, even though I prefer to keep the scale of my paintings down. But her painting just kept coming out too big; I couldn't help but make her larger than life."

Cramer seemed to consider this some professional failure on his part, as though his hand had failed to restrain his brush. If it's some consolation, Barbara Jordan's images have always had a way of becoming larger than life. For example, here are some verbal portraits painted of her lately by journalists and other politicians: "a genius"; "a hero"; "the best politician of this century"; "the salvation of American politics"; "a mythic figure"; "the main inspiration for a troubled time"; "a woman of high destiny"; "a cross between Lyndon Johnson and Mahatma Gandhi." Her reception at the Democratic National Convention in New York City this summer dwarfed that of every other politician, with the possible exception of Jimmy Carter. A legitimate American hero like John Glenn was given short shrift by a crowd eager for her magic, like an audience impatient with preliminaries and ready for the main event. When her filmed introduction began, and her disembodied voice was heard saying, "If there are any patriots left in this country, then I am one," the convention roared into life. This was the woman whose eloquent speech ("My faith in the Constitution is whole, it is complete, it is total") for the impeachment of Richard Nixon elevated that grave process to the level of a national rite. To a country wracked with the longest war in its history, torn by racial division, unsure of its institutions and its future, she furnished clear hope. A Southern woman from the race of slaves, she dramatically affirmed, in spite of slavery, civil war, and segregation, her faith in our original ideals. She inspires the belief that one day the burden of race may be set aside. The first black state senator since 1882, the first black congresswoman from the South, now bandied about as possibly a U.S. senator, and—who knows?—perhaps the first black president, she has established her place as the symbolic trailblazer of Texas politics.

On the other hand, she says she does not want to be a symbol, the first black this or the first black that. She wants to be seen for her performance on the playing field. "I am neither a black politician nor a female politician," she says. "Just a politician. A professional politician." But no amount of insisting that's all she is seems to work. People don't want to see her as a politician. If she were white, perhaps then they would. Then the ambition would shine clearly through the rhetoric; then the opportunism in her political alliances would be obvious; then she, not John Connally, would be seen as the true heir to Lyndon Johnson's wheeling and dealing skills. To a good politician the symbolism of Jordan's position—being Southern, black, and female—would be prime political capital, not to be risked on quixotic causes, but to be invested wisely for political ends. Among the greatest of political ends, of course, is personal advancement. And not only does Jordan continually remind people she is a politician, she also doesn't make a big secret about wanting to go places. For those who believe her symbolic position as a black woman with power imposes the grave responsibility to consider issues over advancement, this personal ambition does not always sit well. "I have watched Barbara Jordan for almost ten years," says one critic. "And I have yet to see any evidence she is interested in anything beyond the advancement of Barbara Jordan."

Now politicians have been accused of sacrificing principle to ambition and expediency since long before Julius Caesar. In Jordan's case this accusation is made mostly by whites—and a few black militants—who think she isn't doing enough for liberal causes or her people. On the other hand, even her most skeptical black constituents seem to applaud not only her performance but also her ambition. They say they are tired of political kamikaze pilots who crash and burn against the warships of the establishment. They want someone who can hold his own with the toughest movers and shakers, someone with staying power. Barbara Jordan has staying power. Although they can point to a few concrete examples, they continue to believe she is using the establishment, and not the other way around. This gap between what she says she is and how she is perceived is a paradox; almost everything about Barbara Jordan is. That's what being larger than life is all about. Her personality ranges from frosty, devastating dignity to warm, humorous folksiness. Her distinctive voice seems without root or place. Personal details about her are few and closely guarded. Much of her time seems spent in rehearsal for some future role, but only she knows what it might be.

## GONNA BE SOMEBODY

The best place to begin understanding Barbara Jordan is with a brief tour of black Houston. The primary black neighborhoods are Third Ward and Fifth Ward. Barbara Jordan had her portrait painted in Third Ward, which is just west of the University of Houston and southeast of downtown. Fifth Ward is north of the Ship Channel, northeast of downtown. Until the Elysian Viaduct was built in 1955, Fifth Ward was connected only tenuously to Houston. It was the poorer neighborhood, the brawn to Third Ward's brains. Like black communities in every Southern town, it was built and owned primarily by whites, who expected at the bare minimum a 20 percent return on the block after block of shotgun houses (so called because you could fire a shotgun through the front door and hit everything in the house). Since the city fathers proceeded on the dubious assumption that blacks paid no taxes—and since until 1945 fewer than 5 percent of the city's blacks were registered to vote—paved streets, street lights, sewers, and other municipal services were slow in coming.

Even the cramped poverty of black Houston shone like a beacon for the rural blacks of East Texas and West Louisiana. From 84,000 blacks in 1940, it grew to more than 350,000 in the seventies, more blacks than Atlanta, more than New Orleans, the largest black population in the South. There are more blacks in Houston today than the entire 1940 population of the city. The old black neighborhoods were steadily swallowed up into the larger boundaries of the expanding black city. And as Houston grew by annexing the white suburbs that surrounded it, blacks took over virtually the entire east side of old Houston. From well north of Fifth Ward, threading across the Ship Channel and warehouse district to Third Ward, then spreading south to Sunnyside and beyond, black Houston stands like a large expanding hourglass in the center of Houston, cutting the city north to south and separating the more prosperous west side from the industrial east side, the port, and the chemical plants of the Ship Channel.

Even though some black leaders worry about a loss of community identity amid such growth, black Houston has at least as much center to it as white Houston does. The old neighborhoods of Fifth and Third Ward still provide the character. Texas Southern University, the black newspaper, and most business and professional offices are in Third Ward. The black elite lives there, in the former mansions of the Cullens and the Weingartens, along MacGregor Bayou; so does the black middle class, mostly in the abandoned Jewish neighborhoods just east of Main Street and north of Hermann Park. Still, there has not been in Houston the sort of second- and third-generation inherited black wealth which has dominated black communities in Atlanta and New Orleans. Black Houston has been a more open place, just as white Houston has. That is true of Fifth Ward as well, which remains the grassroots heart of the black community. The labor unions are there, as are the largest and most fundamentalist black churches, the largest black funeral parlors, and the wealthiest blacks like Mack Hannah and Don Robey. Wheatley, the Fifth Ward high school, usually wins in football and basketball; Yates, the Third Ward high school, usually excels in academics and debate. Fifth Ward is a poorer and tougher place.

Barbara Jordan is from Fifth Ward. A few years after her birth in 1936, her father, B. M. Jordan, became a Baptist minister. To help support his family, he kept his job as a warehouseman. When Barbara was in her teens, the family moved to Campbell Street, just east of Lockwood near the corner of Campbell and Erastus; she and her mother still live there. Most of the houses on the street are shotgun shacks, house after identical house about sixteen feet wide and five feet apart, each constructed with a center door, a small porch, and a window to either side. Since the houses are so small, a good deal of the life on Campbell Street occurs in front yards. Everybody knows everything about their neighbors; it is a small-town feeling that much of white America, with its air conditioning and fixed-glass windows, has unwittingly let slip away. Immediately behind the houses across the street is the vast expanse of the main Houston freight yard, where thousands of trailer trucks and hundreds of railroad cars are constantly in motion, supplying Houston's booming commerce. But Campbell Street, with its corner bar, Lou's Beauty Nook, and the Tornado Motel, might as well be light-years away from that cosmopolitan prosperity.

The distinctive qualities of Barbara Jordan—her speaking ability, her ambition, her charisma, and, of course, her size—all developed early. Reverend Jordan's churches were solidly missionary and fundamentalist, the churches that for three hundred years had promised black Americans salvation from a world of tears and travail. On Sundays, Barbara and her two older sisters would get up behind their father after his sermon and sing gospel music, the old-fashioned kind where they clapped and swayed and affirmed the joyous promise of their religion. The father prided himself on speaking correctly, in full, rounded, unaccented tones. To him correct speech was a mark of good breeding and class, and he insisted his daughters speak correctly. The common assumption that Jordan developed her speaking style at Boston University Law School could not be more wrong. "She had it in the cradle," says Tom Freeman, her debate coach at Texas Southern University (TSU). "She did get a little JFK cadence in her voice from Boston," says her old friend Andrew Jefferson, a former state district judge and a talented politician. "Those of us who knew her well noticed a little extra when she came back from Boston—a sort of embellishment, a little frosting on the cake." So far as Jordan herself is concerned, "I don't have an accent. I just talk like me. I have talked this way as long as I can remember."

Jordan's attitude is disingenuous, at the least, since her voice is much of her image. It underscores her aloofness and dignity, it lifts her beyond region, it masks any fuzzy thinking or lowly ambition, and it scares the hell out of people. On hearing it for the first time, one awed young woman said, "I turned on my television set and thought I was listening to God." It sounds, as Congressman Andrew Young of Georgia says, "like the heavens have opened up." The religious parallels are apt, because the voice is an evangelical voice, a voice designed to bring to the fold the presence of the Lord. For that voice, for much of her ambition, and for her exacting standards of excellence, she can thank her father.

Reverend Jordan wanted his three daughters to become music teachers; two did. In a segregated society, being a music teacher was one of the best ambitions a young black woman could have, and Reverend Jordan insisted on the best. "I would come home with five A's and a B," Barbara Jordan told Molly Ivins of the *Texas Observer,* "and my father would say, 'Why do you have a B?'" She wanted to please her father, to meet and even exceed his standards; but she wanted to be more than a music teacher. "I always wanted to be something unusual," she says, "I would never be content with being run of the mill, I was thinking about being a pharmacist, but then I asked myself, 'Whoever heard of an outstanding pharmacist?'" When she was in the tenth grade at Phillis Wheatley High School, a Chicago lawyer named Edith Sampson addressed the Career Day assembly. Sampson was crisp, competent, confident. Then and there, Barbara Jordan decided that was what she was going to be. At first, her father told a teacher who encouraged this ambition to "stay out of his family's affairs," that the law was no profession for a woman. But he came to encourage her "to do whatever I thought I could." (Reverend Jordan died in 1972, the day after he attended his daughter's Governor for a Day ceremonies in Austin.)

If anyone who knew her as a girl remembers Barbara Jordan having any doubts about herself, they aren't letting on. "She has always been, even as a little girl, very sure of herself," says Mary Justice York, who has known her since the third grade. "We knew from the very beginning she would do something different from the rest of us. She has always been large. . . . In those days, the kids who were the leaders were usually slim and pretty, with nice, long hair and pretty brown skin . . . but Barbara—it wasn't that she tried to be the leader or strove for it—we just recognized her." A. C. Herald, who was her homeroom teacher at Wheatley, remembers that "she had, even then, such an amazing sense of self." She had a weight problem, she wasn't attractive—"My mother says not to make me pretty," she told her portrait painter—but she was smart, and above all, she had boundless ambition and belief in herself. Apparently the sight of an overweight young black girl (she entered TSU at sixteen) going about the normal business of growing up in the Fifth Ward with this doomsday voice, this fierce sense of dignity, this tenacious idea of herself and her future, didn't seem strange. When people who knew her then are asked if she didn't seem a little, well, phony, with that voice and everything, their response is consistently some variation of: "No, not really. She was just Barbara. That's just how she was. We always knew she was gonna be somebody."

At TSU she was everywhere; she wanted to get to the top of everything. She ran for freshman class president, and lost to Andrew Jefferson; she ran for student body president, and lost by six votes. Finally, she was elected editor of the yearbook. But she really shined in debate, where she was the only woman. Her freshman year, Tom Freeman, the debate coach, told her she wasn't able to speak extemporaneously, and so kept her from doing refutations. "She went on to become one of the best debaters at refutation I have ever had," Freeman recalls. "I think when I told her she wasn't good at it that it really challenged her." While she was at TSU the debate team was spectacular. They toured the country, beating everyone, including Harvard. They integrated the Baylor Forensic Tournament and won the first three years they competed. From TSU, Jordan went on to Boston University Law School, where she was the only woman in her class.

At this point a certain perspective might be helpful. Until she went north with the TSU debate team, Barbara Jordan had lived *completely* in the segregated society of black Houston. Even when the debate team integrated the regional meet in Waco, they couldn't stay at the hotel with the other teams. Instead they were put up at all-black Paul Quinn College. The city Barbara Jordan left to attend Boston University in 1956 had segregated taxis, restaurants and lunch counters, restrooms, hospital wards, swimming pools, churches, labor unions, and schools; the handful of black policemen could not arrest whites or eat in the segregated city cafeteria; blacks could not vote in the Democratic primary—the only election in one-party Texas that mattered—until 1944. In 1956, black Houston was a separate city of 200,000 people. Its leading citizens were small businessmen and the leaders of the segregated institutions—the ministers, the educators, the union officials. These men also served as ambassadors to the white society—they lobbied to get a road paved or a library built. In such a society, if you were young, gifted, and ambitious, you had to become aware, in a way no white could really understand, of the limits on your ambitions. You could rise only so far. You had to stay in the black society since the great opportunities of the larger white world were closed. That was what "knowing your place" meant.

The accepted current view of this system, as expressed by the Supreme Court, is that it created a "badge of inferiority"; the white society's claim that separate could be equal was false: Separate was inherently unequal. But the vast effort to dismantle this system has obscured certain of its more positive elements. For example, today many Houston blacks believe their schools have lost something crucial. "Give us back our black principals and teachers," they say. "The new white teachers don't understand our children, they don't enforce discipline or values, they don't make them learn." When Barbara Jordan was at Wheatley High School they taught *pride*. "They taught us dignity," says one of her contemporaries. The segregated black society was ironically a breeding ground of the very fundamental values white Americans were coming to question. Houston blacks were pro-military, pro-education, and, in their own way, pro-American. "I can still get goose bumps when I hear the 'Star Spangled Banner,'" says Jordan, who is fond of reciting the Pledge of Allegiance in her speeches. While blacks most likely burned with a common rage at the humiliation of segregation, they also made the best of things within it. And they were proud of their schools, proud of their athletic teams, proud of their churches, proud of themselves.

Barbara Jordan, for one, has never given the slightest indication she feels "a badge of inferiority" because she went to Wheatley and TSU, or because she grew up in a segregated society. In fact, there must be few pleasures sweeter than going to a debate tournament and beating all the teams you aren't good enough to stay in the same hotel with. And when TSU traveled north and beat the best debate teams America had to offer, that must have dispelled any doubts she might have had about just how good she was. But ability was one thing; ambition was another. Satchel Paige was one of the best pitchers who ever lived, but he only got to play in the major leagues in the twilight of his career. Barbara Jordan was to become the Jackie Robinson of Texas politics, but it would not be easy. When she returned home with her law degree from Boston University in 1959, the first black to win elective office in Houston since Reconstruction had been on the school board for less than a year. The system of segregation was still in effect (after political meetings, if she and her white allies wanted to eat or get a drink in public together, they would have had to go to black Houston). It's one thing to play in the black leagues when that's all it seems can be done. But Barbara Jordan had supreme self-confidence, she had a boundless capacity for hard work, and she had her eye on bigger things.

## JUST BARBARA

When she returned to Houston, Jordan started her law office on the dining room table of the house on Campbell Street. She also started doing nuts-and-bolts political work with the Harris County Democrats. This coalition of labor minorities and white liberals was the mainspring of Houston liberal politics. It had its own office, its own leaders and candidates, and its own platforms; in almost every respect it was a separate political party. The struggles with the Johnson wing of the Democratic party were pitched battles. The liberals had great heart, tremendous esprit, high principles—and they almost always lost. With remarkable resilience they would get up to fight again. Since they openly courted blacks, they were the only place for an ambitious black office seeker like Barbara Jordan to start, just as debate was the place to make her mark at TSU. In the 1960 Kennedy presidential campaign she stuffed envelopes and licked stamps, went on to set up systems to identify block and precinct workers, then was asked to speak at a small rally when the scheduled speaker didn't show up.

If there is anything Jordan has never wasted, it is an opportunity to speak. Soon she was as prominent in the Harris County Democrats as she had been at TSU. She became vice chairman; she helped screen candidates; she seemed in every respect a committed liberal. When the Connally-backed black political organization set out to keep the endorsement of the Harris County Council of Organizations (HCCO, the key black political group) from going to liberal Don Yarborough in the 1962 Democratic gubernatorial primary, Jordan went to bat for him. Some members of the HCCO still remember her speech that day, although the Connally blacks did succeed in blocking Yarborough's endorsement. By then she was running on her own. She borrowed money for her filing fee and persuaded Al Wickliff (who had himself run unsuccessfully for the Legislature and who had managed Mrs. Charles White's successful campaign to be the first black on the school board) to be her campaign manager. The only problem was that blacks made up less than 20 percent of Houston's electorate, and all state representatives had to run countywide. White ran for reelection that same year, got 34 percent of the white vote, and won with a plurality; Jordan got 23 percent of the white vote and came in third.

As she took stock of her defeat, in a subtle but significant way, she crossed the Rubicon, from black politician to politician. Principles weren't worth much if you had no power. A black might win election to the Houston School Board, but its politics were byzantine and unrelated to most everything else. But it seemed unlikely that a black, strictly with liberal support, could win a countywide race. What Barbara Jordan had to do, in practical political terms, was expand her base. She had to keep her original black and liberal allies, but she had to find more. She decided to leave the friendly womb of liberal, black Houston and venture forth into the heartland of her opposition. In her own words: "It was clear then that if I was to win . . . I had to persuade the monied and politically influential interests either to support me or to remain neutral." In 1964 she increased her white vote by 50 percent, but that, along with her now customary 97 percent of the black vote, was still not enough. And, in the wake of her second defeat, Governor John Connally vetoed her nomination to serve on the State Democratic Executive Committee, on the grounds it wasn't ready for a black.

And so, her efforts to court the establishment had been unsuccessful; her law practice was barely off the ground because of her political efforts; and ahead seemed to lie only an endless series of losing campaigns. Barbara Jordan contemplated her future. Again, in her words: "I considered abandoning the dream of a public career in Texas and moving to some section of the country where a black woman candidate was less likely to be considered a novelty. I didn't want to do this. I am a Texan; my roots are in Texas. To leave would be a cop-out. So I stayed." This story, of course, has a fairy tale ending. The next year the Voting Rights Act extended the franchise, and the "one man, one vote" Supreme Court decisions led to the equalization in population of legislative districts. And there, in the twinkling of an eye, were not only 25 percent more registered black voters, but also a brand-new Texas Senate district almost 50 percent black. Barbara Jordan had been out front first, she had worked hard, and that seat was hers.

She won 66 percent of the vote in the primary (including 34 percent of the white vote) and brushed aside a token Republican opponent to become the first black to serve in the Texas Senate since 1882. When she was elected, the civil rights movement was splintering into separatists, militants, and moderates. The vestiges of segregation were everywhere. Yet this first black state senator had not a single item in her platform designed specifically to benefit blacks. She came out for traditional bread-and-butter liberal and union issues like the minimum wage, fair labor practices, and better teacher salaries. She also strongly supported limits on oyster dredging and played political expediency with welfare, calling for its expansion on the one hand and getting cheats off the welfare rolls on the other. It was a solid, traditional political platform. It was also a pale reflection of her extraordinary rhetoric and presence. Because of her charisma, she led people to expect that she would set things right, and they didn't have oyster dredging in mind.

But black issues did not go without their champion in 1966. A young black businessman named Curtis Graves was elected to the

Texas House of Representatives the same year. Graves was a vocal black activist who had been arrested in a Houston sit-in demonstration in 1961. When Graves got to the Legislature, he made it clear that he was a black man interested in black issues, and woe betide white racists. As the sixties continued to unfold, Graves started talking of "honkies" and the "oppressors"; he began building a coalition with the New Left and with hippies; he called Vietnam a racist war. The contrast with Jordan could not have been more direct. Graves was passionate and impulsive, she was aloof and calculating; he was angry, she was conciliatory; he made whites feel personally guilty for the sins of segregation, she emphasized common problems; he would have nothing to do with the establishment, she courted it. While he made herculean efforts to become an effective day-to-day politician, Graves's real ambition was to make the transition from civil rights activist to politician with principles intact: same strategy, different tactics.

Looking back from the perspective of the mid-seventies, it seems obvious that Jordan's approach made more sense. At the time, however, it was not so clear. The changes most affecting the lives of blacks were being inspired by black activists, not black politicians. These blacks—mainly students and young ministers—were the new leaders of black Houston. They could point to concrete accomplishment; blacks who worked within the system came back with their hands empty. Quiet voices didn't get action. Loud voices did. In 1960, the year after Jordan returned from Boston, the sit-ins began, and continued until 1962, the year she made her first race for the Legislature; lunch counters were integrated, and some firms began hiring black employees. Three years later, the focus switched to the slow pace of school desegregation. Ten thousand blacks led by Reverend Bill Lawson marched on the school board; there was a school boycott. Black Houston seemed up in arms.

Through this epic period in black Houston's history Barbara Jordan ran for office. She was a member of the NAACP, the most conservative civil rights organization. She took part in no sit-ins, marched in no demonstrations, carried no signs. And although there were fewer than thirty black lawyers in town, she did not volunteer to defend any of the jailed protesters. In spite of the practical effects of the attacks on the system, she never wavered in her burning desire to find a place in it. And as the sixties wore on, she attacked black power and made no bones about her intentions to continue working with the white establishment. For someone of her age and ambition, this behavior might well have earned the epithet Uncle Tom. But it did not, in part because of the sheer power of her rhetoric, but also because as a woman and a lawyer she was not expected to be a fighter. Just as her childhood friends had accepted her uniqueness ten years before, so the leading civil rights leaders of black Houston—some her former TSU classmates—accepted her uniqueness in the sixties. She was "just Barbara," and she had her own role to play.

It was not a "black" role. Barbara Jordan can count votes; to achieve power she would have to expand, not jeopardize, her white support. The "black" issue she has most consistently fought for is voting rights. When she filed in the state Senate race she brought along the black dentist whose lawsuit in 1944 had won blacks the right to vote in the Democratic primary. She made a rare display of calling in her political chips to prevent the Texas Senate from considering a bill to restrict the franchise by compounding the difficulties of voter registration. She took the same risk in Congress when she went against both the Texas establishment and the congressional black establishment—the two normal sources of her strength—in her successful effort to expand certain provisions of the Voting Rights Act to cover Texas. The blacks were against expansion on the grounds it would jeopardize the act being renewed for the South; in this case, contrary to the accepted stereotype, they were timid and she was bold. She considers the Voting Rights expansion her most significant legislative accomplishment. The franchise is her sort of issue; its exercise is decorous, restrained, impersonal—but effective. It is the cornerstone of the system she believes in. She wasn't raised to rebel or to make a scene; she didn't learn that at home, and she didn't learn it at Wheatley. And, as far as she knew, most blacks were as uncomfortable with those methods as she was. But the militants paved the way for her. They made her seem moderate, respectable, and safe. As Everett Collier of the *Houston Chronicle* says, "Barbara worked to prevent any violence or radicalism that would cause trouble." And there could be no more pure political tightrope artistry than the ability to make a Collier think she is keeping the blacks in line, while making a Reverend Lawson think she is manipulating the establishment.

"The civil rights movement," says Lawson, the leader of the school boycott, "brought to prominence a different sort of person than Barbara. The civil rights leaders were angry, passionate, impulsive people who drew attention to an ancient wrong in a dramatic way. In the language of the Olympics, they were the dash men; for the long haul you need distance runners. Barbara is a distance runner. It's simply not her style to get out with a sign, or to be disruptive. It is no accident that the impulsive and eloquent voices of the civil rights movement did not make the transition to positions of power and responsibility. Those sorts of positions belong to people like Barbara, people with a purpose but also with the ability to hold their own in political infighting with the establishment's best."

And so, when the clash between Graves and Jordan came in 1972, it would be Jordan who would win. After the census of 1970, Houston was redistricted; a new congressional district, the Eighteenth, was drawn for Jordan. She had, however, left Graves the impression he would get her senate district when she moved up. Instead, it was cannibalized into other districts, making it virtually impossible for a black to win. Graves held her responsible for losing it. It was the last straw in what he took to be a long string of compromises and deals with the establishment. He decided to oppose her for Congress. Jordan had worked hard on labor issues, and had the unions sewed up. She also had the financial backing of the Houston establishment. Graves was the underdog; labor unions threw him out of endorsement meetings, he had no money, his old friends didn't seem to mind that the richest blacks and whites were backing Jordan—her money men were old black conservative Mack Hannah and white Houston booster Gail Whitcomb. Those were the sort of people Graves and his allies had always fought, but his allies seemed to be slipping away. The hippies and the New Left radicals he had courted were little help.

Graves then did the only thing he could: He attacked. He called Jordan a "tool" and raged about "an open attempt to buy the Eighteenth District" as she sat tight-lipped on the same platform. This was his case, which has been the standard case against Jordan: "The congressman from this new district must be someone who owes his allegiance to the people who are in the district and not to the corrupt politicians who have brought our state to shame and ridicule. If you are looking for someone who goes along to get along, one who plays politics with your lives, one who is long on speaking but short on delivering services, then don't vote for Curtis Graves." As his position became more desperate, some of his supporters began spreading rumors about Jordan's sex life. It was a tough campaign, an unprecedented battle between two prominent black politicians. Jordan never attacked Graves, and simply repeated that the issue was "who can get things done, who is more effective." She received 80 percent of the vote. Graves got 13 percent, and left Texas for good.

Why did she win? There are several answers, but the most important is she was simply a better politician. She had carried water for key supporters like labor unions, she had gathered new supporters among the Houston establishment, and she had protected her base in the black community by appealing to its abiding conservative instincts. Although Graves played an important role in the protest movements of the sixties, he didn't know, as another black politician said, "when it was time to put his dashiki in the closet, stop raising hell, and start getting things done." The politician with a low civil rights profile beat the militant. In the words of Reverend Lawson, who is also a friend of Graves: "She had a vision back in the sixties. Most of us couldn't see it. She saw beyond the conflict to the enduring institutions, and she saw that most people, even black people, wanted to believe in them, if only they could be made to work. Within these institutions she saw that people like Sam Rayburn and Lyndon Johnson got more done. So she wed her philosophy and purpose to their practical skills. But she kept her purpose. The rest of the civil rights movement is far behind her in making that transition."

## THE HEIR OF LBJ

The transition from the civil rights movement to Johnson-Rayburn politician was actually not that difficult a transition for Barbara Jordan to make. She had never really been in the civil rights movement. She had always, from her days at TSU, been in politics. Johnson-Rayburn politics were the big-time campus operator writ large, and the first opportunity Jordan had to practice them since her student days was when she arrived in the Texas Senate in 1967. As a freshman, she had to earn the support—in student terms—of the seniors. "The Texas Senate was touted as the state's most exclusive club," she wrote in *Atlantic Monthly*. "To be effective I had to get inside the club, not just inside the chamber. I singled out the most influential and powerful members and determined to gain their respect." Barbara Jordan was the perfect freshman to integrate the school: She was bright, she did her homework, she had great talent; she loved the institution, gave deference to its elders, and made them feel that it—and they—were the most important things in her life.

Since no black face had been seen in the Senate chamber since 1882, and since that body had its share of unreconstructed Southerners, there still was a certain period of adjustment. Back then it was traditional for Claude Wild Sr., the Humble Oil lobbyist, to give a little dinner dance for the Senate before the session began. Wild thought he had a bit of a problem, so he called Don Kennard, a liberal senator from Fort Worth, who was rumored to know a few blacks personally. Kennard tells the story: "Don," Wild said. "I've got a little dilemma with Senator Jordan." "What's that?" Kennard asked. "Well, it's about [late Dallas senator George] Parkhouse and Mrs. Parkhouse, not to mention some others. What if Senator Jordan brings along a big black man from Houston? How will everybody react? What if her date tries to dance with Mrs. Parkhouse? What then?"

"They were breaking new ground, and no one knew what would happen," Kennard recalls. "So my wife and I invited Barbara to go to dinner with us. Within three minutes after she arrived she had charmed everyone and was the center of the stage. Just by being so gracious and charming she literally compelled even the biggest racists to be gracious and charming too. It started that night, really. She obviously respected them and didn't make them feel evil or guilty. And they had never been confronted with an intelligent, imposing, witty black person before; so they warmed to her. I know it sounds silly looking at it all from ten years later. But those were different times. She was the first, and she ended up beating all of us at our own game."

The game, of course, was politics. Jordan studied the Senate's procedure so closely that within weeks she was recognized as one of its leading parliamentarians, not above using, as she puts it, "the trickers' tricks." Among politicians political skill is respected apart from ideology, and Jordan quickly demonstrated that she had great technical skills. She only spoke when she knew what she wanted, she didn't preach or harangue, she concentrated on a few subjects and became the Senate expert on them. She never embarrassed a fellow senator; she always gave the impression she understood his own political situation and left him room for self-respect. She shattered stereotypes about blacks: To racists she wasn't shiftless and dumb and she didn't smell bad; to guilt-ridden liberals who believed that all blacks would be liberal, pure of heart, and anti-establishment, she proved to be a hard-nosed politician who gave no hint that she had suffered under segregation.

She also shrewdly combined her exacting and aloof sense of dignity with warm good humor. Since it softens the abrasiveness of conflict, humor is among the most valuable political skills. Few politicians appreciate a somber ideologue, even if he is on their side. Jordan came to the Senate as a female and a black, an inevitable damper for the club's easy sexual and racial humor. It didn't work out that way. "There have always been jokes told on the floor of the Senate," Kennard recalls. "Sexual, racial, good taste, bad taste. No one would have ever thought of including Mrs. Colson [a previous female senator]; no one would have ever thought of not including Barbara. She had a superb sense of humor and could even top old Parkhouse when she wanted to. We'd clean it up a little bit for her, because she just required by God respect. I'm sure the antics of the Senate frustrated her, seemed too frivolous. But she never let on. She put up with it, participated in it, and she used it." (Extemporaneous political humor doesn't always translate very well, but here are two examples: Senator Chet Brooks, addressing Jordan: "Senator, the only thing missing in this portrait is your voice; without your voice, it just isn't you." Jordan, in reply: "Senator, these walls have been needing a touch of color, and when my painting hangs amid the august people on the walls of this chamber, believe me, it's gonna talk." Reporter: "Senator Jordan, congratulations on your election to Congress." Jordan: "Thank you, but that's premature. I still have a Republican opponent in the fall, but since none of you seem to know who he is, I'm not about to tell you his name.") She was, in short, one of the boys. She would joke with them, drink with them, stay up late, play the guitar and sing songs with them. But there was something at the center she always held back. In both her personal and her political life, there was no way to assume you knew her, or to take her for granted.

"Even though Barbara was with us on almost every crucial issue," said one liberal senator, "somehow you never could assume she would be. If you had a real good bill, you know, that did everything right, that had in it all the sort of things she had been supporting, you still couldn't just check off her vote on your scorecard. You had to go see her, reason with her, make her understand what you wanted to do. The same was true of her personal contacts. While she had the easy banter and could be one of the boys, few politicians felt they really knew her. If they tried to get too close, she would cut them off cold. Land Commissioner Bob Armstrong recalls one occasion, when he was in the Legislature: "It was one of those parties Charlie Wilson used to give. Barbara was there, and she and I stayed up almost all night—laughing, joking, telling stories, playing the guitar, and singing songs. It was one of the happiest nights I've spent. I really felt I knew her—she was like my sister. The next day or so I ran into her in the Capitol and went rushing up, and—nothing. She was polite, but everything I thought was there between us just wasn't. I don't regret that experience we had together. I was just surprised."

Now some politicians are committed people, as are some friends. Many committed Texas liberals and conservatives believe that if someone is against you on one issue of principle, then he is automatically against you on all issues of principle; that he is, in short, either a friend or an enemy. If a man is your enemy on civil rights, so this sort of absolutist political approach goes, then he will be your enemy on environmental matters, gun control, education, taxation, labor issues. Jordan's political ideology, however, was not a seamless fabric. She approached issues one at a time, and she took her allies where she found them.

In her three regular sessions she introduced more than 150 bills and resolutions, about half of which were the apolitical meat and potatoes of legislation, from creating a new court and establishing a new medical school to closing off the street that ran through TSU and setting safety standards for people who go into manholes. But the rest were solidly liberal: extending the minimum wage to cover non-unionized farmworkers and domestics; a fair labor practices act; pollution control; a whole range of workmen's compensation acts (her specialty); equal rights and anti-discrimination. She fought for liquor by the drink and against extending the sales tax. But she insisted on not being taken for granted, and she had the charisma to make that insistence stick. She always ended up in the corral, but damned if she didn't have to be rounded up every time.

In the Senate, then, her political techniques were the same ones she would later perfect in Congress: deference to leadership, loyalty to the institution, hard work, humor, an unwillingness to be typecast, all wrapped up in the power and mystery of her personality and topped off with that old standby, her voice—which could either create an easy intimacy or intimidate, seemingly at will. At the end of her first session, her colleagues unanimously passed an unprecedented resolution expressing the Senate's "warmest regard and affection. . . . She has earned the esteem and respect of her fellow citizens by the dignified manner in which she conducts herself . . . and because of her sincerity, her genuine concern for others, and her forceful speaking ability, she has been a credit to her state as well as her race." The thirty men then rose and gave her two standing ovations. To call a militant like Curtis Graves a "credit to his race" in the emotion-charged years of the late sixties would have been patronizing and unthinkable; he would have been outraged. Barbara Jordan was pleased. "I have not been treated with any more respect by any group of men anywhere," she said, apparently unambiguously; when she left in 1972 she said, "Nothing that can happen in my lifetime will equal the memories I have of my years of service in this chamber."

The dazzling show she was putting on for her fellow senators caught the eye of the protean godfather of Texas politics, Lyndon Johnson. It was not a good time for the president. The prodigious outpouring of Great Society and civil rights programs was behind him, and the Vietnam War, no matter how much he wheeled and dealed and plotted and planned, steadily kept pulling him beneath the political waves. His protégé in Texas, John Connally, didn't care about the Great Society and in fact had done some impressive foot dragging on antipoverty programs and civil rights. This pained Johnson deeply. To LBJ, these programs were more than just legislative accomplishments; they were his legacy, they were what would go beside his name in the history books. All the political operating in the world wasn't worth a damn if you didn't do something with it. So far as Johnson could tell, both Connally and his protégé Ben Barnes had inherited his skills but none of his heart.

Barbara Jordan was different. She had many of the qualities Johnson admired: She had a deep respect for legislative bodies and the legislative process, she was uncomfortable with ideologues, and she had great humor and political skills. She admired and recognized what a political accomplishment the Great Society programs were, how much arm twisting and cajoling and convincing and political chips they had used up. But she also knew what they meant to real people. She told him the Voting Rights Act had been crucial in getting her elected. His Texas cronies didn't appreciate that, and other prominent blacks didn't appreciate what he had done either—they just kept yelling "More! More! More!" or encouraging separatism, riots, God knows what. When black riots swept Washington and other cities after the assassination of Martin Luther King, Johnson took it personally. "Don't they realize what I've done for them?" he would ask. Barbara Jordan realized what he had done, and told him so. After he had renounced his reelection campaign because of the war, she went to the 1968 Democratic Convention in Chicago, announced she would support him over anyone should he change his mind and openly fought to keep the Texas delegation solidly behind the plank endorsing LBJ's Vietnam policy. In the King Lear fantasies of his final year, with John Connally a Republican, Barnes's political career in ruins, and Nixon dismantling the Great Society, she was the one child who never wavered, who kept his legacy and promised to carry it on. When he died, she said simply, "He was my political mentor and my friend. I loved him and I shall miss him."

LBJ was a great help to her. He opened establishment doors, attended her fund-raisers, touted her to influential politicians and businessmen, helped get her a seat on the Judiciary Committee when she went to Congress. John Connally, however, was another story. She had spoken passionately against his gubernatorial campaign in 1962; he had vetoed her for a place on the State Democratic Executive Committee in 1964. But beyond those earlier clashes was a fierce clash of egos. Connally maddened Jordan by simply ignoring her. She was the star attraction of the 1967 Senate, but he acted as if she didn't exist. They both had LBJ's backroom magic, but Connally had Lyndon's poor-boy materialism and she had Lyndon's New Deal heart. Blended together, they made a pretty good LBJ. But like half siblings, she and Connally were fated to clash.

When Connally led the Texas delegation to the Democratic Convention in 1968, Jordan announced from the beginning that she would not support him as a favorite son. She was for Humphrey. Then Connally changed his mind and wanted to lead the delegation into the Humphrey camp. Jordan then changed her mind and wouldn't go along (she did end up supporting Humphrey). Whatever Connally wanted, she opposed. In 1972, when one of Connally's key political operatives, UT Regents chairman Frank Erwin Jr., sent her a $1,000 campaign contribution as a peace offering, she sent it back. However, she did testify as a character witness at Connally's bribery trial, for some or all of these reasons: because it put the Houston establishment even deeper in her debt; because beneath the deepest of differences politicians share a basic mutual protection society so far as prison is concerned; and because—less likely—as a lawyer she believed her testimony would help him get a fair trial. At the trial, she testified, "As far as I know from my personal experience, he has a good reputation for honesty." When asked if she had any political differences with Connally, she replied, "I have had spectacular . . ." At that point the prosecution objected, and she was not allowed to finish. Full circle on irony: He helped keep her off the State Democratic Executive Committee in 1964; she helped keep him out of prison in 1975.

Until Jordan came along, the line of succession was to have been from LBJ to Connally to Ben Barnes. Barnes was a real comer, the major star—Jordan had a supporting role then—of late sixties Texas politics. He was the youngest Speaker ever of the Texas House of Representatives, and in 1968, when he was thirty, he was elected lieutenant governor by carrying every county in Texas. Barnes and

Jordan were both natural politicians, and they got along well. They understood each other. Jordan knew what Barnes was up to, and he knew that while she was in the full flights of her oratory on the Senate floor he could catch her eye from the podium, wink, and she would wink back. They almost never agreed on issues, but they had one thing in common: towering ambition. In the spring of 1971, he helped her carve out a congressional seat for herself; she gave him the impression she would support him for governor. She made it, he didn't.

## THE REVENGE OF AUNT JEMIMA

The election of Barbara Jordan to Congress in 1972 continued an undeniable personal achievement. She had come home from the East at 23, a black lawyer with few prospects in a segregated society. She was returning to the East at 36, a U.S. representative and the protégé of the former president of the United States. Her traditional approach to politics had been overwhelmingly vindicated against a black militant. Her ambition, her intelligence, her sense of personal destiny, her voice, and her charisma—combined with her shrewd political skills and her penchant for hard work—would make the Congress her personal national stage. But while Jordan has tirelessly sought office, she has not so obviously sought acclaim. She has consistently gone after power, but recognition came to her. She worked hard to get where she is, but she became a celebrity almost effortlessly. Before taking a final look at her personal and political achievements, the real and symbolic sources of her national appeal, and the reasons she seems to strike such a deep chord in America, it would be wise to reconsider just how she got there.

Barbara Jordan brushes aside high-flown descriptions of her symbolic significance and insists she is just "a practical politician." In judging politicians, means are often as important as ends: How a politician reaches his goals can be as important as the goals themselves. Jordan's means have been the classic politics of her mentor, Lyndon Johnson; some of her liberal critics call her "a black LBJ." Those politics can be characterized in many ways, but above all they are the art of the possible: the practical craft of knowing how things work, what buttons to push, who has power and who doesn't. Such a politician is popularly known as "someone who can get things done." The reduction of politics to the level of the practical makes good, hard-nosed sense in most cases; there are times, however, when it backfires.

Being practical means avoiding unnecessary risks. The line between political prudence and political timidity is very thin; the danger lies in settling for less than you might have gained had you fought harder. When Barbara Jordan used good old political horse trading to create a congressional seat she could win, somehow her old Senate seat got lost in the process. "Either that was part of the deal with Barnes or she just felt she had to give something up to get something, but it wasn't necessary," recalls a former Senate colleague. "If she had used her muscle to keep the Senate seat for blacks, she could have had both. They would have cratered. That's exactly the sort of thing they are most afraid of her about. But she didn't make a peep." "It just wasn't in the game plan," says Jordan. Safe, practical politics. The result: While each state senator represents about 400,000 people, there is no black state senator for Houston's 350,000 blacks, which is the rough equivalent of dividing up Fort Worth to be represented by Dallas, Abilene, and Wichita Falls.

Being practical also means knowing where the power is and cultivating it. The trap here is confusing the trappings of power for power itself. When Jordan let Barnes believe she would support him for governor, she confused his power in the state capitol, which was near absolute, with his power in the state, which had dissipated in the wake of the Sharpstown scandal. (Barnes seemed "clean," but he was then the state's most prominent wheeler-dealer politician, and the political mood was "throw the rascals out.") Both conservative and liberal political outsiders smelled blood. Frances Farenthold was the liberal candidate for governor. To Jordan, Farenthold must have seemed a political lightweight: she was only a state representative, she didn't understand how practical power worked, she was, in short, yet another quixotic, maverick liberal doomed to defeat. But when Jordan went to the Harris County Democrats endorsement caucus, she got a surprise. It was a heated meeting. The liberals were disillusioned with Jordan. They wanted to know where she stood on the governor's race; they wouldn't stay neutral in her congressional race with Graves unless she endorsed Farenthold. For an excruciating moment, the chickens were home to roost. Then Jordan made her choice: Without naming Farenthold, she pledged to support the candidate of the Harris County Democrats. No one knows what she told Barnes, who got 17 percent of the vote and came in third. Farenthold made the runoff, losing finally to Dolph Briscoe, another outsider.

Being practical means playing the game with the people in power. In the intraparty squabbles of Texas Democrats, Jordan customarily comes down on the side of the "ins," which means the conservatives. "Party issues are power issues," says one committed liberal. "Barbara's devotion to the conservatives means she keeps the party's power on the side of the people who oppose her legislative goals. She's been vice chairman of the State Democratic Executive Committee for four years, and as far as I know she's never attended a meeting. That means blacks and liberals really have no voice, which is how the conservatives want it. She doesn't seem to care that her inaction means important issues like voter registration and party finances are in the hands of conservatives. In party politics, she is truly a token. They use her, and she gets nothing for blacks or liberals in return."

Being practical is making the most of what you've got. The most immediately obvious thing Jordan has is being black. What should have been an obstacle she has turned into an asset. One longtime liberal recalls that no one even thought to scrutinize Jordan's intentions or character when she first became active in liberal politics. "I had no idea she would turn out an establishment Democrat," he groused. "Back then we didn't question the motives of blacks. It didn't occur to us that one of them might be using us for her own ambitions. It sounds naive, but then we thought, well, blacks were better, more pure and honest, than white politicians, that they had a cause bigger than themselves. If she had been white, we would have seen her as just another ambitious politician." The source of white admiration for Barbara Jordan, this theory goes, is akin to the admiration white audiences had for an entertainer like Al Hibbler, a blind black pianist. Hibbler was good, but the applause was out of proportion to his performance, because white people were so proud of him for overcoming his handicaps. "Barbara makes it easy for mossbacks to like her," says one white political reporter. "They get buddy-buddy with her and in one fell swoop they can convince themselves they aren't sexist or racist." Admiring Barbara Jordan, in other words, solves the problem of how to deal with all these blacks and women clamoring for recognition. "Black politicians who try to follow Barbara's footsteps are doomed to failure," says one black politician who has tried. "The establishment only needs one black to be cozy with, and she's it."

Being practical also means trading off today's issues for power tomorrow. It means, for example, going with the establishment on energy to get their support on other issues. A better example, however, was Jordan's support for the plank in the 1968 Democratic platform praising President Johnson's Vietnam policy. As early as 1966 Jordan had been opposed to the Vietnam War, but in Chicago she rigorously defended it. Why? Here's what she told the *Wall Street Journal:* "That plank probably resulted in further killing and dying, but I felt it was important for Texans to be supportive of their man." These values—that supporting "their man" is more important than killing and dying—are odious. They are an extreme example of how the Rayburn-Johnson practical politics can function as moral blinders, blocking out conscience by political expediency. These values of "Texans supporting their man" may well also have contributed to her decision to testify for John Connally.

Now no one seriously wants politicians to be "impractical," and no doubt subjecting the careers of other ambitious politicians to similar scrutiny would yield at least as many, and probably more, lapses, missteps, errors in judgment. Such performance is disturbing in Jordan's case, however, because in spite of her protestation that she is only a politician, she is universally thought to stand for something more. In her behalf, her supporters say, as Reverend Lawson did, that she *has* tied Rayburn-Johnson techniques to higher purpose. Further testimony comes from black state representative Mickey Leland, whose Houston district includes Jordan's home: "Barbara uses the system for blacks; it doesn't use her." But Andrew Jefferson says it best: "Barbara will listen to the establishment about their problems, and she'll take the time to understand divestiture and the natural gas shortage. She won't oppose them just because they are the establishment. But when it comes down to some long-standing demand, some long-standing principle, she can be counted on to help the establishment understand it just as she tried to understand their energy problems. She gets her leverage that way, and she's not afraid to use it."

The central dilemma about Barbara Jordan is that while almost everyone believes she has this central core beyond politics, this ultimate devotion to long-standing principles, no one really knows what it is. No one can point to many long-standing principles she has made the establishment recognize. Given her constituency, she should be expected to vote liberal, and she does: she rolls up 80, 90, 100 percent scores on all the tallies kept by black, liberal, feminist, and environmentalist groups. She votes virtually down the line with the Black Caucus on black issues, although she will occasionally oppose them on energy. In Texas she did work for the minimum wage, workmen's compensation, fair labor practice, antidiscrimination. In Washington she passed the Voting Rights Act expansion and extension. But these voting records and these legislative accomplishments are simply straight liberal politics; they are not the core. The remark is, "Well, they're part of it, but they're not it."

What "it" is, is of course the mystery. The same aura that surrounded her as a young girl surrounds her as a mature politician. That elusive quality of being beyond definition, of being "just Barbara," defies the analysis of skeptical adult observers just as it defied the analysis of teenagers. More than anything else, this accepted inevitability of her greatness is her biggest asset. "Barbara has that rare mental capacity to have a master plan for her life, a sense of high destiny," says Reverend Lawson. "Gandhi had that. Martin Luther King had that. John Kennedy I believe had that. When you have it, other people can sense it. It's both a knowledge of how much only you can do and how little time you have to live to do it in. I suspect it's what makes her work so hard, drive herself so much. It's a destiny not so much for herself, but for a people; not black people, but a whole coalition of suffering, yearning people. I can't define it, and she might not be able to, but I am sure she understands what it is."

One of the most important reasons she inspires such hope is because she is a Southerner, and understands as well as anyone the significance of the New South. While she may rigorously avoid being typecast as a black, female, or liberal politician, she takes pains to insist she is a Texan and a Southern one. "I am a Texan," she wrote. "My roots are there. . . . 'Texan' frequently evokes images of conservatism, oil, gas, racism, callousness. In my judgment, the myths should be debunked, or at the least, should include the prevalent strains of reasonableness, compassion, and decency." Her friends say she is really only comfortable with Southerners, including blacks like Georgia's Andrew Young but also some of the most reactionary members of Congress. Jordan says she has a "very good relationship with old, establishment white conservatives. Maybe I have a natural affinity for Southerners because I am a Southerner." Part of the reason, of course, is her application of the same charm, deference, and humor she used on the same sorts of men in the Texas Senate.

Barbara Jordan's rapport with white Southerners is also testament to the basic political change in the South since the Voting Rights Act of 1965. Representative Andrew Young of Georgia, the influential Atlanta black who has thrown in his chips with Jimmy Carter, describes the process: "It used to be Southern politics was just 'nigger' politics, who would 'outnigger' the other—then you registered 10 to 15 percent in the community and folks would start saying 'nigra' and then you get 35 to 40 percent registered and it's amazing how quickly they learned to say 'neegrow' and now that we've got 50, 60, 70 percent of the black votes registered in the South, everybody's proud to be associated with their black brothers and sisters." That is the language Jordan understands. Although blacks are only 20 percent of the voting-age population of the South, that still makes them the largest cohesive voting bloc, except on those increasingly rare occasions when whites vote together. It is not rare for candidates to get more than 90 percent of the black vote; in political arithmetic, that means with only 40 percent of the white vote the election is won. In urban areas where blacks are more than 20 percent, the arithmetic is even better. The result is a Fred Hofheinz or a Jimmy Carter, a Barbara Jordan or an Andrew Young.

But beyond politics, back in the nooks and crannies of a society's most basic psyche, the South has made an even more fundamental change. Blacks now openly talk about preferring the South to the North, of feeling a greater trust and understanding for their fellow white Southerners than for even the most bleeding-heart Northern liberal. Black support for Jimmy Carter is of course one manifestation of that trust, but it goes deeper. Black voices make this point best. This is Eddie Bernice Johnson, a black state legislator from Dallas: "In the North, racism has had a facade, a pretense that it didn't exist. People wanted to think that nothing was wrong, that everything was okay and the problem was somewhere else. They didn't want to admit they had it too, and if you don't admit the problem, you can't deal with it. In the South whites are trying to deal with it; the ones that have dealt with it have been through something, and you can generally trust them down the line." And Reverend Lawson: "The South has always depended on the power that brings the harvest and the seasons, something bigger than one's self and one's strivings. That condition reminds us of our common humanity beneath the shadow of larger forces; it breeds a basic compassion and a basic religiosity, an esteem for others even when you don't particularly like them. In addition, white families in the South have always depended on blacks. Black mammies raised their children and taught them manners, black men tilled their cotton and built their houses. Martin Luther King called it a web of mutuality, a binding of the two races together. That isn't true in the North; the black is a newcomer there, and by and large he isn't wanted. Even George Wallace is somehow more aware of the humanity of blacks than is the average white in Grosse Point."

The symbolic dimension of Barbara Jordan's achievement is to link the troubled past with a hopeful future, to bridge from a segregated society to an unsegregated one. She has been called Aunt Jemima by both her friends and her enemies, and, although she doesn't like it, the metaphor is apt. In appearance she conjures up the common memories of a culture—she is every black maid, black cook, black mammy. She comes to us direct from *Gone With the Wind* or *Uncle Tom's Cabin*, an enduring stereotype of the black women who lived closest with whites, who sustained the web of mutuality. The awesomeness of her presence is rooted in her explicit destruction of that image, as if every black mammy and Aunt Jemima had risen up with their rolling pins to take over the world.

The final mystery about Barbara Jordan is, what next? One of 435 United States representatives can only do so much, no matter how great her political skills or symbolic import. Carter had her on his list of vice-presidential possibilities (and rejected her, Carter sources say, not because she was black but because, like Carter, she was from the South), and she is mentioned as a possible attorney general or Supreme Court justice should Carter win. For her part, she considers the Supreme Court a place to retire to. The U.S. Senate? Perhaps. Four years ago she dismissed the idea with incredulity: "Barbara Jordan run for senator? A black woman run for the U.S. Senate in Texas?" Today she knows those old barriers are falling and is now open to the possibility, perhaps against John Tower in 1978. But ultimately, as one friend says, "all she really wants to do is be president." And brothers, that will be the day.

*October 1976*

## THE WARRIOR'S BRIDE

*One month after the battle of San Jacinto, a nine-year-old girl named Cynthia Ann Parker was abducted by Indians and went on to become the wife of the most feared Comanche chief.*

JAN REID

An icon of strength, courage, and tragedy, Cynthia Ann Parker was the most celebrated Texas woman of the nineteenth century, yet she died in obscurity—in her mind, captivity—when she was just 45. Frontier Texans had made a myth of a vanished nine-year-old and the mystery and rumor that for a quarter of the century enclosed her like a plains mirage: She symbolized all the children and women kidnapped by Comanches in a long and brutal war. Those same Texans were shocked to learn that she loved and married a ferocious war chief—her own captor—and she wanted nothing more than to follow the buffalo trail and nurture three Comanche children. Texas Rangers took her back by accident and force in 1860, almost shooting her as a troublesome "squaw" on a racing horse with a baby in one arm. Then for a decade Texan relatives tried in vain to tame her wild ways. All they did was break her heart.

ON THE MORNING OF MAY 19, 1836, a young Comanche Indian rode into Fort Parker, in East Texas, with a band of warriors, snatched a blue-eyed nine-year-old girl from her mother, and galloped off with her and her younger brother on the back of his horse, vanishing onto the prairie. The abduction, as swift and brutal as any during the 120-year conflict between the Plains Indians and the Texas settlers, turned the little girl into a cause célèbre, a symbol of the war against terror, as it were. Politicians invested her with heroic victimhood, mothers used her tale to keep children from straying far, and frontiersmen envisioned an innocent young beauty trapped against her will on the plains. Oh, to be the virile male who rescued her from those savages! Over time, the mystery of the little girl's whereabouts became a treasured and carefully cultivated Texas legend.

Reality eventually caught up with myth. In the late 1840s traders and military men began returning from Indian country claiming to have come across the girl, who had since grown into a woman, and they shared a consistent revelation that flabbergasted Texans. The young woman had married and had children with a Comanche warrior, and she was unwilling to leave him or her family behind. It turned out that he was the very man who had kidnapped her—the most feared and loathed Comanche of them all. Few Texans openly blamed her for embracing the enemy; she was so young when she was taken. Still, she had a choice of cultures and allegiances, and even after repeated chances to return to her God-fearing Texas family, she infuriatingly chose to remain on the plains, the wife and lover of a killer. The girl who had once reminded every Texan why he fought so hard against the Indians now stirred emotions that were powerful, complex, and contradictory. One day, a group of Rangers unleashed a brutal raid of its own, snatched the white woman back, and delivered her to her family. It was a cruel reward. Amid storms of total violence, she was wrenched and stolen from her loved ones twice. And a few years later, sometime around 1870, the blue-eyed prairie girl, once the most talked-about woman of her era, died in near obscurity in the Piney Woods of East Texas.

Her name was Cynthia Ann Parker, and to this day her tale continues to grip and haunt Texans like few others. There is the Alamo, then San Jacinto, and then there is the little white girl who became a Comanche. The facts, though, were long ago intertwined with fiction. Even as Cynthia Ann is celebrated—in histories, novels, movies, children's literature, and opera—she continues to be mythologized. It is said that she was beautiful (in fact the years of hard living had been punishing), that she was a tragic victim (in fact she cherished her life with the Comanches), that she was a slave to an evil warrior (in fact she loved her husband deeply). Indeed, much of what has been said about her is fiction. But looking at the facts of her story now, even without some of these myths, there's a more impressive truth. Strong as buffalo hide, family-loving, and high-spirited despite dire circumstances, Cynthia Ann demonstrated the same qualities that have ennobled iconic Texans from Mary Maverick to Barbara Jordan, Ima Hogg to Lady Bird Johnson. What's more, she offered Texans and Comanches something no man on either side could provide: a means of finally putting 120 years of rage and hatred to rest. Maybe the reason we can't let go of Cynthia Ann Parker is because she was the original tough Texas woman.

THE LITTLE GIRL'S ODYSSEY began on 14,000 acres of choice land near the headwaters of the Navasota River, where her family, immigrants to Mexican Texas in the 1830s, built a stockade that came to be known as Fort Parker. Her family helped found the Texas Rangers, who rode as sentries along the Indian frontier, and during the revolt against Mexico, they fled Santa Anna's army in the rain-soaked ordeal of refugees called the Runaway Scrape. But when that war was won, they returned home in 1836, disbanded the Ranger company, and began to rebuild their life on the frontier. Peace settled over their village, and one morning the Parker men went to work their fields, leaving the heavy gates to their fort open.

The Comanche riders who arrived that morning in May were joined by Kiowas and some local Caddos. Their faces were painted red and black, and they wore helmets of buffalo horns—they were a terrifying mob. Cynthia Ann's father was one of the first men killed. Relatives were raped and scalped before her eyes. She and her six-year-old brother, John, were among a group of fleeing women and children cut off in a meadow and herded like calves. The Parker children's captor was Puhtocnocony, He Who Travels Alone and Returns. Texans later rendered his name Nocona or Peta Nocona. He brandished a tomahawk and threatened to kill Lucy Parker if she didn't hand over Cynthia Ann and John.

How could the Comanches make war on children? For one thing, kidnapping was an effective way of encouraging settlers to move somewhere else. Too, the Comanches found that some Texas families could pay ransom; the going price was about $400. That was a fortune for nomads who calculated their wealth in horses and mules but knew what money could buy. And as perverse as it seemed, there was a human side to the Comanche child stealing. Smallpox, cholera, and other diseases were decimating all the tribes, and Comanche mothers were believed to be unusually prone to miscarriage. The child captives helped a dwindling people believe they might have a future on this earth. John and his sister were split up, and Cynthia Ann was given to a couple who raised her as if she had been born to them.

By the early 1840s John Parker—who according to one tale was traded off to the Kiowa Apaches—and several other captives taken in the Fort Parker raid had been found and ransomed back to their families. But as the decade wore on, Cynthia Ann was just out there somewhere. One year, a Texas Indian agent named Leonard Williams and two other men finally stumbled across her in a Comanche camp on a High Plains river. Williams offered the Indians twelve mules and merchandise for her, but her adoptive parents said angrily that they would rather die than give her up. The chief ordered the three men out of his camp but did allow Williams to talk to the girl. He said she kept her eyes on the ground and said nothing but that her lips trembled as he spoke. Some years later, a trader named Victor Rose said that he too had seen and spoken to her. He quoted her devotion to her husband, Nocona, and two small boys with sympathetic if dubious Romantic phrasing but described Nocona as "a great, greasy, lazy buck."

In East Texas Lucy Parker heard these stories and was desperate to have her daughter back. She sent her son John out to the plains to retrieve her. Some historians scoff at this claim—John would have been in his mid-teens at the time of this long horseback ride—but in 1852, in an authoritative report on the headwaters of the Red River for the U.S. Army, Captain Randolph Marcy matter-of-factly wrote: "There is at this time a white woman among the Middle Comanches, by the name of Parker, who, with her brother, was captured while they were young children. . . . This woman has adopted all the habits and peculiarities of the Comanches; has an Indian husband and children, and cannot be persuaded to leave them. The brother of the woman, who had been ransomed by a trader and brought home to his relatives, was sent back by his mother for the purpose of endeavoring to prevail upon his sister to leave the Indians and return to her family; but he stated to me that on his arrival she refused to listen to the proposition, saying that her husband, children, and all that she held most dear, were with the Indians, and there she should remain."

Despite these accounts, Texans continued to spread their own ideas about what had happened to Cynthia Ann. It's not difficult to understand why. At the time, Nocona had emerged as the leading Comanche war chief, a man who led unrelenting raids of vengeance on the outlying settlements north and west of Fort Worth. The news that he had captured the devotion of their blue-eyed white woman was too hard to swallow. In Weatherford a fired Indian agent and fervent Indian hater named John Baylor published a frothing newspaper called *The White Man*. Like other Texas men at the time—even as Cynthia Ann learned to put up and take down tepees and trailed after the bison herds and gave birth to her Comanche children—Baylor nurtured a more rapturous idea. In November 1860 Baylor ran on the front page a wholly fictional tale by a former Texas Ranger that stripped the clothes off a common sexual fantasy:

"We could not distinguish the traces of the woman's flight for some distance up the ravine," the frontiersman reported. "I could not help observing the delicate smallness of the wet foot marks she left upon the stones. . . . Poor creature! Her naked feet have been cut in the rapid flight." Later: "I saw at once, from the fairness of her complexion, not only that she was not an Indian, but felt that hers must be the face that had so possessed my imagination. I could distinguish that she was a clear brunette, and evidently a foreigner. . . . She sharply asked me in French, '*Qui êtes-vous?*'

"I speak French very lamely, and answered, as best as I could, 'Texans, Americans, *et amis*.' She smiled brightly . . . and came bounding down the rocks to join us." Still later: "That night her small, graceful head lay upon my shoulder, while the long and silken hair streamed in a raven cloud to my feet. She was very lightly clothed, since the only garments of civilization her captors had left her was something like a chemise of fine linen, which left her breast exposed and the arms naked; she, however, had thrown over her shoulders, as a cape, the brightly rosetted skin of an ocelot, but this had now fallen off. From an instinct of delicacy which does not desert even rude backwoods men, I swept her long hair as the most appropriate veil over her bosom. It was sacred to me!"

A Texas Ranger who spoke French! In his rush to use Cynthia Ann as rhetoric to stir up the anger of white frontiersmen, Baylor had no idea that his paper was close to breaking a stunning exclusive about the comely captive. This time the tale would actually be true.

IN LATE 1860 Nocona led a huge raid that set ablaze the settled frontier from Jacksboro to Weatherford. Afterward, a hard rain set in, and it was easy for the Texans to follow the Comanches' horse tracks. A few weeks later, two companies of Rangers and a cavalry troop approached the Comanche camp on the Pease River. It was one of their favorite places; just north were the four sacred Medicine Mounds jutting up from the plains. A scout with the Texans was Charles Goodnight, the future trailblazer and Panhandle cattle baron. One of the young Ranger captains was Sul Ross, who would go on to become governor and the first president of Texas A&M University. Near the Pease, Goodnight found a Bible that had belonged to a young woman named Sherman. In a raid a few weeks before, the woman had been pregnant when the Indians surrounded her farm in the Palo Pinto country; they raped and scalped her and shot several arrows into her body. She lived long enough to have a stillborn baby, then died. For the Comanches, the stolen book was nothing more than tough packing material for their shields.

Enraged, the Texas avengers rode through the camp and just laid bodies in a heap. Ross took part in the killing of a chief who warbled his death song and tried to fend them off. Ross was convinced that the man he killed was Nocona. The Comanches later jeered at this account. They claimed that Nocona, his sons, and most men of fighting ability were engaged in a buffalo hunt; the camp was now just an outfitting station. But if Nocona lived, he vanished as a war chief after that day.

In the meantime, a figure wrapped in a buffalo robe and riding a fast gray horse led the Texans on a chase from the camp through the river bottom and trees. Concealed in the robe was Cynthia Ann's two-year-old daughter, named Prairie Flower. Seeing that Ross was about to shoot her, the woman pulled up the horse, raised the infant, and called out, "Americano! Americano! Americano!"

Goodnight later wrote that he was the one who saw that the hysterical woman was blue-eyed, but Ross swore that he made the discovery, yelling at a lieutenant, "Why, Tom, this is a white woman! Indians don't have blue eyes." The angry and exhausted lieutenant yelled back: "Hell, no! That ain't no white woman! Damn that squaw! If I have to worry with her anymore, I will shoot her!" They captured the woman and her infant and returned with her to a cottonwood grove along the river to camp. "We rode right over her dead companions," Goodnight recalled. "I thought then and still think how exceedingly cruel it was."

Ross always said that he suspected and verified that she was the long-lost captive. Others, however, claimed that a cavalry officer sent for Isaac Parker, Cynthia Ann's uncle, who was a member of the Texas Legislature for its first twenty years. Living at Birdville, near Fort Worth, Parker rode out to see her. According to one witness at the interview, a neighbor of Parker's, the woman "sat for a time immovable, lost in profound meditation, oblivious to every thing by which she was surrounded, ever and anon convulsed as if it were by some powerful emotion which she struggled to suppress." Parker tried to question her in English but got little response. He turned to the neighbor and said, "If this is my niece, her name is Cynthia Ann." The woman stood up, struck herself on the chest, and cried, "Me, Cynthia Ann!"

THE STORY RACED FROM *The White Man*, which broke the exclusive, to a Dallas newspaper and then all over the state. Cynthia Ann's mother was eight years dead by then, and her uncle took her to his farm, but first he practically roped her into sitting for a photographer in Fort Worth. She was no delicate maiden now, if she ever had been one. She was 34, and the years of extreme physical hardship had worn hard. The portrait was a grim, haunting image of an intently staring woman with a breast bared for a nursing infant. Her hair was hacked short—a Comanche demonstration of grief. She'd been separated from her two boys, and she would never see them again.

At Birdville, her kin and neighbors feared that Prairie Flower's soul had been carried off by the "demon of barbarianism"; rigorous Bible study was required. Meanwhile, her mother continually tried to escape. In the end, the most idealized Texas woman of her time couldn't fit in. The Texans couldn't get through to her, couldn't make her realize how much better off she was. In bitter irony, they became her captors.

At wits' end, in 1862 Isaac Parker turned her over to her brother Silas Parker Jr., who moved her to Van Zandt County, hoping the deep Piney Woods would convince her of the futility of longing for the plains. But Silas was drafted into the Confederate army, and Cynthia Ann's sister-in-law was overwhelmed. Cynthia Ann and Prairie Flower were moved once again, this time to a house nearby built by relatives. There, Prairie Flower began to assimilate, just as her mother had among the Comanches. The girl spoke English more than Comanche, and she was doing well in school. But she caught the flu and pneumonia in December 1863, and she died the next year. Once more the wall of incomprehension shot up. Desperate with grief, Cynthia Ann wailed a keening song and, to the horror of the Parkers, slashed her arms and breasts with a knife.

Even then, the mythologizing of Cynthia Ann never relented. In telling the story of her life, most accounts claim that she passed away right after her child's death—gave up and died of a broken heart. But in truth, she lived on at least until 1870. Probably she died of the flu.

IT WOULD BE A STRETCH to now make Cynthia Ann into a protofeminist who lived in a culture of extravagant machismo. In fact, she may have accompanied her husband on some of his ferocious raids. The wives of leading warriors were useful at managing horses and captives, and the buildup to the stealing and fighting was said to have an erotic charge. Still, something about her character did inspire the Comanches. She was torn from her family at a young age, yet she had become a survivor, one who had learned to live among them and had held up with a winsome quality. She named her first son Quanah, which translated as Fragrant (he was said to have been born in a bed of wildflowers), and her second son Peanut, in honor of her favorite treat when she was a child. The Comanches gave Cynthia Ann a name that reflected their respect: Naduah, which most often translated as She Who Carries Herself With Dignity and Grace.

Almost in spite of themselves, Texans came around to sharing that same opinion. The Ranger company that caught up with her witnessed a mother who could ride a galloping horse bareback while holding a child secure in one arm. Neighbors who lived near her after her capture recalled a woman who could chop wood as ably as a man, who had a gift for sewing and weaving, and who was good-hearted, always eager to help. And she was stoic, a mother who was forced to endure the death of one child and the unknown fate of two others. Even under the worst of circumstances, Cynthia Ann Parker managed to remain tough, strong-willed, and a devoted wife and mother.

After she died, Cynthia Ann's legacy lived on through her elder son, Quanah. (Peanut had died years earlier of smallpox.) Like his father, Quanah had a brief reign as the Comanches' principal war chief and fought bravely to keep his people off the reservations. But after losing the decisive battle at Adobe Walls in 1874 and suffering relentless pursuit all winter, Quanah and the last holdouts surrendered in 1875. The strapping Comanche resolved that he had to walk the White Man's Road and became lionized in peace by cattle barons Charles Goodnight and Burk Burnett, and eventually even President Theodore Roosevelt. With friends like that, he received an $800 grant from Congress to move Cynthia Ann's remains to the reservation prairie of her chosen people.

In 1910 he spoke emotionally at the reinterment service, praising education, farming, and the white man's God. Certainly there was meanness and more on both sides of that bitter Texas conflict, but the note Quanah struck that day was one of reconciliation and tribute. "Forty years ago," he said, "my mother died. She captured by Comanches, nine years old. Love Indian and wild life so well she no want to go back to white folks. All same people anyway, God say." All Cynthia Ann had wanted was the freedom to love and be left alone, to the good of her family. It was a sentiment that still goes to the heart of what defines Texas women.

*February 2003*

# THE QUEEN IS DEAD

*Selena Quintanilla Perez, tejano's first superstar, was about to become an international pop sensation. Instead, she's another victim of gun violence in Texas.*

JOE NICK PATOSKI

**Not many Anglos in Texas had a clue who Selena was when I sat down to interview her on her tour bus in 1994, despite the fact that she was selling more CDs in Texas than Willie Nelson and ZZ Top. But to Mexican Americans in Texas, she was already a superstar. The tragedy of her death at the hands of her best friend and fan club president may have made her world-famous posthumously. I'm convinced her star would have shined far brighter had she been alive for the crossover she'd spent her career preparing for. Regardless, no Mexican American woman in Texas comes close to being the role model she still is today.**

## BLACK FRIDAY

The tragic news arrived the way tragic news often does: by phone. The call came just after lunch from my friend David Bennett, a reporter at the *San Antonio Express-News*. "Selena has been shot. In Corpus Christi at a Days Inn motel. The woman who did it is sitting in a pickup in the parking lot, holding a gun to her head." I waited for Bennett, a font of sick jokes about current events, to deliver the punch line. It was, after all, March 31—the day before April Fool's. But no punch line came when he called back a few minutes later: "She's dead. She passed away at 1:05 P.M. at Memorial Medical Center."

I had met her only once, but it was as though someone close to me was suddenly gone. Selena Quintanilla Perez was a 23-year-old Grammy award–winning singer and the undisputed queen of tejano music, a Texas specialty that is enjoying unprecedented popularity around the country and the world. A year ago, I'd talked with her on a tour bus in Austin for a *Texas Monthly* story. For most of the interview, she sat next to her mother, Marcella, who often traveled with her band, Los Dinos, and her father, Abraham, the band's manager. At one point, her husband, Chris Perez—who was also her lead guitarist—stopped in to say hello. Around midnight, Selena's sister, Suzette—her drummer—and her brother, A.B.—her bass player, chief composer, and producer—would join her and the rest of the band onstage.

Selena's family crossed my mind when I heard about her death. She may have dressed provocatively onstage, but after sitting face to face with her in the company of her kin, seeing her without makeup or her sexy costumes, I pegged her for a good girl—not the sort of person who would be involved in a shooting, especially a shooting involving a jealous woman in a crime of passion.

That, of course, was what the early rumors suggested. A radio deejay somewhere wisecracked that the assailant was "Emilio's wife"—the spouse of Emilio Navaira, the popular tejano singer who was Selena's only real box office competition. That scurrilous suggestion spread so fast that Navaira's office and home were besieged with death threats. To get the truth, I tuned in two of San Antonio's Spanish-language stations, KXTN-FM (Tejano 107) and KEDA-AM (Radio Jalapeño), and stayed close to the phone. Soon, another friend called to say that Ramiro Burr, the *Express-News* syndicated tejano columnist, had heard from Selena's record company that the woman in the pickup was Yolanda Saldivar, a 34-year-old nurse whom everyone knew as Selena's number one fan.

By five that afternoon, San Antonio TV stations—including the affiliates for the Spanish-language Telemundo and Univision networks—had reporters and satellite uplinks at the crime scene. Selena y los Dinos songs were all over the radio. Grieving callers to radio stations read poems on the air. Other tejano artists, such as Stefani, the All-American Sweetheart, phoned in to share memories. Dances at tejano venues were called off in cities across Texas.

When I heard that Tejano 107 would be holding a candlelight vigil at the open-air Sunken Gardens Theatre in San Antonio at seven that night, I jumped into the car. My first stop was Selena's boutique and salon, Selena Etc., on a tony strip of Broadway by Brackenridge Park. Last year, Selena had opened this boutique and one in Corpus Christi; music may have been her living, but fashion was her life. When I pulled into the parking lot, four other cars were there. Two had messages painted on their windshields in white shoe polish: One read "Selena Lives On," the other "Missing You Selena." A bouquet of flowers had been placed by the door of the boutique, alongside a picture of a smiling Selena and several notes. A few adults, four teenage girls, three younger boys, and an *abuela* (grandmother) were milling about, studying the flowers, reading the notes, peering in the boutique's window at the photos and posters of Selena that hung among the designer outfits. Their faces were not animated or emotional but solemn and blank. They wanted to see, to touch, to connect somehow.

Across the park, Sunken Gardens was filling up fast. A small truck, the Tejano 107 mobile studio, was parked in the middle of the stage. Two life-size cutouts of Selena holding a Coca-Cola were placed nearby. The event had been haphazardly organized—when someone from the station began handing out candles, a small stampede broke out—and at first, it seemed as though it might never come together. Then disc jockey Jonny Ramírez emerged from the truck to tell the nearly five thousand people in attendance that they were there because "somebody stupid had a gun." A few people laughed when he recounted first meeting Selena ("I said to myself, 'Yes! This lady makes me want to go home and take a cold shower!'"). Then he said what almost everyone else who had ever known her had said: "She never behaved like a superstar."

By seven-thirty, candlelight illuminated the whole place. Kids still skittered under their parents' legs, and friends still greeted friends with smiles. But a sober, respectful serenity prevailed. Facing the stage, a teenage boy and girl (brother and sister? boyfriend and girlfriend?) stood rigidly, holding a candle and clutching a white banner that read "Honk If You Love Selena." I didn't realize it then, but the veneration had begun.

## WHO SHE WAS

On Saturday Selena's death came up during a conversation with a neighbor in my predominantly Anglo Central Texas community. "I never heard of her," she told me, "and I'm from Refugio. I grew up around those people." Her reaction echoed that of many Texans, who saw this as just another senseless shooting.

Yet to "those people"—the five million Texans of Mexican descent—March 31 was a darker day than November 22, 1963. To "those people," Selena was more than a celebrity. She was an icon. Her status as an entertainer who was a millionaire at age nineteen; her positive personality; her devotion to God, family, and home; and her willingness to talk to kids about staying in school and avoiding drugs made her a hero to brown-skinned people—especially Hispanic girls—who had precious few role models.

Her music validated the cultural duality of the majority of her fans, proving you could embrace the traditions of the land you came from while still being hip and modern. Like most Mexican Americans who have assimilated into the mainstream, Selena's first language was English—and yet she opted to sing in the native language of her parents, proving that who you are and where your family came from are sources of pride, not sources of shame.

Selena was a total package. She could work a crowd. She could dance. She was sexy. She knew how to make time for industry types backstage. And, of course, she could sing. She was equally comfortable with the fancy streamlined polkas that are the backbone of all Tex-Mex music, the histrionic boleros from northern Mexico (such as "Qué Creías," in which she scorches a lover who has taken her for granted), and the mambo-derived cumbias popular throughout Latin America. She reinterpreted the sixties-era Japanese pop song "Sukiyaki" into a sentimental Spanish-language version. She reworked the Pretenders' eighties rock classic "Back on the Chain Gang" into "Fotos y Recuerdos" on her latest album, *Amor Prohibido*. She was savvy enough to write and record the nonsensical but eminently hummable "Bidi Bidi Bom Bom," which received heavy airplay here and in Latin America last year but would have been a hit in any language.

Despite those accomplishments, it was the forthcoming release of Selena's first English-language album that had her fans and business associates giddy with anticipation. Instead of competing with Emilio Navaira (tejano's George Strait), La Mafia, Grupo Mazz, La Diferenzia, or Gary Hobbs (tejano's Vince Gill), she would be taking on the likes of Whitney Houston, Gloria Estefan, and Madonna. Her rivals were cheering her on. She was going to lift all of tejano with her.

Then the dream ended—at the hands of the one person outside her family who stood to benefit most from her success.

## THE KILLER

Yolanda Saldivar fit the classic stereotype of *la dueña*, the faithful chaperone or assistant. Neither attractive nor charismatic, the short, pudgy registered nurse from San Antonio was Selena's constant companion. Her devotion and loyalty were beyond question. With the Quintanilla family's blessings, Yolanda founded the Selena Fan Club in 1991. Whenever Selena y los Dinos played San Antonio or nearby communities, Yolanda was at Selena's side. She was Selena's eyes and ears, friends said—so trusted that she gave up her fan club position last fall to run Selena's boutiques.

But some members of Selena's circle spoke of another Yolanda. She was possessive and controlling, says Martin Gomez, who designed fashions for Selena until, he claims, Yolanda's obsessiveness drove him to quit. She was a loner who had lived with her mother until recently and had few friends. She had once been accused of embezzling funds from a previous employer, and she had defaulted on a student loan. A woman who moved into an apartment with Yolanda discovered that Yolanda didn't just have pictures of Selena on her walls—the whole place was "like a shrine." Spooked, the woman moved out after two weeks.

Word reached Abraham Quintanilla in January that something had been amiss with the fan club. Several fans had complained that they had sent in their $22 but had never received the promised T-shirt, CD, picture, or biography. About the same time, employees at the boutiques began to raise questions about Yolanda's actions.

Abraham began quietly investigating the matter and didn't inform Selena until he felt he had concrete evidence.

In early March, Abraham, Selena, and Suzette met with Yolanda and demanded a full accounting. Yolanda denied the accusations and said that others were intent on making her look bad. Still, she must have seen what was coming. The person she had devoted her life to was going to cut her loose.

On March 13, after undergoing a background check, Yolanda bought a snub-nosed .38-caliber pistol from a San Antonio gun dealer. She then traveled to Monterrey, Mexico, where Selena planned to open a boutique, taking Selena's business records with her. At some point during Yolanda's trip, Selena phoned her and told her to bring the records back.

Subsequently, Yolanda resurfaced in Corpus Christi. On the night of Thursday, March 30, Selena and her husband, Chris, went to room 158 at the Days Inn, where Yolanda was staying, to pick up the records from her—despite the fact that Yolanda had asked Selena to come alone. When Selena got home, she realized some bank statements were missing, and she made arrangements to pick up the remaining records Friday morning.

On the morning of March 31, Yolanda asked Selena to accompany her to Doctors Regional Medical Center, claiming that she had been raped in Monterrey. When test results were inconclusive, Yolanda changed her story: She hadn't been raped after all. Selena and Yolanda then drove back to the motel.

Once again, Selena asked for the bank statements. Apparently, she also attempted to sever their professional relationship. Harsh words were exchanged. Yolanda demanded that Selena return a ring she'd given her as a gift from her employees. As Selena removed the ring, Yolanda pulled out the gun. When Selena ran out the door and yelled for help, Yolanda screamed, "You bitch!" and shot her in the back.

Selena crossed the courtyard and collapsed. The bullet had entered her right shoulder and severed an artery. By 11:49, when she crawled to the lobby door, she was bleeding to death.

"I've been shot," she cried.

"Who shot you?" asked a motel employee.

"Yolanda," Selena said. Then she passed out, clutching the ring in her hand.

An ambulance arrived within three minutes to take her to Memorial Medical Center. Notified almost immediately that Selena had been in "an accident," Abraham and his family raced to the hospital, but the message had gotten confused: They thought she had been in a car wreck. A doctor met them in a waiting area near the emergency room and told them she had been shot. When he said he had administered four units of blood and had been able to restart her heart, Abraham became frantic and interrupted him. Because of her religious beliefs, he said, Selena would have objected to the transfusions.

But it was too late. The transfusions hadn't helped, the doctor said. Selena was dead.

## THE CRIME SCENE

I woke up early on the morning of Sunday, April 2, with an urge to be in Corpus Christi. The outpouring of emotion on the news the night before was unlike anything I'd ever seen.

On the way to pick up David Bennett, who would come along for the ride, I tuned in KEDA-AM's weekly Spanish-language mass from San Fernando Cathedral in downtown San Antonio. The priest was talking about Selena. "It isn't this woman who senselessly killed her," he said. "It is this whole culture of death we're promoting." He criticized the urge to retaliate. He begged the congregation to "say no to the spirit of getting even."

When we got to the Days Inn in Corpus, we met up with about one hundred people, almost all of them Hispanic. Some were taking photos of themselves in front of the motel's marquee, which read "We Will Miss You Selena." Others were hanging around the lobby, where Selena spoke her last words. Still others were standing stoically near room 158, posing for cameras and video recorders. At the foot of the door were a bouquet of carnations, some roses, a pink oleander blossom, a votive candle, and several notes.

Many people seemed to be combing the site for something—evidence, perhaps, or a memento. Several young men hovered around the wooden trash container by the lobby, inspecting every square inch for flecks of dried blood. Two teenage boys in Dallas Cowboys jerseys ran their fingers through the thick blades of grass in the courtyard, where Selena had collapsed. Near room 158, three boys carefully picked up wood chips from the flower bed, studying each one for traces of blood.

Retracing Selena's final steps, I felt the same cold chill I'd felt at Dealey Plaza in Dallas. I looked around for David, who had wandered off. I found him kneeling near the lobby, joining two men in silent detective work. After peering underneath an empty planter, he rose, his face paler than before. "I think I'm going to lose it," he said. He had found a rust-colored spot that the cleanup crew had missed.

## HOME

From the motel, we drove south on Navigation Boulevard to Bloomington Street, where the Quintanilla clan lived. Traffic was stalled for five blocks as motorists lined up to cruise by. The three modest brick homes, surrounded by a single chain-link fence, were among the newest structures in the blue-collar, largely Hispanic neighborhood, and each had a paved driveway that took up most of the front yard. The house on the corner was Chris and Selena's. It was small and unassuming—not the sort of place you would identify as the domicile of a superstar. The two-story house next door was Abraham and Marcella's. The next house belonged to A.B. and his wife, Vangie.

Scores of fans stood in front of the fence, which had turned into a canvas of poster boards, banners, photos, flowers, colored ribbons, balloons, and teddy bears. There were flags of the United States, Mexico, and El Salvador. There were messages from Puerto Rico and Wisconsin, Dallas and Deer Park, Laredo and Three Rivers, and La Feria. One especially touching note was simply addressed, "To: Heaven, From: Houston."

Staring at a picture of Selena on the fence, a toddler gleefully tugged at his mother's skirt: "Look, Mommy. Bidi Bidi Bom Bom."

## THE LONG GOOD-BYE

Downtown, for nearly a mile, people lined the sidewalk of Shoreline Boulevard on their way to Bayfront Plaza Auditorium. They were waiting to see Selena's closed casket, which was surrounded by five thousand white roses—Selena's favorite.

The fans started showing up as early as four in the morning, though the doors didn't open until nine. Still, things went smoothly until a rumor spread through the crowd late in the afternoon: The coffin was empty; Selena's death was a publicity stunt. To calm the well-wishers, the family had the casket opened. The body was Selena's. Her hands, folded across her chest, clutched a single red rose. By ten, when the doors finally closed, almost 60,000 people had paid their respects.

I drove home that night but the next morning impulsively decided to drive back to Corpus. It was too late to attend the private funeral service, but since it was being broadcast live by San Antonio TV and radio stations, I listened while driving down the highway—with my headlights on. Minister Sam Wax, a Jehovah's Witness, preached in English about the resurrection of Jesus according to the faith. "Jesus said, 'Do not marvel at this.'" The service lasted less than twenty minutes. At the family's request, each of the six hundred mourners placed a white rose on the coffin. Before long, a two-foot pile of roses rested atop the casket, which was eventually cleared and lowered into the ground.

I pulled into the parking lot of the Days Inn precisely 24 hours after my first visit. Just as many people were walking the grounds and searching for traces of the crime, but the facade of room 158 had been transformed. Messages scribbled in ink, pencil, and felt-tip marker covered the door, the window, the sidewalk, even the limestone block exterior. From a distance, room 158 looked like an altar.

When I first heard Selena had been shot, I thought I was witnessing the end of an era and the shattering of the great American crossover dream. Now I wasn't so sure. At the very least, my Anglo friends finally knew how to properly pronounce "tejano." And I was getting a life's education in the art of grieving, the power of family, and the cycle of life and death. How sad it all was—and yet how vibrant and full of life this send-off was. These people, most of them strangers to Selena, had gathered to say their good-byes. I heaved a deep sigh, wiped the tears from my eyes, and took one last look around.

## THE WISDOM OF ABRAHAM

It was midafternoon when I arrived at Q Productions, an old auto body shop along Corpus Christi's Leopard Street industrial strip that the Quintanillas had transformed into a company office and recording facility. Most of the mourners had already cleared out, and Eddie Quintanilla, Selena's uncle, was happy to regale me with tales of his childhood and of his brother Abraham's high school group, Los Dinos. Abraham loved street corner doo-wop music and rhythm and blues, Eddie said, but he played traditional Tex-Mex fare—polkas and waltzes with Spanish lyrics—to pay the bills. He recalled how Abraham took a good job, working for Dow Chemical in Lake Jackson, to support his family. With the money he saved, he opened a nice Mexican restaurant, quit the plant, and re-formed Los Dinos with his older children. Selena began singing in the restaurant when she was eight. Then oil prices slumped, people quit eating out, and the restaurant went under.

In 1982, Eddie said, Abraham moved the family back to Corpus Christi. Music provided them with sustenance as they traveled across Texas and the United States in a battered van pulling a broken-down trailer. "That was a long, long time ago," Eddie added with a smile.

I found Abraham Quintanilla sitting in a chair in the studio control room while a TV crew packed up its gear. A broad bull of a man, Abraham had impressed me at our previous encounter as a classic band manager, a streetwise type who instantly sends the message that he's not to be trifled with. He certainly knows the rules of survival on the tejano dance hall circuit: how money at this level of show business is generated (in gate receipts and merchandising, not CDs and cassettes), who was most likely to steal it from you, which disc jockeys can sell an extra 10,000 copies of an album, which promoters skim off the door.

Above all, he knows talent. Even when the shy Selena was

singing country music in English or, later, when the members of Los Dinos were jumping around in shiny space suits, Abraham saw something. And, indeed, in 1989 he managed to sign a breakthrough six-figure deal for the band to cut Spanish-language records for EMI's new Latin division. Then came last year's English-language contract with SBK Records. The beat-up van and rickety trailer were replaced by a tour bus and a semi full of production and staging equipment. Selena y los Dinos had become a mini-empire. I couldn't help but wonder then if Selena would someday ditch her father and sign with a big-time management firm in New York or Los Angeles. Now it was beside the point.

Since Selena's death, Abraham had been on automatic pilot—talking to reporters, overseeing funeral plans, conceding that he had always been wary of Yolanda Saldivar, even lamenting the death threats that Emilio Navaira's wife had received. But as the crowd began to leave, he spoke with dread about the future. "When I see that empty place and I know she's not there, I'm going to start missing her," he said. "It's a tragic thing that happened. It's a reality."

We talked of respect, of family, and of the senselessness of the crime. Abraham railed against the concealed-weapons bill that the Texas Legislature would likely pass: "We live in a dangerous world. Why make it worse? My God, everyone's armed to the teeth. Anybody is liable to kill you for a minute thing."

But life would go on, he vowed. He manages six other bands, and his other children are certainly gifted enough to perform on their own. Selena had already recorded four tracks for her English-language debut, and four more songs in English are on the sound track of the new movie *Don Juan DeMarco,* in which she has a cameo appearance. There was enough material for a new album. "Of course, it would never be the same," he said. "There will never be another Selena. But we'll go forward with it."

I told him what I had seen, how people were looking for answers. Were there any lessons they could take from the tragedy?

He paused deliberately. "Parents, it's time to go back to the old-fashioned way of teaching our children," he said. "About morals, about the dangers of life. They're too trusting. They don't think there are bad things out there. I hope that a lot of young people see this and grow cautious. I don't think Selena knew how popular she was getting. I would tell her, 'Mi hijita, don't go to the store by yourself at night. Don't go to the mall alone. There are people who will kill you for no reason, just because you are famous.'"

Abraham Quintanilla knew all that, but he also knew his daughter was old enough to make her own decisions. She would listen, then tell him, "Dad, you think all people are bad. I can take care of myself."

Abraham talked about the band's first Mexican tour. The promoter warned them that the media there thrived on sensationalism. Yet Selena disarmed everyone at Los Dinos's first Mexican press conference by walking in and hugging every single journalist. "By the time she started doing interviews, they were in the palm of her hand," Abraham said, smiling. "The next day, all the articles praised her. They said she wasn't some prefabricated blonde. Several remarked about the color of her skin." It was the brown tone of the masses, not the pale white of the Castillian Spanish. "They called her *una mujer del pueblo*—a woman of the people. She never forgot where she came from."

You may soon have a problem, I told him. The veneration of Selena was taking on a life of its own.

He shook his head. "Selena wouldn't want that. She believed worship should go only to the Creator. Just remember her as a good person who loved people and loved life. I don't think Selena would be pleased to be part of any form of idolatry."

I told him how sorry I was for him and his family and hugged him in an *abrazo*.

Moments later, I was back on the highway, holding back sniffles, ready for the long weekend to end. I turned on KEDT-FM to listen to the news when an announcer broke in, saying there had just been a shooting at a refinery inspection company in Corpus Christi. Five people were shot by a former employee with a pistol. The company was only about five miles from Q Productions. It happened at the same moment Abraham Quintanilla and I were talking about guns and violence.

*May 1995*

## LIP SHTICK

*At the Neiman Marcus in NorthPark Center, more women buy more makeup for more money than anyplace else in Dallas—maybe in the world. No wonder I couldn't resist.*

PAMELA COLLOFF

**The focus of this story is not one woman, but a place: the makeup counter. The idea—like most of my best story ideas—came from *Texas Monthly* senior editor Skip Hollandsworth, who had heard that the NorthPark Neiman Marcus cosmetics department in Dallas sold more makeup than any other location in the country. Before I spent some time there, it had never occurred to me that a woman could—and would—spend thousands of dollars a year on cosmetics. But at Neiman's, the makeup counter is not just a place to buy lipstick. Women come to talk about their problems, to be listened to, to get fussed over, to have their self-esteem boosted, and they leave a little poorer, but happier, for the experience.**

FIRST, A CONFESSION: I do not like to wear makeup. Whether this is a consequence of living in Austin, where flawless, full-coverage foundation can mark you as a hopelessly unhip out-of-towner—"That's so Dallas," Austinites like to sniff—or simply my own failure as a woman, I'm not sure. Only when it was forbidden by my mother, in junior high, did I wear makeup with abandon. Back then, my vision of worldly sophistication involved gobs of electric-blue eyeliner and bubblegum-pink lip gloss, which I gooped on at school in the girls' bathroom. Later came an unfortunate smudgy-black-eyeliner phase, and then a brief but theatrical flirtation with a vivid shade of red lipstick that I hoped made me look French.

That all came to an end when I went off to a liberal arts college in New England, where mascara was considered proof of a less-than-rigorous intellect. I've used makeup sparingly ever since, and in sandal-wearing, Frisbee-tossing Austin, that's the norm. Only as I've entered my thirties, as the fine lines around my eyes have begun to multiply at an alarming rate, have I started to wonder if maybe there isn't something redeeming in all those compacts and tubes and bottles.

With this in mind, I found myself drawn to the nerve center of all that is cosmetic, the city where the Mary Kay empire was born, the place where women lip-line and shadow and contour-shade before going to the gym. Yes, Dallas. My precise destination was, naturally, Neiman Marcus—not the flagship downtown store but the trendier NorthPark Center location, which happens to sell the most cosmetics of any of Neiman's 35 stores in the country. So far-reaching is its influence that many high-end cosmetics companies choose to roll out their new lines here after introducing them in New York. Bobbi Brown debuted in New York at Bergdorf Goodman, then ventured into the national market by offering ten shades of lipstick at the NorthPark Neiman's. The rest is history.

I arrived a few minutes before the store opened to find that a handful of women were already standing outside its glass doors, exquisitely dressed and coiffed and powdered as if they hoped to be photographed at any moment for *W*. Was there an event at Neiman's? I asked a sleek young Asian woman perched atop impossibly high heels. "No," she said, as if I had asked a very stupid question. And so I stared at the window display—a basketball hovering, inexplicably, above a three-inch-high Manolo Blahnik pump—and waited. Before long, a security guard turned the lock and swung open the doors ("Good morning, ladies!"), the lights brightened, and we all rode the escalators down one floor to Cosmetics: a florid world so rooted in fantasy that Neiman's saleswomen privately call it the Land of Oz.

What waited for us below was an expanse of cream-colored marble, roughly the length of a city block, where row upon row of gleaming countertops were lined with lipsticks in every shade and hue: Pink Sugar and Grenadine and Mauve and Warm Apricot and Caramel and on and on, reflected in what seemed to be an infinity of mirrors. There were lip plumpers and eye balms and bronzers too, and hydrating serums and night creams with "age-defying" properties. Promenading down the aisles was Neiman's A-list clientele: well-groomed Junior Leaguers, couture mavens clad in Prada, snowy-haired doyennes in pearls. One woman toted her fluffy white bichon frise in its own Louis Vuitton bag. Soon the place was humming with conversation and laughter as women settled into the makeup artists' chairs, a few, despite the early hour, sipping complimentary glasses of white wine. Roaming the department were saleswomen, all dressed in black, who nodded sagely, advising women about summer colors with the intensity of Zen masters. No sign of the faltering economy was evident here; $500 sales were commonplace. At the Chanel counter, a longtime customer told me that she had recently spent $1,000 on makeup in one visit to Neiman's.

"So is that your yearly supply?" I asked.

She squinted at me, searching for any discernible signs of intelligence. "No," she said after a moment, patting my arm.

A few paces away, seated at the Yves Saint Laurent counter, a girl wearing a frilly pink dress and Mary Janes was receiving a lesson in beauty. A makeup artist hovered over her, smoothing pale blue eye shadow across her lids. The girl's mother, a striking, immaculately dressed blonde, took a step back to appraise her. "Oh, my!" she cooed. "Don't you look like a model now?" The little girl giggled. Blush already brightened her cheeks, and her lips shimmered with pink gloss. I stood beside the counter and watched until my curiosity got the best of me. "How old are you?" I finally asked the girl.

She smiled, revealing a missing tooth, and held up her hand, extending each of her fingers one by one. "Five," she said.

I was a long way from home.

EVERYONE SEEMS to have a theory about why Dallas women are crazy about makeup. There's the hot-weather theory, which holds that the sun is somehow stronger in Dallas, so women must more aggressively combat the elements with powder and base. "Anything that's beautiful in Dallas was either planted, dug, erected, or willed into being," observes Ellen Kampinsky, who created the fashion section of the *Dallas Morning News* in the late seventies. "The same philosophy carries over to women's grooming." There's the status theory, which maintains that wearing the right kind of makeup, like having the right plastic surgeon, is essential for membership in the right social circle. ("Really, it's very tribal," says journalist David Feld, a longtime observer of Dallas society who wrote for the *New York Times* before becoming the creative director of *D Magazine*. "You can practically tell what country club a woman belongs to by the shade of her lipstick. If she's wearing coral, she belongs to Brook Hollow or the Dallas Country Club.") And then there's the inferiority-complex theory, which links the city's preoccupation with makeup to its insecurity over not being an international city, a port, or a fashion capital. "We desperately want to prove that we're cosmopolitan," a friend from Highland Park e-mailed me on condition of anonymity. "So we wear makeup and clothes that scream, 'Look! We have high fashion! Look! We can overspend on designer products too!'"

Neiman Marcus, which has catered to this anxiety in Dallas for nearly a century, can be partially credited (or blamed) for the city's fascination with exterior beauty. "I think it's a chicken-or-the-egg question," says Leonard Lauder, the chairman of the cosmetics giant Estée Lauder. "Did Stanley Marcus make Dallas acutely aware of appearance, or was Dallas just the logical place to found a store like Neiman Marcus?" Lauder notes that while plenty of people in Dallas do not, of course, shop at Neiman's, they do see its newspaper ads featuring fashions straight off the Paris runways; these ads have raised the fashion bar for Dallas women for decades and given birth to the trickle-down theory. According to this hypothesis, the heightened awareness of haute couture made Dallas a natural cosmetics mecca. Neiman's will not reveal sales numbers, but Lauder confirms that his company does a brisk business in Dallas; the Estée Lauder spa inside the NorthPark Neiman's cosmetics department—yes, there is a full-service spa inside—is the busiest and most profitable Lauder spa in the world. "Dallas is a bellwether market for cosmetics," Lauder says. "From a per capita standpoint, it beats New York City and Los Angeles hands down."

It follows, then, that the "Dallas look" requires a great deal of makeup. But what is the look, exactly? At Neiman's, its model is less the street chic of Jennifer Lopez than it is the cool perfection—

 still, after all these years—of Dallas native Morgan Fairchild: part soap star, part Highland Park Methodist. Among the women who frequent the cosmetics department, there is a certain sameness to their faultless faces. "New York has a more European appreciation for idiosyncrasies," says Kampinsky. "In Dallas, the flaws are smoothed over." There is the scrupulously made-up mouth, lined just above the lip and polished to a high shine; the contour-shaded eyes, fringed with mascara; the palette of vibrant reds and corals. And then there is the base. "The dead giveaway that a woman is from Dallas is foundation—and lots of it," my Highland Park friend wrote. "We wear lots of base to cover up our blotchy skin, which we get from wearing lots of base. It's a dreadful cycle." This style is most entrenched in white, middle- and upper-class Dallas, in parts of the city where the lawns are groomed with a similarly exacting attention to detail. "In the Park Cities, women's makeup is so perfect that it looks almost invisible, even though it's applied through an extraordinarily complex, Kabuki-like process that can take hours," says Feld. "As you head farther north, it gets a bit heavier and less polished. You could almost add an extra layer for each exit you pass on the Dallas North Tollway."

My friend from Highland Park reads great meaning into the fact that she wore her makeup to bed for years and wonders if it's the plight of Dallas women to be afraid to look imperfect, even in the dark. "I read that Angie Harmon, who went to my high school, used to sleep in her makeup too," she wrote. "I wonder if more Dallas women go to bed with their faces on? I think we all knew exactly what Mary Kay Ash meant when she used to say, 'I go to bed looking like Elizabeth Taylor and I wake up looking like Charles de Gaulle.'"

THE GRANDE DAME of the NorthPark Neiman's cosmetics department is a short, stoop-shouldered 64-year-old saleswoman named Christina Gilbert who wears quite possibly the largest glasses in Dallas. Their colossal brown frames arch above her false eyelashes, where they brush against her copper-colored bangs, and dip below the bottom of her nose, magnifying her green eyes to such a degree that whenever she peers at customers, she appears to be gazing at them with rapturous interest. Women who can't remember her name invariably ask for "the lady with the glasses," sometimes illustrating who they are talking about by cupping their hands around their face in two gigantic parentheses. She is a curious fixture in a place where the rules of beauty are so uniform, but she understands her customers well; they are competitive, and her glasses obscure what is a very pretty face. Because she is fond of wearing leopard-print headbands, baubles, loud sweaters, and an array of gold pins shaped like bumblebees, it would be easy to assume she is just an eccentric. She is, in fact, a shrewd saleswoman. After 24 years behind the counter—currently she sells the Sisley Paris line—she is one of the top sales associates in the makeup department, which sells untold millions in cosmetics and skin-care products each year.

Keep in mind that it takes a particular talent to summon women into a department store to buy products that are not essential, that are wildly expensive, and that can be purchased over the phone or online—and then to retain these customers, and sometimes their daughters and granddaughters, as loyal clients for decades. Christina shrugs off any suggestion that she must have special intuitive powers. "I listen," she said. "Most women don't get listened to." Indeed, throughout my time at Neiman's, Christina was often huddled in conference with various well-heeled women as they unburdened themselves over the shiny glass cases of moisturizer. Or she was slipping off a giant earring so that she could press her ear a little bit closer to the phone receiver, all the while nodding vigorously in communion with the caller. Like a good hairdresser, she knows. She knows whose husband is cheating, whose teenager is struggling with addiction, whose wife is getting ready to file for divorce. It's all in the name of customer service, though the purchase often seems an afterthought. "Oh, I almost forgot," women will say, returning to the counter after an involved conversation that ended moments before with an embrace. "I wanted to get the Botanical Night Complex."

The mix of commerce and confidences is not unique to Christina; it's part of the fabric of the cosmetics department, where vanity and hope and self-doubt are all interwoven. "Anytime you let someone touch your face, it's very intimate," said saleswoman Carol Anderson. "Women tell us about their face lifts and intimacy with their husbands. We know things their own families don't know."

Christina, to her credit, was too discreet—and too astute—to let me eavesdrop on such conversations. My only glimpse of this kind of exchange came by accident one morning, when I was talking to saleswoman LaDonna Powers; suddenly, a petite blonde who had been scanning the room from afar strode up to us. "LaDonna!" she cried. "Thank God you're here. I *had* to get your opinion." She squeezed LaDonna's hand as if they were old friends. ("I love LaDonna because she doesn't put any pressure on me," she told me. "She shows me what's new and how to look good.") LaDonna smiled warmly as the woman debriefed her on her life post-divorce and her various cosmetic adventures. "The plastic surgeon you suggested was fabulous," the woman said. "Look! I got my tummy tucked again two weeks ago." Beaming, she tugged on her jeans to show how loose they were at the waist.

"You look great!" LaDonna marveled.

"And guess what else? I'm in love!"

"That's wonderful!" LaDonna said.

"I'm just crazy about him. Really! He's the one." She smiled for a moment at her own good fortune. Then, without missing a beat, she got down to business. "So I need one of these," she said, extracting a tube of lipstick from her purse. "And I need something to make my face look less shiny."

"La Prairie?" LaDonna offered, naming one of the priciest cosmetics lines Neiman's carries.

"Don't you think?" the woman said.

LaDonna gave her a significant look—*You want the best, don't you?*—and nodded, ushering her to the counter.

This scene plays out, with variations, seven days a week. Women are pampered, affirmed, empowered, and made to feel beautiful, all while vast amounts of merchandise are moved off the shelves. No one is spared; not the Middle Eastern royals who buy here, nor Angie Harmon, nor the Bush twins. It would be easy to be cynical about the whole thing, but in the end, everyone wins: The customer feels elated when she walks out the door with a bit of the Neiman's mystique, and the saleswoman has made another 9 percent commission. (A top salesperson in a good year can make a six-figure salary.) Christina does not fawn over her customers or offer up false flattery to make her sales; she simply gives them her undivided attention and good judgment. Her clients want to be nurtured, and so she nurtures them. She sends them bouquets and chocolate-covered apples on their birthday and flowers when there has been a death in the family. Throughout the year, she calls periodically to check in and pens cheery notes on homemade cards festooned with feathers and sequins. And still, business is never too far away: "Would you like to charge this to your Neiman's account?" is her constant refrain, the chorus to almost every love song she sings to a client.

Whether or not the beauty products Christina sells actually do what they say they do—the literature on one $350 elixir claims that it "revitalizes, repairs, restructures, rehydrates, and renews" the skin as it "plumps the dermal layer"—is beside the point. The beauty business has always, in the famous words of Revlon founder Charles Revson, provided women with "hope in a jar." One of Neiman's best-sellers is La Prairie's Creme Cellulaire Radiance, a facial moisturizer that purports to improve the skin's elasticity; it is displayed atop an illuminated platform, as if it were a talisman, and runs $500 for a 1.7-ounce bottle. Rather than discouraging customers, its price has become its selling point. "We can't keep it in stock," Christina said. "It sells itself." The reasons for its popularity are simple enough. "Women want to stop time," she observed on my last visit. "Beauty is what makes us powerful, and so we try to buy our immortality." She was in a philosophical mood. Then, out of reflex, she switched into sales mode. Her voice softened and she leaned a bit closer, her gaze washing over my face as she drew me in. With great earnestness, she began to make the pitch: "And you know, good skin care can make all the difference . . ."

I'D LIKE TO SAY that I was immune to the notion that I could somehow buy beauty at the cosmetics counter, but I was no different from any woman who walks into Neiman's. I did successfully withstand the urge to purchase a $250 jar of moisturizer that carried the intriguing claim that it was "made entirely by hand in a monastery." I also passed up the chance to buy various masks and creams laden with exotic ingredients such as "pure diamond powder," "crushed Polynesian pearls," "wild yams," "sea wrack," and "powerful caviar extracts." And I refrained from pulling out my credit card after the maestro performance of a natty fragrance salesman who, with great dexterity and care, massaged my hand, misted me with a heady blend of "citrus-sandalwood notes," and then blew softly on my wrist until I was certain he would pass out from a lack of oxygen. But it didn't take long to break down my resistance. Once I got a makeover, I promptly spent more money on makeup in a few minutes—$136, to be exact—than I did all last year.

It was an unusually slow afternoon, and so the Neiman's makeup artists had passed the time by working on me as we talked. They dusted and drew and smoothed and polished and contoured and shadowed, stopping now and then to take a step back and assess their work. A woman with smoky eyes gave me smoky eyes; a woman with peachy lipstick and lip liner applied peachy lipstick and lip liner. At some point, my hair acquired significant amounts of hairspray, which gave it a sturdy sheen, and I was spritzed in lemony clouds of Acqua di Parma. Bronzer lent my pallid skin a healthy glow. Under the diffuse lights of the cosmetics counter, I looked good. Not wildly different, just better. *Enhanced.*

The most stunning woman among the makeup artists, a dead ringer for Sophia Loren, told me as I began making my round of good-byes that she wanted to put makeup on me the following day. I thanked her but said I would have to decline. I was returning home to Austin. "Really?" she said, surprised. She did a quick appraisal of my face—the full-coverage foundation, the perfectly drawn flourishes of black eyeliner, the peachy lipstick so glossy that it was practically reflective—and then offered her assessment: "I thought you lived in Dallas."

*September 2003*

# HALLIE AND FAREWELL

*Rancher, judge, teacher, and mother:*
*When Hallie Stillwell died in her hundredth year,*
*Texas lost its last link to the Old West.*

HELEN THORPE

**My great lament was that I got to see Hallie Stillwell after she had stopped telling stories. By the time I met her, she was in a nursing home, and she wasn't talking anymore—not even to her closest friends. While I was visiting her there, I remember noticing that the nursing home had written her name on the bottom of her slippers, to prevent them from getting lost. It was a reminder that all of us, no matter how legendary, are made humble again in the end.**

HALLIE STILLWELL was wearing a Western-style plaid blouse and a denim skirt when I went to see her last July, the kind of clothes she had worn for years, and that made it easy to imagine she was about to get up and walk around. She was wearing pink terry cloth slippers instead of shoes, though, and she was sitting back with her legs up on a wheeled bed, and it had been a long time since she had walked on her own. I was visiting her at the nursing home where she lived out the last ten months of her life, a brick building on a hill in Alpine. Stillwell was 99 when she died, on August 18. In the weeks before my visit she had retreated into an interior world. She rarely spoke anymore, even to family members, and she had nothing at all to say to me. I wondered what she was thinking as we sat together under a tree in a garden behind the main building, looking out at one of those burning West Texas days: the striped red hills, the spiky sotol plants, the bare sky.

She loved that land. It had always comforted her to look at it. When Hallie married and first moved to the Stillwell ranch, down near the Big Bend, she used to sit outside to regain her composure after a long day, particularly if she had failed at some task, disappointing her husband, Roy. "Soon after the evening meal," she wrote in her autobiography, "as I was sitting on a rock, looking into the far-away beautiful mountains in Mexico and enjoying the lovely evening shadows so typical of West Texas at dusk, my emotions were calmed and I felt peace and happiness."

When that book, *I'll Gather My Geese,* was published six years ago, it confirmed Stillwell's status as a living Texas icon. She became emblematic of the Big Bend region of West Texas, a person who epitomized that part of the country—or rather, what that part of the country had once been like. Stillwell reminded people of a lost time—the frontier era—and at this safe remove from its actual hazards, those days seemed like a particularly romantic time. In fact, Stillwell never claimed that she was a living symbol of anything, let alone West Texas in its wild and woolly days. When she arrived at the Stillwell ranch in 1918, she was a stranger, uncertain of the rules and constantly transgressing them. In her book Old Texas appears in the figure of Roy, a cowboy to the bone, the embodiment of what the Big Bend once was. Hallie was many things throughout her life: a schoolteacher, a rancher, a newspaperwoman, a beauty parlor operator, a justice of the peace. Some of her choices, such as getting into newspaper writing, were considered odd in West Texas ranching country, where discretion was prized above communication. It was her outsider status that enabled her to write about the place so well.

Hallie Crawford was born in Waco in 1897. Her father had a hard time staying put, and over the next twelve years, the family made five moves, stopping in various West Texas towns and then homesteading in the New Mexico Territory. The Crawfords moved to Alpine for the school facilities, among the best in the region. One of Hallie's schoolteachers was J. Frank Dobie, and her daughter, Dadie Potter, believes that Dobie probably inspired Hallie to write.

Hallie went on to become a schoolteacher herself; in 1916 she began teaching in the border town of Presidio. Pancho Villa's army had recently captured Ojinaga, and Presidio was full of refugees when Hallie arrived. Her parents, worried, had urged her not to accept the job, but she did what she wanted. "I found the days hot, the sand deep, the Mexicans strange, and the U.S. soldiers curious about an Anglo girl moving there," she wrote in her book. "There was only one other white girl there . . ." Though she took refuge in the federal fort when Villa was rumored to raid, the greatest threat Hallie faced came from U.S. troops stationed along the border; one afternoon she was chased by two drunk soldiers.

The following year Hallie taught in Marathon. It was there that she met Roy Stillwell, a rancher who had grown up in Mexico, where his father had owned land. Stillwell owned a 22,000-acre ranch 46 miles southeast of Marathon, just northeast of the land that, decades later, would become Big Bend National Park. In 1918, after a courtship that consisted of automobile rides, picnics, and midnight serenades performed by a blind Mexican guitarist Stillwell had hired, the two became engaged. Hallie was twenty, Roy was twice her age, and he was known to drink and gamble. Again Hallie's parents opposed her decision, so she and Roy eloped.

Hallie's move to the Stillwell ranch transformed her. She had always been an avid rider, a good shot, and a girl who lived to please her father rather than her mother, a Southern lady who thought Hallie's tomboy ways made her a fright. Even so, she was not prepared for ranch life. First, there was the ranch house itself: "I really hadn't expected much but I was somewhat surprised at its size, one room about twelve feet by sixteen feet." Upon her arrival the three cowhands moved out into the barn. No woman had stayed at the ranch before, and they viewed the development with disdain. Hallie took the cool reception as a challenge, deciding to prove herself useful. She didn't have much of a choice—her husband considered it unsafe for her to stay at home. He expected Hallie to ride with the cowhands. When she showed up the first morning in a riding skirt, Roy said she would spook the horses and insisted she wear men's clothes. "I found out quickly that I was to live like a man, work like a man, and act like a man, and I was not so sure I was not a man when it was all over."

Learning to be useful was complicated by the fact that Roy, an often difficult man, seldom gave explicit directions. "For cowboys, the life of a ranchman is nothing to brag about, their problems are nothing to discuss with other people, and their business is very confidential," Hallie wrote. "[F]ew have much to say, and most expect others to know what they are thinking at all times. Roy was certainly this type of person. This made life on our ranch somewhat complicated at times."

Motherhood changed Hallie as much as the ranch did. Married life had seemed an adventure, a liberation from the constraints of her parents. But once she discovered she was pregnant in 1919, Hallie realized her days of independence were over. Her first child, christened Roy but known as Son, weighed twelve pounds and was born after 48 hours of labor, endured without anesthesia. His arrival transformed the atmosphere of the ranch house; the cowhands, who had been so distant to Hallie, melted around Son. Two more children followed, Dadie and a second son named Guy. The cowboys finally warmed to Hallie.

Over the next twenty-plus years, Hallie tended to the children, worked alongside Roy, and watched the children work alongside him as well. The ranch was plagued by a series of hardships. Everyone fell sick during an epidemic of Spanish influenza; Roy got tuberculosis; Son left to fight in World War II; a dust storm that looked like a crawling blanket smothered the ranch; drought choked the land. Hallie took it upon herself to modernize the ranch—usually over Roy's objections. One of the first improvements she wanted to make was to install running water in the kitchen. Roy, stubborn in his old ways, refused to install the sink, saying it would just get clogged up. Finally one of their nephews did the work. When Hallie wanted to build a bathroom, Roy balked again; this time she did the work herself. Later on, when a man drove up in a pickup carrying a gleaming new gas-burning refrigerator that Hallie had ordered, Roy became apoplectic.

"How is everything, Roy? Had any rain?" the refrigerator salesman asked.

"Nope. It is hotter than blue blazes and dry as hell," Roy shot back, "and you can take that thing right back to Alpine."

Like any true cowboy, Roy considered appliances unnecessary and a sign of going soft. Hallie was a generation younger and more open to change. But she wasn't soft. In 1948, just as Texas was sinking into the grip of its most prolonged drought on record, Roy set off for town for a load of hay. Hallie thought of going with him, but she was watching her granddaughter at the time. Instead, she asked him to mail some letters and to bring her two loaves of bread.

"I later heard that Roy made the trip into town safely, got his hay, ran my errands, and made a last stop at the general store," wrote Hallie afterward. He also visited their house in town to look in on Dadie.

"I don't think your mama and the boys realize how serious this drought is," he said to her.

"Oh, yes, they do," Dadie told him. "Mama just always tries to cheer you up. She realizes how bad it is. She knows we're in for rough times."

Roy's truck overturned on the way home. When Hallie got to the scene of the accident, he was unconscious, but she thought he would be all right. It never occurred to her that Roy, who was so tough and had weathered so much, might be fatally hurt. But doctors discovered massive internal injuries, and he lasted only 24 hours more. In the aftermath of Roy's death, the drought worsened, and Hallie managed to hang on to the ranch only by leaving it in the hands of her sons and taking on a series of other jobs.

The job that she held the longest, and that she seemed to find most satisfying, was that of justice of the peace in Alpine. From 1962 to 1977, Hallie drove all over Brewster County, the largest county in Texas, performing marriages, serving as the coroner, and judging misdemeanor cases. That job, along with her Ranch News column, which she began writing for the *Alpine Avalanche* in 1955, made her a local celebrity. Finally, when it was clear that the cattle business was becoming less and less profitable, in 1969 Hallie opened a general store and an RV park on her property just six miles from the northern entrance to Big Bend National Park. "That was one of the smartest things she ever did," says Dadie. In a sign of the changing times, the store and park soon generated more money than the rest of the ranch. To the campers who arrived every year, Hallie became something of a tourist attraction herself. In 1991 Dadie opened a museum called Hallie's Hall of Fame, which features exhibits like the Colt .38 pistol Hallie carried in Presidio, photographs of Roy on a white horse named Red, and the crude bedroll they once shared.

Toward the end, visiting Hallie was a different experience. She stayed at the nursing home in Alpine after a stroke made it extremely difficult for her family to take care of her. As we sat outside watching the hills rise beyond Alpine, I told Hallie that I was reading her book, but I got no response. I tried several other openings; all failed. Eventually Hallie closed her eyes and dropped her head. I began to think that visiting Hallie hadn't been a good idea. She was old, and I should have left her in peace. But I had hoped that by meeting her in person, I might get a glimpse of the individual behind the folksy legend displayed in the Hall of Fame.

Just then a small, spry woman with short white hair and sporting Wrangler jeans, a Resistol hat, and a cane, stepped up. "Hallie? Good morning! Good morning! Hello, darling!" she yelled. "I'm Faye, Faye Yarbro. We've had a lot of good times together!" Yarbro, a funny, salt-of-the-earth retired schoolteacher, had known Hallie for years, but she believed that Hallie no longer recognized her. This did not faze her. She went on chattering at top volume, and Hallie soon brightened visibly. "I found a picture of you," announced Yarbro. "It was taken when you came and talked to a group of retired teachers, and you told about being in Presidio. You had a pistol that you put in your teacher's desk. Sometimes Pancho Villa would raid over on this side, and the soldiers would come and take you to that fort."

The significance of Yarbro's words struck me later. I had gone to see Hallie hoping she could uncover some original truth hidden inside the myths of her life, and instead I found myself listening to somebody tell those stories back to her. I realized then that Hallie was almost gone—not just that she was losing her hold on life but also that we are losing the reality of what her life once meant. There is no stopping the accretion of myths about her; a community hungers for legends and heroes. She knew West Texas when it was young. She knew Roy when he was a cowboy, when he raced horses and roped cattle and they slept under the stars on a bedroll. It did not matter that she was really more representative of the New Texas than the old one. The store and the campground, strangely public enterprises to mix with the solitary occupation of ranching, are exactly the kind of accommodation that ranchers all over West Texas are having to make these days. One can only imagine what Roy would have said about it all.

*October 1997*